OSCAR'S
BRAZIL

OSCAR'S BRAZIL

A JOURNEY TO THE HEART OF A NATION, ITS PEOPLE, PLACES AND PASSION FOR THE GAME

Tom Watt

with **Tim Vickery** and
Fernando Figueiredo Mello

BLINK
bringing you closer

BLINK
bringing you closer

Published by Blink Publishing
Deepdene Lodge
Deepdene Avenue
Dorking RH5 4AT, UK

www.blinkpublishing.co.uk

www.facebook.com/blinkpublishing
twitter.com/blinkpublishing

ISBN: 978-1-90582-584-4

A CIP catalogue record of this book is available
from the British Library.

Design by www.envydesign.co.uk

Printed and bound in Slovenia
by Svet Print, d.o.o.

Colour reproduction by Aylesbury Studios Ltd.

1 3 5 7 9 10 8 6 4 2

Tom Watt © 2014

Papers used by Blink Publishing are natural,
recyclable products made from wood grown
in sustainable forests. The manufacturing
processes conform to the environmental
regulations of the country of origin.

Blink Publishing is an imprint of the
Bonnier Publishing Group
www.bonnierpublishing.co.uk

CONTENTS

I grew up in a suburb of São Paulo called Americana. Life was very different in a neighbourhood like mine compared to life in the centre of the city. You know, there are drugs and crime everywhere, and the threat of violence, but Americana was a calmer, more relaxed place. The problems weren't anything like they are in the poorer neighbourhoods of São Paulo. I have three sisters, one a half-sister on my dad's side. I liked where we lived – it was a good place to be a boy, a boy who liked football. Americana was safe enough that I could go off and play on my own in the park. Perfect: a little pitch to play on, with floodlights and everything. I could be out there all day, every day!

I lost my dad when I was three. He died in a traffic accident. My dad used to buy and sell things; you could call it re-cycling. It's a very normal profession in Brazil. My mum was always a housewife, at home and there for us, but she used to make and sell clothes after Dad died. Mum raised us on her own but because, like her, my dad's family were from Americana, she had help from them, too. We were like one big family in many ways. Life wasn't easy: we weren't rich, my mum was on her own, but we were happy and Mum looked after us really well. In different circumstances our situation might have been much more difficult but we had a house to live in, we had family around us. I'm aware, though, that there are lots of children in Brazil growing up without the support we had: in the *favelas* there are a lot of boys and girls who are having to try and find their own way, without guidance or help, and in social and economic conditions that are much worse than I experienced as a boy. Knowing how tough things are for thousands of kids growing up in São Paulo, I know how important a place like Casa do Zezinho can be and what a difference it can make in a young person's life.

★ ★ ★

There is a very difficult area in the south of São Paulo where the borders of three *favelas* meet: Capão Redondo, Parque Santo Antônio and Jardim Ângela. There is very little of the social structure, like healthcare, transport, green space or recreation facilities, which most people take for granted. And most kids need them at some time when they're growing up. There are many very poor families living in those neighbourhoods, many mothers trying to bring up families on their own and having to work to survive, leaving boys and girls to fend for themselves when they're not in school.

Those children are often just forgotten by many of us. They live along alleys where crime and drug dealing and violence happen every day. Because their families aren't able to support them and because there isn't any kind of safety net for them, they turn to the streets as a way of making their way in the world. They are drawn into the life of the gangs or they simply become the victims of violence and crime. It's almost as if everybody assumes that is what is going to happen, that it's those kids' destinies. How can they escape? How can they change the story that's been written for them almost since the day they were born?

There's a woman in that particular neighbourhood, a teacher named Dagmar Garroux. But she is better known to thousands of local boys and girls – and their families – as *Tia Dag*, 'Auntie

Dag'. *Tia Dag* started out by looking after a few kids who were
in trouble, letting them come to her house to play and to learn;
and to be safe from life on the streets. The numbers of young
people needing – and wanting – her help grew and grew: all
ages, from the very young to older teenage boys and girls.
Tia Dag found a building and, nearly 20 years ago, she set up
the Casa do Zezinho. Just three rooms to begin with, it's a lot
bigger than that now! Since the Casa first opened, over 10,000
children and young people have had their lives made better
by being there. As the Casa has grown, so has the waiting list.
Now, 1500 Zezinhos, aged between 6 and 21 and all from the
favelas, come to the Casa after school during each year.

Tia Dag would be better than I can be at explaining how she
works with the Zezinhos. It's not just about being a place to
come and hide away from life in the neighbourhood. Casa do
Zezinho offers the children and teenagers all sorts of courses
and activities: from painting and drawing to *capoeira*; from
computer science to playing in an orchestra; from English
lessons to filmmaking. Of course they can play football, too.
And there's even a swimming pool at the Casa now. They come
along after school and learn what they want with support from
Tia Dag and the other teachers and volunteers.

It's an amazing place: bright, warm, friendly, lots of little rooms
just like at home. The idea behind Casa do Zezinho is to let
the boys and girls discover their own path instead of having
to follow the path that poverty and poor social conditions
had otherwise mapped out for them. *Tia Dag* believed in the
children of the neighbourhood when nobody else did. And now
they can believe in themselves. So many of them finish school
and then have the confidence and the inspiration to go off
to college or to start work in a job that will lift them out of
poverty and fulfil them as people.

In many ways, I have been lucky in my life: I had the support
of my family around me when I was growing up; I was a boy
in a neighbourhood where I was free to go out and run around
in the fresh air without my mum worrying about where I was;

and I had football, which I loved and which has given me the chance to fulfil my dreams. Every child should have the same chance; whether their ambition is to be a dancer or a musician, a journalist or a businessman, an artist or a teacher. Casa do Zezinho is there, thanks to *Tia Dag*, to give boys and girls – children who have had the most difficult starts in their lives – the chance to fulfil their potential and to take control of the rest of their lives for themselves.

Casa do Zezinho receives some funding from the state government and from the Brazilian government; it also partners with individuals and companies who want to make a difference for the next generation growing up in the *favelas* of south São Paulo. I want to do a little to help the work of *Tia Dag* and everyone else who works so hard at Casa do Zezinho, too. I love my country and I'm proud to be a Brazilian, especially if I have the chance to represent Brazil at a World Cup here at home. I'm very proud as well – and grateful – that places like the Casa exist to help more young people enjoy the kind of opportunities in life all of us should have, whoever we are and wherever we come from. That's why I have taken part in this project: *Oscar's Brazil*. I want to express my love for Brazil and for the generation that's following on from mine. Buying this book means you have helped the next generation, too, because funds from *Oscar's Brazil* will be passed on to Casa do Zezinho. Thank you. Enjoy this book, enjoy our country and enjoy the World Cup. And pray for the Zezinhos who are pursuing their dreams!

Oscar dos Santos Emboaba Júnior, 'OSCAR'

INTRODUCTION BY OSCAR

13

A World Cup in Brazil

It was an incredible thing: the defeat against Uruguay at the Maracanã in 1950, the game they call the *Maracanazo*. I've never actually seen the pictures but it's as if I still know exactly what happened that day. I understand the effect it had on the Brazilian people; we went on to win the World Cup after that, five World Cups. And we've won them everywhere else but, because Uruguay beat us, we've never won one at home. It just makes this year that much more important, for the people and for the players, too: a World Cup here in Brazil again.

I can't say I know a lot about what Brazil was like, back in 1950! But I know the country has evolved and changed a lot. Football has changed, of course, but so too has everything else. The thing about 2014 is Brazil is known all over the world as the home of football, a particular kind of football: football that makes people happy. It's not just the players, either. Brazilians are known as a happy people and people who are big fans of football. That will all be on show to the rest of the world at a World Cup in Brazil: our football, our country and our people.

Brazil is a very, very big country. I'm not sure people realise just how big! And each area, each city, has its own character, its own culture. You know, Brazil is where I was born and grew up. I've played football in lots of different Brazilian towns and cities but even so, there are so many parts of Brazil that I've never been to, so many places I don't know. For a World Cup, all of those different regions and all those different people come together, though. Especially for a World Cup being held in Brazil. It's another reason 2014 is so important for all of us. The excitement is amazing. Everywhere! And for me. I've never played at a World Cup before but I know what happens: the whole of the country stops to watch when the *Seleção* play. So you can imagine: for me it has always been a dream, to play at a World Cup for Brazil. There's pressure as well – playing for your country brings that. But the pressure is felt by our sup-porters, by the Brazilian people, too. It's as if they share that pressure with us; it's about all of us together as hosts of the tournament.

What's important is to recognise our reponsibilities and take them seriously as players. But not to let the pressure inhibit us. When the whistle blows for kick-off, we have to make sure we let the joy in our football come through. If we do that, we know we'll have 200 million Brazilians on our side, cheering us on. We have to be true to ourselves and true to our football ideals and not let the scale of the event, the importance of a World Cup in Brazil, stop us playing the way we all want football to be played.

So many Brazilian players now play overseas. It will make a World Cup back at home even more special. I've been playing in London, with Chelsea, for two years but I know what it feels like to play in front of Brazilian fans, a Brazilian crowd. All of us are the same: we're passionate about our country. Whenever we have a holiday, we go home to Brazil, home to our families and our friends. So, now, to have a World Cup there? That will be a very special kind of homecoming indeed!

1. THE FIRST TIME

YELLOW AND GREEN, a splash of blue … Flags, pennants, bunting and banners hanging from window sills, railings, aerials, balconies; wristbands, bandanas, T-shirts and hats; walls, pavements, children's faces, the bodies of grown-ups: any surface that will take a brush will be brought alive with improvised paintings and messages of good luck and good hope. Yellow and green will be fluttering, glistening and shimmering in glorious sunshine across Brazil during the summer of 2014. Every four years, as if for some kind of tropical Jubilee, Brazil decorates and dresses up, throwing itself into the spirit of the World Cup. This is a Jubilee with a difference, though. It is not a celebration of an aristocratic family's place in the way of things. This summer – and every fourth summer – the royalty that's celebrated and celebrating could very well have been born next door.

As the national anthem plays and the world looks on, the camera pans along the line of players, the *Seleção Brasileira*, the Brazilian national team. What you see are the real faces of this giant of a country. Most of them are young men from humble, modest backgrounds. They might have been born as pawns but now, in gold and green, they feel like kings. For the next 90 minutes and then until the tournament ends – in triumph or disaster, there are no half measures for this team – this handful of players are Brazil's most visible

and important citizens, representatives of a population touching 200 million in 2014.

It is all too easy to take this for granted; the connection's been made a million times. 'Brazil' and 'Football' might these days seem synonymous, two faces of the same glittering coin, but it's not always been that way. Not so long ago, before *Futebol* became the heartbeat of a nation, it was a foreign invader, a reminder of times colonial and past, and because of that met resistance along the way.

'Football will never catch on, you can be sure of it,' wrote Graciliano Ramos, one of Brazil's great men of letters, just over 90 years ago. 'It is a temporary enthusiasm, a craziness, an obsession for many people, lasting perhaps a month. We have lots of our own sports. Why should we want to go poking our nose into foreign ones?'

Ramos was writing in the early 1920s, from the remoteness of Palmeira dos Índios, a small, lost inland town in Brazil's impoverished North East. But at the same time, down in the South East, in the booming, cosmopolitan cities of Rio de Janeiro and São Paulo, a very different story was being told. Two years earlier, as tournament hosts, the Brazilian national team had won the South American championship for the first time (and would win it again in 1922). Songs had been written in celebration, poems composed. Parties had spilled out

across the city's streets. Here, football had started to take a grip on a country's urban psyche, a grip that's shown no sign of loosening ever since.

In 1949 Brazil were once more victors in the *Copa América* – the South American championship – winning a final playoff against runners-up Paraguay 7–0. The following year, though, the stakes were altogether higher for the *Seleção*. In 1950 the country wasn't just playing host to teams – and neighbours – from elsewhere in South America. This time the world was coming. Off the pitch – and, even more so, on it – the 1950 World Cup was Brazil's chance to make a powerful statement about itself, its future and its place on the international stage. How had it come to pass, then, that – in the space of just three decades – football had become so vital to the nation's identity, its image of itself?

★ ★ ★

Introduced by the British, the game arrived with the cachet of First World prestige. Almost from the off, it was re-interpreted by the locals. Originally the preserve of a wealthy elite, football quickly caught on because of the game's essential simplicity. Here was a game with very few barriers: given a round object and a space, anyone could play. And in Rio and São Paulo, lots of people wanted to play. The rapidly growing cities, with immigrants pouring in from Europe, the Middle East and other parts of Brazil, were an environment in which change was embraced. And so Brazilians – South Americans, indeed, because the same process was taking place in cities such as Buenos Aires and Montevideo, too – came to the game with fresh eyes and open minds. Instead of the hard-running, 'Muscular Christianity' tradition of the British, they developed something far more sinuous and balletic, an artistic style of play ideal for a player with a low centre of gravity.

Crucially, the South American re-interpretation of the game very quickly led to international triumphs and with them, to recognition for a region of the world

usually starved of such acclaim. It is no surprise that Uruguay were the first to make a mark. Brazil's little southern neighbour was a global pioneer in enlightened social policies, organising its own version of the modern welfare state during the early years of the twentieth century. On the football field, the country's clubs and its national team drew on talent from all sectors of society, irrespective of racial or economic background, almost straight away. When Uruguay won the inaugural *Copa América* in 1916, the tournament's top goalscorer was Isabelino Gradín, a black player from a poor neighbourhood of Montevideo.

In semi-feudal Brazil, meanwhile, where slavery had only been abolished in 1888, the idea of a black player representing his country would have been unthinkable. Arthur Friedenreich, hero of the Brazilian team that won the 1919 *Copa América*, had a black mother but his father was a German businessman, and only his extraordinary talent – and hairdressing designed to hide his Afro-Brazilian heritage – enabled him to kick-start the process of inclusion that had already enriched the Uruguayan game. But change, when it came during the 1920s, was as steady as it was irreversible.

In December 1932 Brazil played World Cup winners Uruguay in Montevideo. The visitors won 2–1. Their best players were two young working-class blacks, defender Domingos da Guia and centre forward Leônidas da Silva. Uruguayan football had just turned professional and, after the game, the Montevideo giants swooped: Domingos signed for Nacional, Leônidas for Peñarol. Other Brazilians were already playing in Europe – and being paid to do so. The next barrier to fall was the one defended by those still wedded to elite, amateur ideals. The loss of the country's brightest talents decisively strengthened the hand of those promoting change. By the mid-1930s a professional career in Brazil was open to any player with talent.

Come the end of the decade, an inclusive and professional game was firmly established in Brazil, triggering a great leap forward in standards. A team of outstanding talents stood ready to represent Brazil in time for the World Cup on home soil in 1950. The star turn was attacking midfielder Zizinho, idol of the young Pelé. 'This is a genius. A man who possesses all the qualities that could be imagined for a professional to get close to perfection,' wrote journalist Willy Meisl, at the time one of the most respected thinkers in the game, after watching Zizinho in action. A correspondent from Italy's *Gazzetta dello Sport* waxed even more lyrical. Zizinho, he claimed, was 'the maestro, his football reminiscent of Da Vinci painting something rare.'

Alongside Zizinho was another artist of the game, Jair Rosa Pinto, a small, slightly built figure, who over the course of a 25-year club and international career had a reputation for damaging goalkeepers' hands with the astonishing force of his left-footed shooting. Zizinho and Jair were the supply line for centre forward Ademir, quick, strong and a proficient finisher off either foot and in the air. Behind, directing play from deep was Danilo Alvim, known as *Principe*, 'the Prince'. Further back was the lithe, athletic Barbosa, rated the best goalkeeper Brazil had ever produced. What could possibly go wrong? Prepared for the tournament by a well-respected coach, the debonair and authoritative Flavio Costa, this generation of players looked ready to represent a nation being talked up as the country of the future.

Rio de Janeiro, 1950

Brazil had taken huge strides forward since the Wall Street Crash of 1929, which, after the initial shock, had turned into something of a blessing for the growing and industrialising nation. The country was shaken out of its traditional role as a simple supplier of raw materials. With the collapse of external markets for its natural resources, Brazil was forced to develop from within. Between 1930 and 1945, it was governed by Getúlio Vargas, first as a president and then during the years of the *Estado Novo* – Brazil's 'New State' – as a dictator. A

podgy, avuncular figure, Vargas introduced an initially benign version of tropical fascism that would continue to influence Brazil's political agenda long after his death.

Vargas was an able and insistent populist and moderniser. He used the glamorous new medium of radio remorselessly to help consolidate a new sense of national identity, aiming to unify a disparate population defined by successive and recent waves of immigration. Along with the President's nationalist

Maracanã Stadium, Rio De Janeiro, 1949

propaganda, radio took football coverage all over Brazil and helped establish samba as the national soundtrack. The Vargas regime appropriated Carnival, handing out subsidies in return for control of the content samba schools took to the streets on parade. The theme now had to be Brazil. And the Vargas version of it: social criticism was frowned upon and eventually outlawed. The longstanding image of Brazil as an all-singing, all-dancing, all-smiling land of perpetual happiness dates from the years of the *Estado Novo*.

That impossibly optimistic portrait of the country was,

of course, a honey-coated myth. But, post-World War II, a conflict in which Vargas eventually managed to side with the victors, there were genuine reasons for Brazilians to be cheerful. In many respects the nation and its people had never had it so good: the industrial sector was growing and Vargas announced a wide range of labour legislation which – though nowhere near universally applied – introduced paid holidays, pensions, an eight-hour working day and other benefits. There were fresh ideas in Brazilian cinema and, especially, in architecture: spearheaded by Oscar Niemeyer, a new generation took the stern lines of European modernism and added sensuous tropical curves. Built specially for the 1950

World Cup, the Estádio do Maracanã was a stunning example: just north of Rio's city centre, the new stadium dominated the landscape, an imposing statement of intent from Brazil about its future and its football team.

It was in the Maracanã that Brazil gave perhaps its finest ever performances in the white shirt, which preceded the later and now instantly recognisable yellow one. Unlike previous tournaments, the 1950 World Cup was not played to a knock-out format. Instead, the four group winners met in a final pool. Brazil were apparently unstoppable, playing with a breathtaking combination of style and athleticism, and blasting seven goals past Sweden before overwhelming Spain 6–1. Their final opponents were Uruguay, who had squeezed past Sweden after only drawing with Spain. A draw, now, would be enough to see Brazil crowned world champions for the first time in front of a capacity home crowd on the afternoon of July 16.

In the build up to their final game, the team's training base was moved. Earlier in the tournament, Brazil's players had enjoyed the relative tranquillity of a facility on the outskirts of the city. Now they were near the centre of Rio, at Vasco da Gama's stadium just across a park from the Maracanã. This was election year: the campaign – ultimately successful – to win a further presidential term for Getúlio Vargas was in full swing. Brazil's training base seemed to be doubling as the epicentre of national politics. The players were forced to gather to listen to speech after speech, with most of the candidates already hailing the Seleção as world champions. The local media did the same. So too the Mayor of Rio, Ângelo Mendes de Moraes, on the pitch before the game kicked off:

> You, players who in less than a few hours will be hailed as champions by millions of compatriots; you, who have no rivals in the entire hemisphere; you, who will overcome any other competitor; you, whom I already salute as victors!

The reward for such hubris would be tragedy. Uruguay, after all, were still Uruguay: a team who had never lost a match at a World Cup. They had played Brazil in three warm-up matches shortly before the tournament started. The margin of victory each time had been a single goal, with Brazil winning twice and Uruguay once. Forgotten in the excitement of the occasion was the fact that this was a game between two well-matched teams. As it turned out, La Celeste were, as expected, on the back foot for much of the game and, early on in the second half, Brazil's pressure finally told: Ademir and Zizinho worked the opening for winger Friaça to score. Reflecting nearly half a century later, though, Zizinho would remember that triumph as the moment when Brazil started to lose their grip on the game: 'It seemed that we had a collective drop in pressure. Our team stopped. It seemed that we had carried out our duty in the game. Our responsibility had ended there, when we opened the scoring.'

On the touchline, coach Flavio Costa was worried. Those easy wins against Sweden and Spain had not prepared his players to withstand hardship in games. He would later remember how 'in a team where he sees no weaknesses, the coach pats the players on the back and hardly has anything to do'. Now, with 40 minutes still to play, Uruguay were obliged to press forward. They found a weak spot down Brazil's left, according to Costa:

> Bigode was having problems marking [Uruguay's right winger] Ghiggia, who did the same thing four or five times, beating Bigode and going on freely to the bye-line. A defender, Juvenal, wasn't giving cover to the marking of Ghiggia. Perhaps he was worried by the crowd. He hid from the game in the middle of the others.

There were, of course, no substitutions permitted in those days. Costa tried desperately to shout instructions and encouragement to his distracted players. Inside the Maracanã, though, 200,000 people were already celebrating, waving their handkerchiefs in the air – an *adiós!* to their opponents – and chanting triumphantly. The coach went unheard. Until, suddenly, the stadium fell silent. Ghiggia set up an equalising goal for the Uruguayan centre forward, Schiaffino. Costa later described it as 'a silence which terrorised our players. They felt responsible for this, and didn't react.'

Less than 15 minutes later – and with only ten remaining – Ghiggia raced away once more. Anticipating another cross, Brazil's keeper, Barbosa, came off his line only for the Uruguayan winger to surprise him with a shot inside the near post. The underdogs in front, Brazil roused themselves and once more laid siege to the Uruguayan goal. But the crowd appeared to have lost all belief. Afterwards players from both sides commented on how quiet it remained around the huge and tightly packed bowl as Brazil went in search of an equaliser. Time, as always for the losing side, seemed to tick by with alarming and unforgiving speed. Uruguay held on. At the final whistle, the home crowd streamed away, most of them in tearful silence. Some sought ways to vent their frustration and anger, however. Newspapers were set on fire, as were pieces of timber left behind from recent building work. A bust of Rio's mayor, the hapless and overconfident Ângelo Mendes de Moraes, which had stood at the entrance to the Maracanã, was found next morning floating in the nearby river that had given the new stadium its name.

Disappointment and pain transmuted into an orgy of recrimination and self-hatred. Brazil's crushing defeat, it seemed, hadn't just been inflicted on its footballers, but on the whole nation. Most of the blame was attributed to the black players, especially left-back Bigode and goalkeeper Barbosa. Many Brazilians took the result to be confirmation of an innate inferiority that seemed always to undermine the best efforts of the country and its

Maracanã Stadium, Rio de Janeiro 1950

people. Over the course of 90 minutes, the self-proclaimed 'country of the future' had been re-described as the home of a mongrel race, a people condemned to perennial and self-inflicted disappointment. Brazilian sports journalist João Máximo summed up the sense of doom:

> Gigghia's goal was received in silence by the whole stadium. But its strength was so great, its impact so violent, that the goal – one simple goal – seemed to divide Brazilian life into two distinct phases: before it and after it.

A nation mourned and the players paid a heavy price. Zizinho wrote in his autobiography: 'I played for 19 years and won titles but, along with the other players of that campaign, I'm remembered as a loser.' Jair confessed that he worried about the prospect of someone coming at him with a knife because he'd been part of the team that lost to Uruguay. Many years later, Barbosa held a ceremonial burning of the goalposts used in the game at the Maracanã. But even this didn't bring closure: he died in 2000, still lamenting that, despite the maximum jail term for criminals in Brazil being 30 years, he himself had served a 50-year penalty for the crime of being caught out by Gigghia's winner.

★ ★ ★

Although the sense of inferiority and its accompanying racist undertones have lifted, the 1950 World Cup is still looked back on as a national tragedy of epic proportions. Perhaps, more than 60 years later and with a Brazil World Cup having focused the world's attention, the time has come for a reappraisal of what that generation of players represented and what they – almost – achieved. Although scorned at home, the 1950 team was highly valued abroad, nowhere more so than in Uruguay. Sharing the intensity of that extraordinary game at the Maracanã forged a bond of affection and mutual respect between the two sets of players. In subsequent years

they gathered for frequent reunions, a quiet example of football's ability to forge friendships transcending international borders.

The *Seleção* of 1950 was unquestionably the finest to wear the white shirt, the strip retired in shame as a consequence of their defeat. Others took stirring memories of them in action away from the tournament. *Gazzetta dello Sport,* for example, declared: 'In the game against Spain, those who had the privilege to watch this spectacle saw everything that could theoretically be imagined in football. There was science, art, ballet and even moves from the circus.' European players and pundits had never seen anything like it. Brazil might not have won the trophy, but the 1950 World Cup made it very clear that they had now earned a permanent place at the world game's top table.

As well as reconsidering the merits and achievements of the team, it's also a good time to reappraise the success of Brazil as the ambitious host nation in 1950. There's a real danger of missing the point if the beginning and end of the story is Uruguay's two goals denying Brazil at the final reckoning. The significance of the 1950 World Cup for Brazilian football – and, indeed, for Brazilian history – reaches well beyond the tragedy of July 16.

When Brazil staged the *Copa América* of 1919 and 1922, all of the games took place in a single stadium: Rio de Janeiro's charming Estádio das Laranjeiras, the home of Fluminense, with its old-fashioned main stand, similar in architectural style to an English cricket pavilion and evidence of the Brazilian game's elite origins. By the time the tournament returned to Brazil in 1949, much had changed. The main stadium was now Vasco da Gama's home ground, the imposing Estádio São Januário, right in the heart of working-class Rio. Matches were also played in São Paulo at the recently built Estádio do Pacaembu. Rio and São Paulo had long since been established as Brazilian football's showpiece

Estádio das Laranjeiras, Rio de Janeiro

cities. At the *Copa* of 1949, however, there were 29 games played: one was taken down to the port city of Santos, another to the north of the capital and a tiny stadium in Belo Horizonte.

A year later, for the World Cup everything was on a different and altogether grander scale. Rio, staging eight games, remained the most important host city. But now it had the Maracanã, many times bigger than São Januário, built especially for the tournament and the biggest stadium in the world. Another new stadium was opened in Belo Horizonte, the Estádio Independência, which staged three games in 1950, including the USA's historic victory against England. Six further matches took place at São Paulo's Pacaembu. But for the first time the tournament was also taken outside Brazilian football's traditional heartland in the South East. To the south, two games were played in Porto Alegre in the state of Rio Grande do Sul, two more in Curitiba, the capital of Paraná. Up in the North East, meanwhile, a match was played at Recife's Estádio Ilha do Retiro.

Already football had gained a real foothold in even the most far-flung of Brazil's provinces but the feeling remained that the top-class game was something experienced elsewhere, notably in the country's two biggest cities. International tournaments were events to be followed on the radio rather than witnessed first-hand. However the 1950 World Cup began to change that mentality. The decision to play games at new venues around the country would eventually lead to the decentralisation of the Brazilian game. A decade and a half after Belo Horizonte played host in 1950 not only to the USA's surprise victory over England and to Uruguay's 8–0 undoing of Bolivia, the city boasted a sparkling new stadium of its own – the Mineirão – a copy of Rio's mighty Maracanã. This celebration of provincial football in concrete and steel coincided with the astonishing breakthrough, on the pitch, of one of the city's teams.

Maracanã Stadium, Rio de Janeiro

In 1966, Cruzeiro, led by a young and rising talent, Tostão, thrashed Pelé and Santos FC's star-studded supporting cast in the final of the *Taça Brasil*, at that time the most important national club competition, the winners progressing to the *Copa Libertadores*, South America's equivalent of the European Cup. Shortly afterwards, the Brazilian national team, defending the trophy won twice in succession, crashed out of the World Cup in England. A despondent Tostão flew home with thoughts of giving up the game and concentrating instead on his medical studies but when he arrived back in Belo Horizonte he was greeted by a huge party: he was the first local player from the local club to be selected to represent the country at a World Cup, a cause for historic celebration irrespective of Brazil's results. Tostão received the boost he needed to continue as a player, something opposing defences at the 1970 World Cup would soon have cause to regret.

In 1971, Brazil launched a truly national championship. Transport – and infrastructure generally – were improving and the military dictatorship of the day saw a new national league, the *Campeonato Brasileiro*, as a means to bind the giant country closer together. The inaugural champions were Cruzeiro's Belo Horizonte rivals, Atlético Mineiro. In the decade that followed, the traditional giants from Rio and São Paulo did not have things all their own way. Against all the odds and everybody's forecasts, teams from Porto Alegre – Grêmio and, especially, SC Internacional – wrote the headlines, stepping up from regional competition in the *Campeonato Gaúcho* to win titles at national level. Clubs with reputations forged in relatively obscure regional club competitions, the state *Campeonatos*, now had the chance to make a mark countrywide, their games broadcast live on TV.

The state of Rio Grande do Sul is probably the most 'European' part of Brazil, its character reflected in its

Santa Teresa, Rio de Janeiro

approach to football. Conducted by midfield general Falcao, Internacional dominated the 1970s. They could play, of course, but they were also big, physical and difficult to play against. Over time this 'European' approach spread throughout Brazil. Many of the country's most important coaches come from states in the far South, not least Luiz Felipe Scolari and both his immediate predecessors as coach of the national team. It's hard not to see this key development in Brazil's football history as a direct result of the decision to stage 1950 World Cup matches in Porto Alegre.

Football in the North East has yet to make the same impact at national and international level. Teams in the states of Pernambuco and Bahia have huge fan bases. Santa Cruz FC in Recife can fill stadiums even when competing in the third tier of national competition as they are today, an achievement all the more remarkable given the sometimes fickle nature of Brazilian fan culture. The power and passion witnessed off the pitch in the North East, however, is rarely seen on it. Teams from Salvador and Recife seldom challenge for the title and are usually happy just to avoid relegation. The traditional big 12 of Brazilian football are the four clubs each from Rio and São Paulo, and two each from Belo Horizonte and Porto Alegre, all from the South and South East of Brazil. Curitiba, also in the South and capital of Paraná state, is currently a city on the rise in respect to football, too. If the states of Brazil's North East are to make a mark on the *Campeonato Brasileiro* – and then, internationally, on the *Copa Libertadores* – the 2014 World Cup will need to act as a trigger for the next stage of Brazilian football's decentralisation, mirroring the impact made on the game by the 1950 tournament.

In 2014, it was decided that World Cup venues would be heavily weighted in favour of host cities in the North and North East. These are the areas of Brazil closest, geographically, to Europe but they enjoy year-round tropical climates. With something like half of the matches at the 2014 tournament played in the North East, the hope is that investment in stadiums and training grounds will see the regional clubs in those states far better prepared to compete with the national game's traditional powerhouses. In footballing terms, at least, this may well prove to be the tournament's most significant legacy.

Questions have been asked about the decision to take World Cup fixtures north to Manaus, close to the heart of the rainforests of the Amazon basin, and west to Cuiabá, the state capital of Mato Grosso, which sits at the dead centre of the South American continent and borders both the Amazon rainforest and the wetlands of the Pantanal. These last are the most controversial steps being taken towards the decentralisation of Brazilian football. Are expensive new stadiums in Manaus and Cuiabá really necessary? Is their viability guaranteed after the World Cup circus has packed up and moved off to Russia and then to Qatar? Many think not and are angry about what some commentators have described as a misuse of public funds; funds which might perhaps have been better spent on much-needed public works and infrastructure projects elsewhere. Alongside the pre-tournament excitement in Brazil ahead of the country hosting its second World Cup, the debate about the means employed to do so rumbled on and will surely continue to rage. After the demonstrations witnessed at the 2013 Confederations Cup, a World Cup being played out against a controversial and potentially explosive political backdrop emerged as a strong possibility.

At the 1950 World Cup, the *Seleção* were held up as icons, representatives of a glorious future for Brazil and responsible for the prestige of a nation in thrall to football. In 2014, there are altogether different expectations: Scolari's Brazil are under intense pressure, of course. Sixty-four years ago there were 50 million Brazilians dreaming of – *demanding* – victory; the population has grown fourfold since then. But the Brazilian team's footballing

Praia da Guarita, Rio Grande do Sul

fortunes this time around are of less significance when it comes to defining the status of the country in its own and the world's eyes. The arguments about Brazil – what kind of country it is, what kind of country it could be – have become part of a conversation taking place outside the confines of the World Cup stadiums: in a free press, on television, across social media and, perhaps, in protests on the cities' streets.

Now as ever, Brazilians wish to take pride and joy from the achievements of the players they celebrate so passionately and colourfully every four years. After all, they're the most successful team in World Cup history, with traditions to maintain, not least in a tournament on home soil. But in the twenty-first century the people of this extraordinary and dynamic nation want to be able

to take pride too in the country they're constructing, a country they know now has an increasing role – and increasing prestige – on the world stage. The World Cup: a carnival, for sure, and a celebration of all that's best about football. Any Brazilian will tell you that although the English may have brought the game there, it was they who elevated and perfected it. A giddy, colourful and inspiring month watching the world's best players in competition; but also the chance to witness a brave, relatively young nation rushing towards the future, struggling to create a shared sense of its own complex and cosmopolitan identity as it does so.

This is a country always more focused on the present than the past: football in the wake of a dictatorship of 1950, football on the crest of democracy in 2014. Without question, on and off the pitch, Brazil can claim progress has been made.

The Best of All Worlds

When I was growing up, home was Americana. Even though it's near the city, it's a completely different sort of place. When I was playing for São Paulo, though, I had a place in the middle of the city. São Paulo is fantastic. People come from all over Brazil: to live, to study, to work. It's seen as an agitated and frenetic kind of place but there's everything you could want there: restaurants, shops, things to see and do. I loved living there; but I was close to home, too; only an hour away from my family. Like everyone in São Paulo, I worked and worked; for me that was training and games. But then I could go out to Americana and just relax: the best of both worlds.

When I joined Internacional, I moved to Porto Alegre. I was amazed at the reception I got, even as a *Paulista*. I loved it there. Porto Alegre is like São Paulo in that it's a busy city: you can find and do whatever you want. But because it's down in the south, Porto Alegre has a very different culture. The people, the *gaúchos*, have their own way of doing things, their own way of life; even their own way of speaking Portuguese. There's a calmer attitude and I enjoyed that: it's a more tranquil place than São Paulo.

At first, I felt like a stranger. We'd go out to a bar, perhaps, and there'd be music on: everybody else would know the songs and the artists, but I'd never heard of any of them! We went to the theatre: a famous play, famous actors from Porto Alegre but, a *Paulista*, I didn't know any of them. Everywhere else in Brazil, we drink coffee but, in the south, everyone drinks *Chimarrão*, a kind of tea made with mate herb. At Internacional, when it was cold, players from the city or from around Rio Grande do Sul would come to training with their own flasks of hot *Chimarrão*. You see people drinking it everywhere: it's a *gaúcho* thing, unique to the south.

Of course, in Brazil, we have our stereotypes depending on where we're from: everyone's the butt of a joke because everyone's from somewhere! Because people from Bahia are laid back, people say: *Oh, Baianos are so lazy!* Because I come from a suburb, they call me a *caipirã*, meaning 'a country bumpkin'. They'll laugh at my accent because ours is different out in the suburbs. If people are from Rio, everyone else says they're just on the beach all day every day. Paulistanos, they say, just work all the time; people from the south are bad-tempered. We all get stereotyped!

São Paulo and Porto Alegre are the two cities I know best. Rio is fantastic, too. My favourite place in Brazil, though? Well, the place I would say to everyone to visit if you get the chance is Fernando de Noronha. We went there for our honeymoon: the most beautiful beaches you have ever seen. It's a little group of islands, out in the Atlantic Ocean but they're part of Pernambuco State up in the North East: you get a boat out from Recife. The landscape, the sea: everything's perfect. But I feel like I haven't been to even half of Brazil; I've never been to Amazonia, to the rainforest, for example. Such a massive country, so many incredible places to see: every state has a different culture, a different atmosphere, a different sound. You could spend a lifetime travelling around in Brazil.

2. *VERDE E AMARELO*: A Journey

IT'S SIX O' CLOCK IN THE MORNING, in the North and deep interior of Brazil. We are in a boat that glides noiselessly across the glassy surface, tiny on the broad expanse of the Amazon River, a kilometre across; unknown depths below us. The sunrise is overwhelming; shafts of sunlight arrow through the treetops on the far bank. Sunshine and the forest, yellow and green, this is Brazil – ancient, timeless, vast. It seems as if the whole earth is awakening. The endless and uncharted forest embraces us with a maternal tenderness, the air damp but warm against our skin. An indigenous, red-skinned mother – descendant of the native inhabitants of the land first discovered by the Portuguese navigator Pedro Álvares Cabral in 1500 – emerges from among the trees by the shore.

A bruise-coloured haze shimmers along the riverbank. The warmth of day beginning draws moisture upwards from the ivy clinging to trees which climb into a perfect sky, greys and pinks swiftly giving way to gold, then azure. On the riverbank the native Indian mother starts her daily chores. Straight black hair frames her painted face: keen eyes, but a guarded smile. Although still in her teens there is a lightly-carried wisdom suffusing her features. The forest is her home and she is perfectly at ease in the familiarity of her surroundings. Children chatter and call. Their mother watches over them: stern,

a smile and then stern once more. She pulls a young boy close and uses her fingertips to draw lines across his forehead with rust-coloured mud; a tradition being practised and passed on.

This young woman's role is clearly defined in native Indian society: she will be tasked with the children's education; selflessly, she will nurture the foundations of her marriage too. She will prepare and cook meals for her family and for the tribe. Her partner, meanwhile, will hunt and fish, using a bow and arrow to down a wild boar or a spear to harpoon a *tambaqui*. He will build their home and protect the settlement from real and potential predators and foes. Together, where a clearing has been made, they will cultivate cassava, corn, beans and bananas. They will weave hammocks and build canoes. Together, too, they will hand down traditional customs to their children, teach by example and perpetuate native traditions which link them, an unbroken chain, back to the lives of their ancestors.

When the first European explorers landed on Brazil's north east coast and navigated their way here into the Amazon Basin, there were at least 2,000 tribes – each with its own territory, culture and identity – living under the forest's canopy: millions of men, women and children. Disease, conquest, slavery … history has taken its toll. Today perhaps 200 tribes survive, fewer

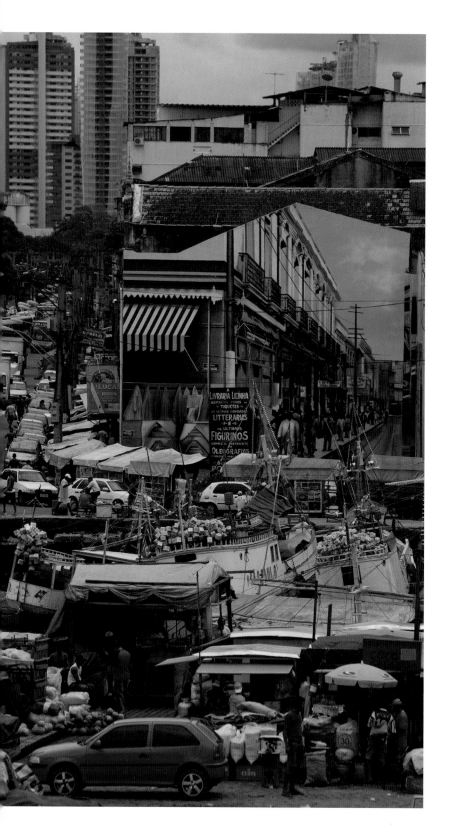
Belém

than 800,000 people and yet *Índios* are in every city in Brazil. Out of a population of 200 million, there are few Brazilians who do not carry at least a trace of Indian blood in their veins. Brazilian Portuguese is given its own character by the inclusion of a myriad of words whose origins lie in the depths of the forest. The cuisine has an Amazon identity, rich in ingredients and cooking methods which have travelled down-river with natives and outsiders alike to grace tables in every corner of a nation that loves to eat. Brazil is Indian at its very heart and the pulse of *povos indígenas* courses through every Brazilian's veins.

A couple of hours down-river lies Manaus, capital of the state of Amazonas, named for *Manáo*, an indigenous tribe and a native word meaning 'Mother of the Gods'. From the peace and tranquility of dawn at the river's edge to the sweat, toil and tumult of a huge and growing industrial hub. Manaus is where the great rivers meet, the black waters of the Rio Negro colliding with the dun-coloured tide of the Solimões, the Upper Amazon. As the waters churn, so too do past, present and future, here at the Amazon Basin's feverish heart. Colonised early, a small native village quickly grew to become a bustling city under Portuguese rule. In the early twentieth century Manaus swept to fame across the world, gathering to its streets and squares, its bars and brothels, its docksides and shanty towns, the ambitions and dreams of millions before affording unimaginable wealth to the very few.

This was the *Ciclo da Borracha*, the Rubber Boom, long since imploded but having left an indelible mark. As the heat of the day builds around us, we walk past a dazzling pastel confection, the Teatro Amazonas: an opera house, almost impossibly gracious, built in 1896 to celebrate Manaus' new-found identity as a city of the Belle Époque, conscious of the world's eyes upon her. Under a blue sky, the theatre's monumental façade, built in perfect Renaissance style with raw materials imported from Europe and across the South American continent, supports a dome covered in 36,000 Italian ceramic tiles in the yellow, green and blue of the Brazilian flag. Within, the interior has been painstakingly restored to past glories and now, this morning, musicians from the Amazonas Philharmonic Orchestra are already inside the auditorium, tuning their instruments before rehearsal for tonight's performance at the *Festival Amazonas de Ópera*.

We move north from the centre of Manaus, away from the shoreline to the engine driving a city two million strong in the twenty-first century, the industrial hub. Here are over 600 factories and workshops. Manaus is no longer just a stopping-off point for the Amazon's natural resources as they head towards the open sea and industrial centres across the world. Now the city itself manufactures, particularly in the technology and electronics sectors. One hundred thousand people and more work here, in a different kind of forest: one of concrete and steel. The sounds of the jungle are drowned out by the roar of machinery, trucks revving their engines and workers shouting to be heard. These workers will sweat the shirts from their backs today – and every day. The relentless humidity and the stifling heat, already pressing up towards 30 degrees, are a reminder that we are in the tropics and the jungle lies everywhere around Manaus. Brazil past, Brazil present: both are here and palpable.

Our boat returns to the water, chugging gently east down-river along the Amazon, which widens – metre by metre, mile by mile – as we head towards the ocean. Sixty miles before we reach the Atlantic, we make landfall in Belém, capital of the northern state of Pará. Skyscrapers pierce the sky as we look up from the old port, but at their feet and spread across the city, pastel-coloured colonial buildings take us back to the seventeenth century when the Portuguese first decided *Nossa Senhora de Belém do Grão Pará* offered them safe

haven. Like Manaus, Belém spread its wings in the early twentieth century when the *Ciclo da Borracha* took flight, powered by a worldwide clamour for the automobile. Profits from the export of rubber paid for a city centre studded with Belle Époque architecture, including what became the jewel of '*Paris N'América*', the neoclassical Theatro da Paz.

Belém is of course 'Bethlehem' in Portuguese and every October the city celebrates its spiritual life when the streets teem with crowds – the whole community is here, involved and inspired – gathered for the 'Christmas of the Amazon', the *Círio*: weeks of preparation and then five hours of colourful procession and joyous celebration as two million line the route between Belém Cathedral and the Basilica of Nazaré. Belém is also known as the *Cidade das Mangueiras*, the 'City of Mango Trees'. The fruit first brought here from India found the perfect conditions in which to blossom. Mango trees grow everywhere, on sidewalks, in parks, in gardens. But the fruit is only one of those we'll find among the colour and chaos beneath the iron arches and turquoise turrets of one of South America's biggest market halls, the waterfront *Mercado Ver-o-Peso*, 'Check-the-Weight Market'. Mango, cashews, passion fruit, açaí, acerola, ciruela, cupuaçu, cupuí, graviola, guarana, jaboticaba, jenipapo, jua, mangaba, pitanga … Fish from the river, fish from the sea. Meat is fresh, salted, cooked and marinaded and there are spices once from Africa, the Indies and everywhere between. In the tropics the land is blessed and you reap whatever you can sow. It's astonishing, this wealth of nature: every taste, every texture, every hue piled high as far as the eye can see.

Now ashore, we head south, perhaps on the flat bed of a truck – people have travelled from the North like this in their millions over the years – towards the state of Tocantins. They call the *Jalapão* a desert. That's what it would be, except this dry savanna – *cerrado* – cut through by rivers, is a natural miracle, a kind of mirage. Dazzling white shrubland, *caatinga*, gives way to sweeping waves of slowly shifting sand dunes, then outcrops of forest, pierced by narrow ravines and breathtaking waterfalls. The greatest of them all is the Cachoeira da Velha, a massive horseshoe of whitewater plunging into pools: swim, and replenish body and soul. Anteaters, armadillos and rheas all scamper across the landscape but the *Jalapão* is eerily quiet after the bustle of Belém: almost uninhabited, tiny hamlets populated by the descendants of fugitive slaves who three centuries ago fled into the unknown from sugar plantations on the coast.

Striking east, through the stately and imposing *Chapadões*, the plateaux of the Serra Geral de Goiás, we return to that coastline first glimpsed by Portuguese navigators half a millennium ago. We see just what they saw: the blessed sea of Bahia. Green, blue, dappled and ever changing to reflect the angle and intensity of the sun, this land is a gift that glitters all year round. On the beaches the light glows on the slender backs of young, black Afro-Brazilian boys practising *capoeira*. They whirl to the haunting, insistent sound of the *berimbau*, an ancient musical bow. The spirit of Africa, the soul of Africa is here: in the dance, in the game and in the shadow-fight of Brazil's own martial art. Here – and across Brazil – whatever can be expressed is expressed in music. Drums are beaten, hands clap and songs fill the air from dawn into the depths of jet-black night, their inspiration in every captivating smile. And those smiles are everywhere on the faces of *Baianos*, the men and women, young and old, who call Bahia home. The boys on the beach gather round to talk: *Where have you come from? Where are you going to? Do you want to play?* There's no ball here, though: this is *capoeira*.

Baía de Todos os Santos was once just the 'Bay of All Saints'; now Bahia is the name of a whole state, up in the country's north eastern corner, closer to Africa in terms of distance than it is to the southern reaches of

Brazil. Here a nation's African heritage, borne across the Atlantic on countless Dutch and Portuguese slave ships, has taken root, inspiring and nourishing a way of life. This is the synthesis indeed that defines Brazil and Brazilian culture. Salvador, the nation's first capital and still its third largest city, stands proud and burns with energy, rejoicing in the unselfconscious beauty of its architecture and people. Everywhere, alongside reverence paid to the Catholicism of the former colonial power, *Baianos* embrace and worship the complex deities of *Candomblé*, a religion transported in the holds of slave ships by the Africans squeezed in so mercilessly below.

The Atlantic has its tales to tell. Today, a fisherman casts his nets out across the bay. Friendly and outgoing, he guides us through the blue-green waters aboard his *jangada*, a traditional fishing boat driven by a single triangular sail. His face is lined and weathered by the sun and wind. Strong but delicately built, he's a man whose body and spirit have been crafted by the ocean. He tells us fishermen's tales and opens our eyes to the life force beneath the waves: marlin, yellowfin tuna, wahoo, mahimahi, sailfish, king mackerel, amberjack, cobia, trevally, African pompano, snook, snappers, groupers … 'Today, there are not so many fish as in past times but we thank God for what we are given each day,' he tells us. Humility, faith, gratitude, indomitable optimism, this is a Brazilian spirit. Each day brings with it the promise of a better tomorrow.

We leave Bahia behind us and nose northwards along Brazil's 4,000 miles of coastline: past Sergipe, Alagoas and on to Pernambuco. Accents and traditions merge and shift as we move from one state to the next. The pace of life slows, becomes more contemplative, even in the larger conurbations. We drop anchor off Recife, drink sweet and refreshing coconut water, taste the rich, salty tang of the mangrove crab. The city's name derives from the reefs, breaking the waves above the rock shelf

Recife

which edges along this stretch of the Brazilian coast and offering safe haven from the buffeting of the Atlantic Ocean. Boa Viagem is the most famous of Recife's beaches, remembered in songs, poems and stories.

Recife poses a question: is this a waterborne city clinging to every little island of dry land where it can, or solid ground cut through with waterways? They call it the 'Brazilian Venice', but it might just as easily be named the 'Brazilian Amsterdam'. Finding our way through the maze of narrow streets and bridges that make up the old town, *Recife Antigo*, we encounter blondes and redheads. But these are not backpacking tourists; they are the descendants of the Dutch, who fought the Portuguese for control of the gateway to Pernambuco in the seventeenth century. The architecture reflects that brief and violent occupation, too. Meanwhile, in the here and now, the sound of the drum, the *maracatu*, is heard everywhere, powerful and relentless. The spirit of Africa pounds through Recife life, a steady bass-note to the heady mix of races, faiths and traditions that give the North East its own extraordinary and diverse character.

It's as everyday as a bus or subway ride, but this is a taxi in the air, taking us high above the expanse of the Ilha do Bananal, the world's biggest river island, an area the size of Wales – or Israel or New Jersey – on which converge the very different worlds of rainforest, wetland and savanna. We have left the North East and descend, over the dusty, rolling high plains of the Mato Grosso, into the Pantanal, squeezed up against Brazil's borders with Bolivia and Paraguay. Here, on the wetlands in the middle and far west of Brazil, we find as dizzying an array of plant and animal life as we saw thriving in the forests of Amazonia. We can ride on horseback out into the heart of the Pantanal: the ancient plain is what remains of a vast inland sea, the Xaraés, which began drying out 65 million years ago.

This land is alive, roamed by jaguars, pumas, oncillas, tapirs, maned wolves, giant otters, howler monkeys, marsh deer and scurrying capybaras. The boss of the

Pantanal, the fearsome caiman, takes his lunch at will from the waters beneath him, which teem with pacu, suribim, bagre, giripoca, piraptanga, cachara and countless other fish besides. Masters of the sky such as the crowned eagle, masters of the lakeside like the giant jabiru, brilliantly-plumed birds including macaws, nandays, toucans and parakeets flock in their

a lunch of dourado, grilled over charcoal, with him: this, after all, is a fish that comes up big enough to share.

From the natural exuberance of the Pantanal we cross to a city whose architecture is as dazzling and flamboyant as the wetland fauna we've just left behind. While São Paulo may be the heartbeat of Brazil's economy and Rio may be the face the country turns to the outside world, this is the seat of political power. Brasilia is the third capital in Brazil's history, a city dreamt up and then sketched out on paper by visionary architects Lúcio Costa and Oscar Niemeyer. Improbable, instinctive lines and shapes combine to fashion an entirely Brazilian setting for the business of government: Congress, Presidency and Supreme Court. Laid out in the mid-1950s, Brasilia is also a temple to Modernism – and a UNESCO World Heritage site because of that.

The most beautiful building in Brasilia – and there are plenty to choose from as we make our way through the grid of avenues laid out to look like a bird or a plane from above – is not one designed to pay tribute to political power. The Catedral Metropolitana Nossa Senhora Aparecida pays tribute to faith, its superstructure 16 concrete columns clustered like a crown. We step through darkness before emerging into the vast, sunlit interior: the Cathedral's glass roof lifts eyes and hearts towards the heavens. Surrounding us, dazzling stained-glass panels. It's a Niemeyer masterpiece, one among many here built thanks to the sweat of *candangos*, migrant workers from the North and North East who moved to the country's heart in search of work and a new life. Inaugurated in 1960, it symbolised a country inventing itself all over again: grandiose, spiritual, resolutely modern; a capital for Brazil like nothing else in Brazil.

We swoop down to the South and East, over the beef ranches and coffee plantations of the *cerrado* of Minas Gerais, towards the state capital, Belo Horizonte. Minas Gerais – 'General Mines' – was named for the natural resources underground which first attracted prospectors

hundreds and thousands across an untouched, unspoilt land. The only human we meet is a Pantanal cowboy, a *peão*, marshalling his herd with the quiet authority of a midfield general directing his football team. He lives a life that's been unchanged for almost 200 years. We enjoy

Catedral Metropolitana Nossa Senhora Aparecida, Brasilia

in the seventeenth century and are still being exploited to this day. Away from the pits and spoil, the state – as big as France – is a synthesis of Brazil, beloved for the mountains and waterfalls of its central, southern and eastern regions. Earth and water appear to coexist in perfect, inspired harmony. So many of Brazil's defining flavours are found here in the cheeses, breads and milk. Everywhere, the smell of chicken and pork being cooked on a *fogão a lenha*, a wood-fired stove – and of course the taste and aroma of Minas Gerais coffee. Sit and sip: take the excuse that's offered to eavesdrop on the daily small talk typical of Minas, typical of Brazil. You might even order up *Café Pelé*, coffee named after the great man who was born in Três Corações, in the south of Minas Gerais.

We find our way into the capital, Belo Horizonte, named for the views of the mountains circling one of Brazil's biggest, busiest cities. Perhaps this is the country at its most welcoming: unprepossessing, hospitable and alive. Belo Horizonte was planned as an art nouveau capital by wealthy landowners and coffee-growers while Minas boomed at the end of the nineteenth century. Just north of the imposing avenues and wide squares of downtown, another Oscar Niemeyer vision unfolds: the Pampulha District and its crowning glory, the church of *São Francisco de Assis*, around which pilgrims and tourist gather, shoulder to shoulder. And there's more: we take to the shade of a bar near the Mercado Central and sip Brazil's other national drink, the sugar cane spirit, *cachaça*. The barman adds crushed lime, sugar and ice and claims the *Caipirinhas* here are the best in Brazil. Who's to argue? As we toast the early evening it would not be hard to convince us right now that everything about Minas Gerais captures the best of the nation it is at the heart of.

We travel down towards the Atlantic Ocean. The Estrada Real – the 'Royal Road' – was first mapped out in the nineteenth century, the route by which treasures of the interior, not least gold and diamonds, could

be carried down to the coast. We start north of Belo Horizonte in Diamantina and continue south through the town of Ouro Preto, '*Black Gold*' in Portuguese, perched amid the mountains of the Serra do Espinhaço. From the early eighteenth century onwards huge amounts of money were made here in gold and diamond mines, thanks to the unbending, miserable toil of the many and the cunning of the very few. However the age of exploitation left behind towns of charm, grace and Baroque beauty, all cobbled streets and elegant architecture washed in white and pastel pinks and blues.

Both Diamantina and Ouro Preto are listed as UNESCO World Heritage Sites. Marvellous towns on the way to the City of Marvels, Rio de Janeiro: *Cidade Maravilhosa*. Before taking a look, we eat! Rice, beans, steak, *farofa* (a traditional Brazilian dish of toasted manioc flour), fried egg. In the centre of one of the world's greatest and most cosmopolitan cities this is a very ordinary *carioca* meal. The *cariocas* – citizens of Rio – have transformed the traditional cuisine of the indigenous Tupiniquim people into a culinary art. Simple, tasty … you can be sure we won't be hungry for a while! To go with the food, an iced beer: always iced, frost clouding the outside of the bottle.

And then we walk out into the streets: Rio really is a place of wonders, somewhere the usual dividing lines between city and nature magically don't seem to matter any more. Look upwards to the city from the famous beaches of Copacabana and Ipanema: skyscrapers rise between the forested slopes of dizzyingly steep mountains. On the sand itself, the spirit of Rio is made flesh by the country's favourite game: amid the laughter and the shouting, a trick or sleight of foot is the answer to any challenge. Beach football, footvolley, *altinha*: the laws of gravity plainly do not apply here – love of football and lust for life see to that. In twos and fours and crowds, the game flows from one player to the next, the ball never touching the ground, via heads, chests, foreheads, heels and toe tips. Rhythmic as a samba

school, vital as Carnival, artful as a pickpocket ... men and women, young and old. Everybody plays. The beach is a hypnotic, ball-playing democracy. A shout goes out: *Você quer jogar?* 'Do you want to play?' Perhaps. Or perhaps we'll just watch and applaud. And survey the infinite and seductive beauty of Rio de Janeiro as another evening falls.

Brazil's second capital is intricate and compelling. Mythology, urban and otherwise, winds through the streets and squares. Inland, once night falls, is where we'll find the city's soul: in Lapa and Santa Teresa, where the sounds of samba spill from every bar, mysteries lurk under every archway and there's a wise-guy story on every *carioca's* lips. The impoverished *favelas*, climbing up the foreboding hillsides and away from the city's wealthier streets, twinkle with light after dark and pick out Rio's extraordinary landscape. Day and night in Rocinha, Mangueira, Cidade de Deus, Vigário Geral, Complexo do Alemão, life is as challenging as anywhere on earth. Poverty, unemployment and crime take their toll and yet these communities are driven by those who moved here from across Brazil in search of work and a better way of life, who refuse to abandon hope. Even here, smiling faces are everywhere, on the faces of old and young alike: misery and hope, despair and joy are woven through life today in the *favelas* just as they have been through ordinary people's lives, it seems, forever in Brazil.

The statue of Cristo Redentor – Christ the Redeemer – blesses the landscape from high on Corcovado Mountain. Our familiarity with a creation so often photographed and replicated does not undermine the overwhelming impact when we climb the staircase to meet Him and share His view out across the city. Built in 1931, 100 feet high and measuring nearly the same from fingertip to fingertip, the statue gazes out – tranquil and benign – from its perch on a shaft

Cristo Redentor, Rio de Janerio

VERDE E AMARELO: A JOURNEY

of rock which reaches skywards from the chaos of the city below. Lit up at night, Cristo Redentor can be seen from almost anywhere in Rio: an inspiration, a meditation in soapstone and concrete. Meanwhile, back at street level, near the geographic and cultural divide between the two Rios, north and south, lies an equally spectacular and equally famous monument, one dedicated to Brazil's secular passion. In 2014, the Estádio do Maracanã will host the final game of a World Cup for the second time. For football fans, across Brazil and around the world, the Maracanã is sacred ground, home to legends and gods of the game. The stadium, when full, is an experience never to be forgotten: sounds reverberate through the body and colour floods the eyes. It's as if every sense, every pore, has opened wide to let the greatest spectacle on earth – *futebol* – flow through us: a true adventure in football.

We travel south now, along the Costa Verde, virgin forest opening onto beaches and the charm of antique fishing villages along the way. Brazil is famous for football, of course. It's famous, too, for 7000 kilometres of coastline and some of the most beautiful beaches anywhere on earth. Whatever your idea of paradise, it's probably to be found somewhere lapping the country's Atlantic shores. The big city beaches are where Brazil comes out to play: football, volleyball, picnics, romance, a day out with the family. They are stages on which all Brazilian society gathers to enjoy itself and put itself on show. On the Fernando de Noronha archipelago, on the other hand, nature hasn't yet learnt to fear humanity: turtles, fish, sharks all swim carefree in the waters surrounding the protected beaches of a cluster of islands off the northeast coast. Around the coastline of Florianópolis, meanwhile, the Atlantic surge draws surfers, sailors and adventurers in addition to those in search of sun. If we're prepared to venture off the beaten track, we can find a tropical cove, washed by perfect blue water and fringed with golden sand, where we'll be completely undisturbed from dawn until dusk,

birds and monkeys our only companions. And, between Rio and São Paulo, lies as perfect a beach as any, perhaps: the Praia da Fazenda, where a bay of pristine sand arcs away from the small, traditional fishing village of Picinguaba. The dense green of the forest, the *Mata Atlântica*, plunges down towards the sea; the sand stretches away, soft and warm between our toes, shimmering the colour of white gold; and the Atlantic breaks on the shore, deep, mysterious and blue.

And, in an instant, we are back in busy streets, amid the crush of metropolitan life. This is still a city landscape but one altogether more explosive, more frantic; more relentlessly urban than Rio. There are cars of every shape and size, motorcycles pressed between them, crowded avenues, jammed streets, busy shops, clattering factories, frantic bars, cosmopolitan restaurants and buses chugging by, wreathed in their own exhaust fumes. And people. So many people: Japanese, Chinese, Italians, Germans, Poles, Hungarians, Lithuanians, Jews, Syrians, Lebanese, Africans, Peruvians, Bolivians, Colombians and all of them Brazilians now. São Paulo is South America's answer to New York. It embraces everything and everybody – immigrants from outside Brazil, migrants from the northern drylands, Amazonia, Bahia and every other corner of this enormous country. It's a melting pot of ethnicities, faiths and cultures that somehow functions as a single, breathing organism amid the chaos. This huge and pulsating metropolis is a city dedicated to hard work, built on hope, its people drawn here by the promise of opportunity.

The *paulistano* – the city native, indigenously urban – is like no other Brazilian. His is a singular character composed of multiple contradictions. He works, rests if he can afford to and then it's back to work again. He is earnest and still – somehow – easy-going; suspicious but generous; harassed but discreet; impatient but cultured; single-minded but craving distraction; capable of right

Rio de Janeiro

or wrong in two sides of a single moment. The *paulistano* absorbs the frenetic pace of the city around him; feeds on it, digests it; is energised by it. And then returns an image of São Paulo to itself in light and shadow. Above all, the *paulistano* is one tough guy. But he needs to be: for most, life in this city is very tough indeed.

In the fever and aggression of São Paulo's daily working life – so little space, so little time, so much to do – urban culture is the breath of fresh air that sweeps through the city, nourishing its soul. There is art on every other wall – graffiti is a rash that blossoms everywhere; brash, colourful, a call across the chaos. Rap, hip-hop – and every other genre of music from around Brazil and across the world besides – have

been absorbed and re-invented here. Listen: music is everywhere; re-imagined, re-mixed, reborn as the city is each day. Every morning, São Paulo wakes to take life by storm but, in truth, lives only for the night. From deep underground to the heights of sophistication, from the most obscure cults to the straight lines of the mainstream, so long as you have energy left, anything goes here. And goes on till dawn.

In a city where every face has a story to tell, its own unique mix of birth, rebirth and adaptation, it should come as no surprise that there's a different temptation for your appetite at every other corner. There may be restaurants to cater for the wealthy and the delicate of constitution – and some of them are very good indeed – but to eat in São Paulo, for most, is to eat on the street. The world is here: pizza, sushi, tortilla, nachos, pasta,

sauerkraut, hot dog, hamburger ... as many tastes as there are ethnicities. Before the street market closes, we can make a stop to eat *pastel*, savoury Brazilian pastries, and take a glass of *caldo de cana*, cane sugar juice, the complement to every Brazilian street meal. 'Pretty girls don't pay, but they don't take anything either!', 'Pay for two and you can take two!' The street merchants put on their own show; fun and laughter in the *paulistano* style. An old lady sighs, starting to pack up her wares. She tells us, 'We wake up very early, carry our stalls here and set them up. Then we take them down and carry them away. Tomorrow, we'll be here to begin it all again.' Every day is a battle but as dusk falls like a cloak over São Paulo's streets, she smiles the smile that's taken her through to the end of another day.

Another capital to visit and here you'll need your coat. Especially now, after dark: it's getting cold. Curitiba is the capital of Paraná, the first state as we head into *o Sul*, the South. It feels as if we've crossed back over the Atlantic and pitched up somewhere in Europe. When immigrants arrived from Germany, Italy, Poland, Hungary and Lithuania – as cheap labour once slavery had finally been abolished – they sought the spirit of the old continent and found it here in the cool temperatures, mountains and rolling fields. They brought their faiths and their customs with them and have kept them alive even if, a century on, the European cultures have often surrendered to a distinct Brazilian twist. And Curitiba itself is all that São Paulo and Rio are not: this is a less sophisticated, less vibrant, less sexy Brazil but life is good for the state capital's citizens with green space, cheap public transport, a roof over one's head and for most, a job that pays.

Heading south from Curitiba, we make tracks along 350 miles of some of Brazil's most beautiful beaches: Santa Catarina state. We can swim on the coast – look to the ocean and you may even see whales and their calves playing in the surf – or head inland to hike or ride through the forests and meadows of the Serra

Geral, where in winter the peaks are topped with snow. Santa Catarina's capital, Florianópolis, is a gateway to the beaches, pine dunes and forests of the Ilha de Santa Catarina and a little urban paradise in its own right: the old town and sophisticated modern city centre are on an island reached by bridges from the mainland, the oldest of which lights up the skyline each night. The tennis star Gustavo Kuerten was born here. Now retired, he's back. In 'Floripa', they wonder: *Why would anybody ever want to leave in the first place?*

Dawn breaks as we find ourselves down where Brazil borders its southern neighbours, Argentina and Uruguay, in the state of Rio Grande do Sul. In the capital, Porto Alegre, they look forward and never back; progressive politics, progressive art, progressive culture. Out on the Pampas, though, traditional life goes on. And even where the gaúcho culture is not lived, it is still deeply respected. We are in border country and those who watch over the vast herds of cattle for which the state is famous ride on horseback wearing their baggy-legged *bombachas de campo* and wide-brimmed *Pampeano* hats. The *gaúcho* has spiritual brothers across on the far bank of the Rio Uruguai but he is Brazilian to his core. From gourd cups, we share his *chimarrão*, hot tea brewed with *maté* herb that warms us through and soothes tired limbs as another sunrise breaks. Shadows fold into the creases on the ageing *gaúcho's* tanned and weathered face; trees and livestock are silhouetted against the brightening sky.

We gaze at our friend's cattle, who gaze back at us in return. It's six o'clock on a chilly morning and once more Brazil comes to life. Wherever you find yourself, you are welcome to be part of it all as the game begins again. This country the size of a continent rings with the echoes of history, but pick up its spirit: here the past must be respected but cannot be dwelt in. Brazil insists you dream of tomorrow with a passion, just as you celebrate today.

Ouro Preto, Minas Gerais

In Our Blood

Everyone in Brazil has a mix of blood in their background and sometimes in football it might help to be able to trace your descendants back to a particular ancestry. Definitely that used to help in the past. Me? I'm just mixed up all the way back through my family – I'm a mongrel! And so I'm just a 'Brazilian' and my family have just been Brazilians as far back as we can go, back to the Indians, probably. But we have a new descendant on the way, we hope: my wife, Ludmila, and I are expecting a baby and that will be something new in both of our family trees.

Ludmila's grandparents, on her father's side, came to Brazil from Japan, to work. Lots did, starting about 100 years ago: there are more Japanese people in Brazil than anywhere else in the world except for Japan. They settled mainly in the South, in Paraná, and around São Paulo. Her grandparents went to Paraná. Maybe they were planning to work, earn some money and go home but they stayed here: they must have liked life in Brazil!

At first, there wasn't so much mixing between different peoples: all Ludmila's uncles and aunts married other Japanese people and her father only married her mother, who's Brazilian, after his parents died. But I suppose those traditions become less strong as each generation passes. And, of course, I'm lucky: I found a Japanese girl I love and I'm just Brazilian so I could marry whoever I liked!

I've been to Japan a couple of times, playing football. I loved it there and I can't wait to go back. The Japanese people made us feel so welcome. There's a strong connection between the two countries: Brazilian players have played in Japan – Zico was a famous coach for the Japanese team – and of course we won the World Cup there in 2002. Like all the different cultures in Brazil, there are Japanese traditions which survive but these days, they celebrate being Brazilians, too. We all celebrate that culture together.

The diversity of Brazil is something we're proud of, I think. Everybody's here: on the same street, you'll see blonde-haired, blue-eyed girls alongside what we call *morenas*: olive-skinned with dark hair and dark eyes; there are black girls, Indian girls, Japanese girls! Maybe it's why Brazilians have this reputation for being happy people: everyone's welcome here. We see everyone as the same, without anybody worrying about your skin colour or where you're from. That's how we are. That diversity is something important in Brazilian football, too. Look at the teams who have won the World Cup, going back to 1958: there is the same mix of people from every ancestry as you see on the street. Of course I know there had to be pioneers to make that happen, for black players to be able to play when football first came to Brazil. And maybe football, over the years, has helped to break down barriers between different races in Brazil.

We have big divisions in Brazil but those are to do with social background. I understand those divisions because I come from a humbler family but now I'm more comfortable. I've experienced it from both sides, how people are different towards you depending on your social class. Our divisions, I think, are about rich and poor: there's no stigma attached to the colour of anyone's skin in Brazil.

3. *CARIOCAS E PAULISTANOS:*
A Story Begins

ALTHOUGH THE FORMALITIES were not completed until a month later in Manchester, the world's first professional football league was born on March 23 1888. The great and the good of the Victorian game were already in London: the following day, West Bromwich Albion caused a major upset by beating Preston North End 2–1 in the FA Cup Final at The Oval. On the Friday evening, representatives of the North's leading clubs had been invited to Anderton's Hotel in Fleet Street by Aston Villa director Sir William McGregor. They met to discuss founding a league competition that might generate a regular income now the Football Association had lifted its ban on the employment of professional players.

The immediate and obvious beneficiaries of the evening's proceedings turned out to be 1888's losing FA Cup finalists: a year later, Preston's 'Invincibles' returned to The Oval and beat Wolves 3–0 to complete English football's first Double, having already sailed through the Football League's inaugural season unbeaten, finishing 11 points clear of Villa in second. Half of the Invincible's team were Scots: much of the pressure to professionalise the game had come from players heading south in search of a game. Thanks in large part to their influence, football was on the way to outgrowing its early 'gentlemanly' tradition as a violent – but strictly amateur – exercise in kick-and-rush.

The Scottish game – and Scottish players – would leave their own legacy further afield in due course. Meanwhile that momentous gathering in Fleet Street, on premises advertised as 'Commercial & Family', pretty much changed the world. We've all got a rough idea what happened next. Humanity had discovered a favourite – and international – pastime; the English had discovered a way to make money from it. Between those poles, modern football has spun now for over a century, celebrated in the most spectacular fashion every four years at World Cups.

That chilly evening in March, the outside world seemed a pretty distant prospect as the gas lamps flickered along Fleet Street, though. The Empire could look after itself for the time being; McGregor and his colleagues weren't thinking far beyond their own profit and loss columns. And, if they were, the only concern would be how to make their way to South London in good time for the following day's Cup Final. Concluding their business upstairs, the founders of the Football League retreated for refreshment to the coffee house occupying half the ground floor at Anderton's.

Which is where Brazil – and Brazilian football – come in …

★ ★ ★

Rio de Janeiro

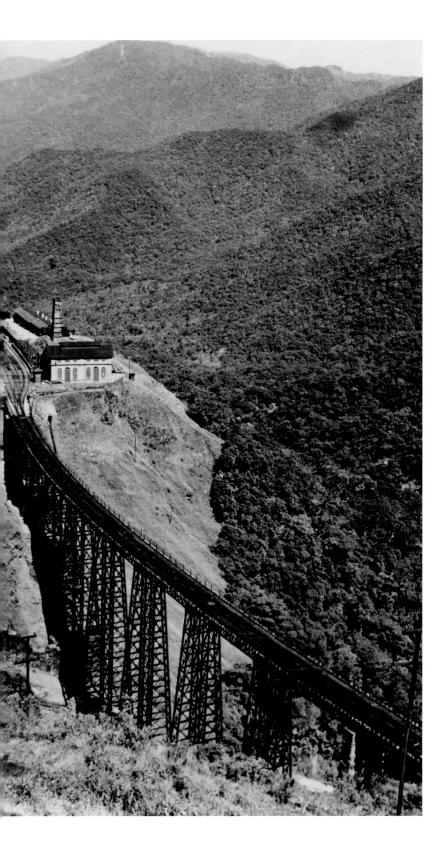

Coffee was the making of São Paulo. Founded by Jesuits in 1554, the city – such as it was – remained a frontier town for the best part of 300 years, a trading post for slave traders and chancers, *Bandeirantes*, on their way into and out of Brazil's interior. That was where the real treasure was buried: in the gold mines of Minas Gerais, Goiás and Mato Grosso. By the early nineteenth century a tide had turned: coffee was replacing sugar as the country's most significant export and São Paulo, as the gateway to the market, became the city where soon-to-be unimaginably rich planters settled, built homes and spent their money. In 1882, it was also where the Portuguese King's eldest son, Prince Pedro, declared Brazil an independent empire – and himself its first Emperor, for good measure.

As São Paulo's star rose, the rest of the world came calling. European migrants – preposterously rich and penniless alike – arrived to work, trade and make money. To get coffee beans into the city from elsewhere in Brazil and then out to a worldwide market with an apparently unquenchable thirst for the stuff, railroads were built. The line running from São Paulo down the steep mountainside of the Serra do Mar to the docks at Santos was a wonder of the age. The construction of the São Paulo Railway attracted designers, managers and engineers from across Europe, not least Great Britain. The cableway that dragged carriages up and down an incline previously climbed only by legions of baggage mules was mapped out by an Englishman, Daniel Fox, and funded by a consortium of London banks.

Among the new arrivals was a Scotsman, John Miller, who not only found work on the railway but also married into an established local family of landowners, the Rudges. John and his wife, Charlotte, had four children: Carlota and Adolph died in infancy, John Henry in his teens. Charles William survived and prospered, though. Born in São Paulo in 1874, he was schooled in Hampshire at Banister Court, where he played for and

São Paulo Railway, c.1930

against some of the great footballers of the Victorian era, gentlemen and amateurs all. Charlie captained his school, represented his county, got at least one game for the famous Corinthians and several more for St Mary's, a club which would later professionalise and become Southampton FC. Football is often described as a religion: well, Miller was a missionary for the game. His life's work would become Brazilian football's creation myth once he shipped back to the land of his birth.

But the story probably begins a few years previously, just weeks after the meeting in Fleet Street that changed English football so dramatically. The English community in São Paulo was small, tight-knit and convinced of its own very influential place in the world. And considered sport – cricket in particular – a perfect expression of the moral and physical qualities that had taken Britain to the top of the imperial tree. Today the Rua São Bento, in the heart of São Paulo, still harbours echoes of its nineteenth-century identity: banks and businesses line up alongside shops, bars and coffee houses. Work and play still share space in the shadows beneath the awnings. In one of those bars, on May 13 1888, a dozen men, including Charlie Miller's uncle Peter, met to discuss the fortunes of their cricket team. By the end of the evening, they had decided to found their adopted city's first sports and social club.

The São Paulo Athletic Club (SPAC) was soon established on premises a couple of miles away on Rua Visconde de Ouro Preto. Six years later, in 1894, Charlie – football-mad – turned up on the Santos dockside with boots, footballs and a copy of the Hampshire FA's laws of the game. His re-introduction to life in the country of his birth was helped by his joining SPAC at the first opportunity. In return, so the story goes, Charlie introduced Brazil to the very English game he'd learnt to love while he'd been away. Until Charlie Miller's arrival back in São Paulo, the Athletic Club had concentrated on playing traditional British sports – tennis, rugby,

Ouro Preto, Miras Gerais

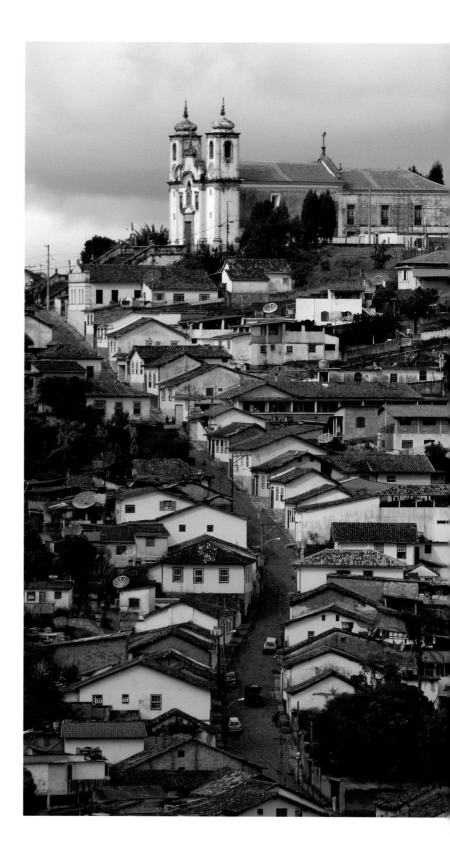

cricket – and serving British refreshments – steak and kidney pudding, Sunday roasts and afternoon tea – in comfortable and exclusively British surroundings.

Miller was happy to take to the crease or swing a racquet and did both very well. A personable and popular young man, he was also a man on a mission: desperate to introduce football to his distinguished new circle of friends. By all accounts, they needed some convincing. Charlie didn't get his way – or a proper game of football – for nearly a year. When he did, it was on a field in between two streets – Rua do Gasômetro and Rua Santa Rosa – on the Várzea do Carmo, flat land near Miller's birthplace in Bras, which was flooded on a regular basis during the nineteenth century by the nearby Rio Tamanduateí. However it was dry enough on April 14 1895 for 22 players to turn up for the first ever match played to Football Association rules in Brazil. A São Paulo Railway XI beat a São Paulo Gas Company XI 4–2. Charlie, unsurprisingly, was the star of the show and scored twice for the SPR team. More to the point, he'd made his first converts. Here was the game that would soon inspire and captivate the newly independent nation that lay outside the polite and exclusive little world encircled by the São Paulo Athletic Club's walls.

★ ★ ★

On the same day in May 1888 British sportsmen were busy dreaming up their Athletic Club in São Paulo, altogether more immediately significant matters were afoot some 230 miles north in Rio de Janeiro. Sitting at a Chippendale desk in a parlour of the Paço Imperial – the Imperial Palace – the Princess Regent, Isabel, slowly and deliberately added her signature to the *Lei Áurea*. Already ratified by her parliament and senate, the Golden Law brought a definitive end to over 300 years of slavery in Brazil. Within 18 months, indeed, the last vestiges of the colonial era would be shaken off, too:

Santos c.1930

Isabel and her husband were packed off home to Europe, deposed by a military coup establishing Brazil as a republic for the first time.

Brazil was the last country in the western world to abolish slavery. African slaves had been key to the exploitation of the vast country's natural resources, not least its countless acres of sugar plantations. In total, some four million slaves were shipped from Africa, about 40 per cent of the entire total to reach the Americas. Abolition was a slow process that began in the early nineteenth century. First, the children of slaves were born free, then all slaves over 60 were emancipated. In 1850, nearly half the inhabitants of the country had been slaves. By the time Princess Isabel signed on the dotted line, that figure had shrunk to 15 per cent of the population.

One of the first – and most obvious – results of Abolition was a flood of cheap labour to Brazil from all over Europe and beyond. The slave market had been replaced by a labour market. Many of the migrants were as desperate as they were capable: not slaves, exactly, but willing to work for next to nothing once they arrived. Others were experienced craftsmen, hoping to prosper in pastures new. Thomas Donahue had followed his father into the textile industry in Busby, a mill town just outside Glasgow. There he'd made his mark by setting up and captaining the factory's first ever works football team. But times were hard, even for a skilled worker like Donahue, and in May 1893, he set sail for Brazil, where he hoped his talents would be in demand and his ambitions might be realised.

Donahue pitched up in the dusty western suburbs of Rio de Janeiro. Bangu, at the time, amounted to not much more than a village: a single street and a single factory belonging to a textile company, the Companhia Progresso Industrial do Brasil. The *Fábrica Bangu* took Donahue on as a master dyer; he'd found work and a new home. And he soon made friends among Bangu's tight-knit expatriate community. What was missing, though, was his game of football at the weekend. The following year, Donahue returned to Britain to collect his wife and young family and bring them to the country where they would spend the rest of their lives. While in Glasgow, he made sure to purchase boots, a pump and a ball.

Donahue arrived back in Bangu ready to take on all comers and, on a Sunday afternoon in April 1894, he organised a six-a-side game between his fellow factory workers on a field next to the Fábrica Bangu. That field has long since been swallowed up in the sprawl of modern-day Rio de Janeiro but in the local museum – the grandly-named Gremio Literário José Mauro de Vasconcelos – replicas of Donahue's boots and that first football take pride of place. When it comes to football, *Banguenses* claim their own hero, their own founding father for the game.

★ ★ ★

In line with the legend, Charles Miller is traditionally identified as the man who introduced football to Brazil. Perhaps Thomas Donahue deserves that distinction, though: his game outside the factory in Bangu happened several months before São Paulo Railway took on the Gas Company down in São Paulo, after all. It's an argument that still matters given how important the game has become to an entire country's identity over the course of the following century. The story that, with all its twists and turns, has brought us to the summer of Brazil 2014 needs somewhere to push off from, too. What's certain is that the conflicting claims of a couple of football-mad Brits from the Victorian era give us a first clue as to what is unique about the game in Brazil, the country that took football to its heart like no other during the twentieth century.

The game Charlie Miller organised on the Várzea do Carmo in 1895 was basically the same as the one he'd played with such success at Banister Court, the same

São Paulo c.1920

Copacabana c.1910

game played at the Estádio do Maracanã and across
Brazil at the World Cup in 2014. It was an 11-a-side
football match conducted in accordance with the
Hampshire FA's copy of the agreed rules which Miller
had brought to São Paulo, along with his boots and his
ball: Association Football according to the laws of the
Football Association. In that sense, Charles William
Miller introduced football to Brazil but Thomas Donahue
should perhaps be remembered as the man who first
introduced a Brazilian spirit to the game.

The game Thomas put together across the road from
his factory was a kick-about: small-sided, informal
and without a referee. The literal translation of the
Portuguese word *pelada* is 'naked'. In Brazil, specifically,
pelada describes the kind of game first enjoyed by those
textile workers in April 1894: pick-up football, played
by all ages, all classes and all races. It's the kind of game
you'll still see played everywhere across the country
today: on squares of concrete in the heart of São Paulo,
in the sand on Rio's Copacabana Beach, across dusty
fields in Pernambuco, along shallow riverbeds outside
Manaus. Informal, untutored, unstoppable: *pelada* is
the heartbeat of football in Brazil, where skills and a
competitive spirit are honed before being harnessed to
the 11-a-side discipline of organised soccer.

There was something else, too – something just as
fundamental – which set Bangu's place in early Brazilian
football history apart. Down in wealthy and exclusive
São Paulo, the organised game was restricted to a
narrow – and very privileged – little band of devotees:
the British kept football pretty much to themselves until
other European communities and elite Brazilian families
decided to get involved. The city was the stage for the
first-ever Brazilian football tournament in 1902, between
teams drawn from those upper echelons of *Paulista*
society: the Associação Atlética Mackenzie College, the
Sport Club Germania, Athletico Paulistano, Sport Club

Internacional and the inaugural *Campeonato Paulista* winners, the São Paulo Athletic Club, for whom Charles Miller finished the season as top scorer.

By the start of the new century, the great and the good of Rio de Janeiro had joined in the fun: Fluminense, the city's first football club, was established by Oscar Cox, an aristocrat born in Brazil to wealthy English parents, who picked up his taste for the game while a student in Switzerland. In 1901, Cox took a team down to São Paulo to twice draw with Charles Miller's SPAC. Cox then established Fluminense FC the following year in the leafy and exclusive Rio suburb of Laranjeiras. Fluminense's first competitive game was an 8–0 thrashing of the now-defunct Rio FC. By 1904, rival clubs in the city, in the shape of America and Botafogo, had been founded to take on Fluminense and Bangu. The aristocrats from Laranjeiras won Rio's first *Campeonato Carioca* in 1906. In those early days, the class and race barrier at Fluminense was absolute. It wasn't until 1914 that a mixed-race player appeared for the team and, even then, the hapless Carlos Alberto smothered his face in white powder to disguise the colour of his skin. Hence one of Fluminense's traditional nicknames: the *Pó de Arroz*, the Rice Powder.

Out in the countryside, at the Fábrica Bangu, Thomas Donahue's *peladas* were altogether less formal affairs. While high society gathered to watch the sons of the wealthy play 11-a-side football in comfortable surroundings on manicured lawns in downtown Rio, the games out in the far-flung western suburb of Bangu reflected the culture of factory life. If you could play – be you white, black or anything in between – there was a place waiting on the football pitch. It's no accident – of history or geography – that the club established in 1904 by Donahue and his colleague Andrew Procter, Bangu Atlético Clube, became the first in Brazil to include a black player, Francisco Carregal, when they beat

Fluminense in a friendly in 1905. The team was a mix of Europeans – Brits, Italians, Portuguese – and a single Brazilian, all of whom worked alongside one another at the Fábrica Bangu. Textile weaver Francisco Carregal was, like his club's founder, a genuine pioneer. Brazilian football may or may not have been born in Bangu. What's certain is that Francisco was the first to set it free.

★ ★ ★

Before Brazil could set out on the path that would see the country conquer world football, football had to conquer Brazil. The game had to reach out across the country and then outgrow its European and upper-class traditions. By the dawn of the twentieth century, the seeds had been sown: doubtless, scratch games preceded organised football in factories and on docksides up and down Brazil before Charles Miller and Thomas Donahue wrote their names into the history books. Wherever Europeans pitched up, so too did their favourite games. Compared to cricket, rowing and rugby, though, football stood apart in terms of popular appeal. And word spread fast once the pioneers in São Paulo and Rio had broken new ground.

Down in Rio Grande do Sul, the 'gaúcho' state bordering Uruguay, a team was established in 1900 by Portuguese, Spanish, German and Italian settlers. SC Rio Grande, indeed, are the oldest club still active in Brazilian football, albeit they now compete in the second division of the local state league, the *Campeonato Gaúcho*, and play their games in a stadium which can hold only 5,000 fans. In the North East, in the state of Bahia, football took hold around the city of Salvador, too. The state championship, the *Campeonato Baiano*, was established a year before its Rio equivalent, in 1905. Local rivalries were – and, to a great extent, still are – the rivalries that count. The sheer size of Brazil – and the cost and difficulty of travel – meant that, for the next 50 years, football focused on state championships and cup competitions between clubs from neighbouring states.

Brazilian football in the early years of the twentieth century was exclusively amateur. Indeed, the game's amateur status helped keep it exclusive. Players were white and wealthy or, at least, sons of the wealthy. The crowds who watched were the same. Football matches were occasions for high society to mix and mingle: dressed to the nines, polite applause interspersed with the occasional 'Hurrah!' This was the kind of select and gracious company in which business could be brokered and marriages were made. AC Bangu's star

man, Francisco Carregal, was the exception rather than the rule: a black face on the pitch was as rare a sight as one in the crowd. Unlike the other sports imported from Europe, though, football couldn't be contained for long. Everything changed; and did so in the course of one man's spectacular career.

Arthur Friedenreich was born on July 18 1892 in São Paulo. His father, Oscar, was German; a merchant who had emigrated to Brazil from Hamburg. His mother, Mathilde, was the daughter of freed African slaves who had worked as a washerwoman before she married. Arthur was an extraordinary-looking boy: his pale brown skin and black, wavy hair offset by piercing green eyes. His love of football was almost certainly inherited from his father, who was involved with one of São Paulo's first clubs, SC Germania. However his style of play was anything but European: every account makes reference to his skill, his pace and his trickery on the ball. Those qualities, matched by a ferociously competitive spirit, were to define the age and spark his country's love affair with its very own brand of football: *futebol*.

Another Scot – and, like his compatriot Thomas Donahue, another textile worker – Archie McLean had arrived in São Paulo in 1913 and immediately joined an ex-pat football club, the Scottish Wanderers. McLean was a bright enough talent in his own right to be selected to play for *Paulista* representative teams in fixtures against sides from Rio. It was the style of play developed by the Wanderers that left the more lasting impression, though. Used to the dribbling, hacking and long balls of the English game, locals were mesmerised by the Scots' use of a short passing game. Archie's Brazilian peers christened the style *tabelinha*, 'the little map': here was a new way to navigate a route from one end of a football pitch to the other. A philosophy which local players and fans took to their hearts, it was a style of play, too, which might have been designed to get the best out of a slim, quicksilver striker like young Arthur Friedenreich.

★ ★ ★

Most black and mixed-race Brazilians, at the dawn of a new century, were too poor to even dream of being involved with organised football. Those with the wherewithal weren't welcome anyway, Brazil's early clubs being almost exclusively the preserve of white players. However, his father's membership of SC Germania and Arthur's European features allowed him to push back the barriers. Here was a boy of evidently prodigious ability already well known to the German émigré members at his father's club. Arthur played his first game for SC Germania aged 17 and found himself instantly in demand, a striker for hire in an amateur age. Then as now, every team was looking for a reliable goalscorer. In 1912, playing for AA Mackenzie College, Friedenreich was *Pé de Ouro* – the Golden Boot – with 16 goals in the *Campeonato Paulista*. He repeated that feat two years later in the colours of CA Ypiranga.

Although football remained, ostensibly, an amateur pastime for the privileged and wealthy, Arthur's early career would suggest a star striker could still make the game worth his professional while. Doubtless the other players at the succession of clubs he turned out for around São Paulo made sure of that: Arthur Friedenreich was, almost certainly, Brazilian football's first 'Ringer'. The *Paulista* clubs he played for, though, were those perceived to be at the lower end of the city's social scale and the question of Arthur's ethnicity remained an issue, if not for his team-mates then for his opponents. And, perhaps, for the man himself, too. Arthur was invariably the last player to take the field: his pre-match preparations included diligent application of hot towels and a pomade – *gomalina* – to straighten out the curls in his hair. In contemporary reports, his skin-colour was referred to as 'tanned' rather than 'black' or 'mulatto'. Nevertheless, regardless of those obstacles, Friedenrich, the toast of São Paulo, was soon to become a key member of Brazil's earliest national teams.

★ ★ ★

By 1910, São Paulo and Rio had become prospective destinations for touring European teams, even though the Atlantic crossing took the best part of three weeks. In that year, the gentlemen of London's Corinthians club docked in Rio to play four games against local clubs, winning them all comfortably. They then travelled south to São Paulo, where they beat Paulistano 5–0 and then, despite a goal from Charlie Miller for the home team, put eight past SPAC. Those games were to have a lasting impact on Brazilian football. Excluded from top-flight football by their working-class origins, five tradesmen employed by the São Paulo railway – two wall-painters, a shoemaker, a driver and a general labourer – saw enough of the English visitors to be sufficiently inspired to start their own club, naming it Sport Club Corinthians Paulista in their honour. The pledge was to create a club 'of the people, by the people and for the people'. Corinthians, one of Brazil's best-supported and most successful clubs, proved as good as the founders' word: they remain *Time do Povo*, the 'Team of the People', to this day.

In 1914, Exeter City – a professional club playing in England's Southern League – undertook a seemingly endless South American tour which brought them, eventually, to Rio de Janeiro. As their boat tied up, the party were amazed, apparently, to witness a kick-about in progress on the dockside. A travelling newspaperman reported the shocking news: the children involved were 'all niggers, as black as your hat, and most of them playing in bare feet.' Proof indeed, if such were needed, that football had quickly put down roots in Brazil. After a couple of wins against club sides, the first official fixture to be contested by a Brazilian national team saw Exeter take on an XI selected from the best club players in Rio and São Paulo. Ten thousand fans gathered at Fluminense's Estádio das Laranjeiras to watch Arthur Friedenreich lose two teeth in a clash with the English keeper before setting up the second goal in a 2–0 win for 'Brazil'.

The earliest organised football in South America was played in Argentina and the Argentine Football

Association was founded in 1893. International competition was only a matter of time: a tournament involving Uruguay and Chile took place in Buenos Aires in 1910. In 1916, a South American Championship – later and still known as the *Copa América* – included Brazil for the first time. In 1919, Arthur Friedenreich scored the only goal – in extra time added on to extra time – to beat defending champions Uruguay in the final. Brazil were hosts and 20,000 fans crowded into the Estádio das Laranjeiras in Rio to witness history being made. Already a hero at home, Friedenreich – 'El Tigre' and 'South America's sweetheart' – had announced his arrival on the international stage: to mark this achievement, his

Pacaembu Stadium, São Paulo

boots were paraded around the streets of Rio before being put on display in a prominent jeweller's shop window.

The decade that followed would see Brazilian football enter something recognisable as the modern era. The 1920s began, though, with a row that proved to be a watershed moment for the game. The 1921 edition of the *Copa América* was played in Argentina. The hosts announced only white players would be welcome to participate, a ruling designed, in all probability, to inconvenience Uruguay, where black players were already involved in the professional game. Since his SC Germania debut, Friedenreich had been passed off as white in the world of Brazilian football but this was an argument which thrust the country's star player into the

world of international politics. To his shame, Brazil's president, Epitácio Lindolfo da Silva Pessoa, concerned a football tournament might be about to turn into a diplomatic incident, decreed no black or mulatto players would join the *Seleção Brasileira*. The controversy sparked by Friedenreich's omission from the team was to change football in his homeland forever.

By the time he was excluded from the 1921 *Copa América* team, Friedenreich had joined the most powerful club side of the day, Paulistano, serial winners of the *Campeonato Paulista*. In both São Paulo and Rio de Janeiro, the upper echelons of the domestic game continued to exclude the vast majority of Brazil's black and mixed-race population – players and fans alike – despite the fact that the game had clearly captured the imagination of an entire nation. Friedenreich's exploits, representing Brazil in 1919, had been celebrated passionately and by every Brazilian, after all. But the tide was about to turn: after the affair of the *Copa América* in Argentina, it had to. AC Bangu had long since opened its doors to non-white players but was essentially a works team, without the wealth, power or influence wielded by the elite clubs in Rio such as Fluminense, Flamengo, Botafogo and America. Instead, a brand new club emerged whose success would liberate Brazilian football and allow the *Seleção's* famous future to unfold.

★ ★ ★

After a meeting at their local amateur dramatics society headquarters, CR Vasco da Gama was established by émigré Portuguese in 1898. In 1904, this new *Club de Regatas* – like several Brazilian clubs, Vasco began life as a rowing club – broke with all convention and elected the first non-white President in the history of Brazilian sport, the popular and well-connected Cândido José de Araújo. In 1913, the visit of a touring football team from Lisbon led to an upsurge in interest in the game among Rio's Portuguese community. Several new clubs were formed and Vasco merged with one of these – Luzitânia

SC – to begin competition in the third tier of the city's metropolitan leagues in 1916. It took the new club just six years to find their way into Rio's top division and, in 1923, Vasco won their first *Campeonato Carioca*. They did so by overturning some of Brazilian football's most firmly established traditions.

While Vasco's rivals, mostly based in the southern suburbs of Rio, drew both players and supporters from among an upper-class and affluent elite, the new club opened its doors to footballers and fans from every community living in the growing sprawl of the city's northern suburbs. From the outset, black and mixed-race Brazilians lined up alongside whites in Vasco colours. It was only when the new club broke the Rio mould by winning the league that the likes of Fluminense and Botafogo realised what was going on. Or, at least, began to make a fuss. And there was more: Vasco were flouting the spirit of Rio's amateur football tradition in finding work for talented players from working-class backgrounds who might otherwise not have been able to afford to play regular games.

The Rio establishment reacted with as much collective bluster as they could. That amounted, first, to withdrawing from the league Vasco had just won and, then, to setting up a new league from which Vasco were barred. The reasons given for the champions' exclusion were plentiful: they had no stadium and they were paying players, for starters. The real issue, though, was made clear when Rio's elite suggested there was a way back for Vasco if the club was prepared to release a dozen named players, all of them poor and either black or mixed-race. Plainly, the affront wasn't simply to Rio's barely credible amateur traditions. Vasco da Gama responded to the offer by way of an open letter, the *Resposta Histórica*: a polite but absolute refusal to comply. In 1925, Vasco were re-admitted to the league anyway – a tacit recognition that football in Brazil had outgrown

Rio de Janeiro c.1925

its elitist, amateur roots – and two years later, the club opened its own stadium, Estádio São Januário, then the biggest in all of South America. The game in Brazil, on and off the pitch, has never looked back.

★ ★ ★

His credibility only bolstered by events behind the scenes in Rio, Arthur Friedenreich had, by the mid-1920s, become a football superstar, arguably the world's first. His club, Paulistano, were carrying all before them in Brazil and, in 1925, set off on a ten-match tour of Europe. A squad of 20 included reinforcements drafted in from Santos, Ypiranga and Flamengo but Friedenreich was the main attraction, scoring a hat-trick in Paulistano's opening game – a 7–1 victory – against a French XI in Paris. The Brazilian tourists were fêted as *Les Rois du Foot* – 'Kings of Football' – by the French press and eight wins in their next nine games followed, with Friedenreich scoring nine further goals. The players returned to São Paulo as all-conquering heroes, outstanding ambassadors for Brazilian football. Paulistano, however, heirs to the Brazilian game's aristocratic roots, were already running out of track; less than five years later the rise of professionalism would see the club fold.

Vasco's fight with Rio's elite clubs had cleared the way for black and mixed-race players to take their place in teams on merit. The same battle, eventually, led to players being paid – above board – to play for their clubs. Paulistano stuck to their traditions, choosing to join a local amateur league in São Paulo rather than join their peers in rising to the challenge of football as a professional game. Boot money and paid appearances in exhibition games became a thing of the past; 30 years of hypocrisy were swept away by a nationwide and ravenous appetite for exploiting the game's obvious commercial potential.

Early on in his celebrated and extraordinary career, Arthur Friedenreich had been a victim of the same racist snubs as millions of his compatriots. Straightened hair and his light complexion – combined with a unique talent – were enough to get him onto a football pitch in mixed company. Just 5'8" tall and weighing not much more than eight stone, he took his fair share of kicks during games: hacking was the English way, after all, and 'the green-eyed mulatto' wasn't really one of us anyway, was he? It's also been said that he found himself barred by elite São Paulo's often unwritten rules and regulations from socialising and celebrating with team-mates after victories in the early part of his career.

As the times changed, so Friedenreich's fortunes changed with them. He wasn't a pioneer in the sense of having taken up the battle; his strength – and credibility – lay in an unquestioned ability and a remarkable longevity. Arthur Friedenreich didn't change football, exactly; instead, he was the perfectly focused lens through which his peers watched the sport they loved transform itself. By the mid-1920s the best player in Brazil was probably the best player in the world: a phenomenal goalscorer who would have succeeded in any era and under any circumstance, not least as the inventor of the curling, long-range free-kick. Arthur was the inspiration for a new way of playing the game, as described by the São Paulo magazine, *Sport*, in 1919:

> Unlike the British style, with the ball being brought forward by all the forwards together up to the opposition's goal, shots were taken from any distance and the forwards moving in a line wasn't necessary. Two or three players would break away with the ball, their devastating speed catching the opposing defence off guard.

As well as playing for a succession of prominent clubs, Friedenreich quickly and spectacularly took to the trappings of fame which football afforded him. He became a regular visitor – and attraction – at nightclubs around São Paulo and, during two separate spells with Flamengo, in Rio as well. He was said to own 120 Irish linen suits, drank only the best French brandy and expensive local beers, and smoked handmade,

sandalwood-scented cigarettes. Friedenreich left struggling Paulistano behind and joined São Paulo FC, founded in 1930 and the city's first fully professional team. It may well have been his abandoning of elite, 'amateur' football that led to him being left out of Brazil's squad for the first ever World Cup in 1930. It may have been that a row between bureaucrats led to the team being picked entirely from among Rio-based players. Or perhaps, at 38, age and injuries were beginning to take their toll on Brazilian football's most celebrated player.

Whatever the reason for him staying at home, the tournament, hosted and won by Uruguay, was the poorer for Friedenreich's absence. And Brazil, unsurprisingly, were the weaker without their star striker, too: despite being seeded, they went out at the group stage. Arthur played just once more for his country, against France immediately after 1930's summer disappointment. Four years later, he was too old to be considered for the 1934 tournament in Italy. By then, anyway, Brazilian football had a new star on the rise in the shape of the 'Black Diamond', Leônidas da Silva. Friedenreich's club career continued long enough for him to reap in full the rewards of the struggles he'd been through, though. He retired in 1935, aged 43, 26 years after his first game for SC Germania.

The youngster who'd tried to hide his black Brazilian roots in order to take part in the rough and tumble of the white man's amateur game had become his country's first professional star, his mixed-race background ensuring he was a hero an entire nation could rally behind. Football in Brazil had begun to realise its destiny as the people's game, inspired by a passion that celebrated difference and crossed every social boundary. And, in doing so, the game brought to South America by the British had itself been transformed, discovering a style all its own.

Arthur Friedenreich's career began with Association Football, it finished with him playing the game Brazilians now called *futebol*.

We Teach Ourselves

There are two towns very close to one another: Americana and Santa Bárbara. Each has a football team: Rio Branco in Americana and União Barbarense in Santa Bárbara. The two clubs are kind of mixed up together and so I was involved with Barbarense when I was young. But the first teaching I had for football wasn't at a club. On the little pitches out in the park near where I lived, there was a soccer school: an *escolinha*. And anywhere around Americana where there was a school going on, I'd go and join in. Run by the municipality, you didn't have to pay – boys like me were picked out from the *escolinhas* to go and play at the football club.

They tried to help us with a little coaching at the *escolinha* but, you know, I was out in the park playing all day, every day, anyway! Already I'd learnt how to play from trial and error, playing on my own, either in games on the pitch in the park or in the hall where we played *futebol de salão*, 'futsal'. When you're little, there are no tactics, there's no idea of teamwork – everybody chases after the ball, wherever it goes. Whoever can dribble the ball and score just does it! And that's what I learnt to do.

I used to play *futsal* all the time, right up until I turned professional at 16. I think Brazilian football has reached the level it has because of *futsal*. The pitch is smaller. The goals are smaller. You have to be faster in everything you do; particularly, you have to make quick decisions. If you're dribbling, you have to do it by controlling the ball in a much smaller space. If you're shooting, you must be much more accurate because the goal – the target – is smaller. There are skills you learn better playing *futebol de salão* and I loved the game. I still play now whenever I get the chance.

Fifty years ago, 100 years ago, there weren't the halls to play *futsal* in. But maybe, back then, kids learned the same sort of skills from playing in the street: close control, dribbling, playing in small areas. Everything that's beautiful in football is in *futebol de salão*, and that's why I like it so much. When you love the game, you'll play anywhere. If it was too busy on the pitch or in the hall near my house, I would just play on the street. The *futsal* hall reminds me a bit of playing in a garden or a backyard anyway; the area's smaller. Out in the street, of course, there could be 20 or 30 boys playing and so the pitch seems smaller then as well, everybody crowding round the ball. You still need those skills you need in *futsal*.

I think it's true for a lot of players in Brazil: we teach ourselves. I learnt football by playing it, in *futsal*, in the *escolinhas*, in the street and in the park. By the time I joined São Paulo, I had already developed my style of play. At the club, they just had to say to me: *Go here and then do what you already know. Or: Do this and then just do what you know*. It was learning the tactical side of the game. There's more coaching involved when you play at the back. Every boy grows up in Brazil wanting to be a midfield player or a forward so the good players will have been strikers when they were young; they have to learn later on how to defend.

4. THE RUBBER MAN

FOOTBALL AND POLITICS have always made uncomfortable but inevitable bedfellows. Not least in countries such as Brazil, where football is so intimately bound up with a sense of national identity. As if he didn't have enough to handle, as a mixed-race Brazilian during those early years of the game's development, Arthur Friedenreich understood and cared enough about what was happening in his country off the pitch to go to war over it. When he scored the winning goal for Brazil against Uruguay in the 1919 *Copa América* Final, Friedenreich had become something of a hero for an entire nation. In 1932 he took up arms in what was a short but bloody revolution – it was enough to make him a hero on an altogether different scale in the city and the state he called home.

1930 saw a bloodless coup d'état in Brazil. Getúlio Dornelles Vargas led a faction representing Minas Gerais, Paraíba and Rio Grande do Sul, states which resented São Paulo's dominance of the economic and political scene. Having lost the election – and with a little help from the military – he ousted the President, Washington Luís, and the President-elect, Júlio Prestes. After a decade and more of Brazil being controlled by vested interests such as the coffee barons of São Paulo, Vargas was determined to nationalise, centralise and industrialise the country. He remains perhaps the most important – and most controversial – figure in twentieth-century Brazilian history. Vargas wielded power until 1954 when, isolated politically and threatened by a military coup, he committed suicide. By then Brazil – and the country's great passion, football – had changed beyond all recognition.

In the early 1930s, though, and confronted by the new – and unelected – President's assumption of dictatorial powers, the state of São Paulo rose up in protest. So too did its most famous footballer. Not only did Arthur Friedenreich sell his precious medals and memorabilia to raise money for the *Paulista* rebels, he also undertook radio broadcasts urging fans and players alike to join the armed struggle. SC Corinthians put their stadium and offices at the fighters' disposal and that was where Friedenreich joined up in July 1932. By August 1, he was on the front line, facing down the Federal Army and State Police at Eleutério, a village on the border with Minas Gerais. The battle lasted 25 days and only ended when Vargas called in the Air Force; it had been another extraordinary chapter in the life of an extraordinary man.

The *Paulista* rebels lost their war but prospered in peacetime. Vargas knew how vital to Brazil's economy São Paulo was and ceded a great deal of autonomy to the state to avoid the possibility of a *Revolução*

Rio de Janeiro

Constitucionalista ever happening again. This was a huge country, after all, trying to find its feet in a modern era, with the potential for conflict seemingly everywhere. The yawning gap between rich and poor was only the most obvious of forces that might conspire to pull the republic apart. There was a divide, too, between the wealthy South and the impoverished North. There was the complex web of ethnic backgrounds – European, mixed-race and Afro-Brazilian – to somehow knit together. Then, in a Brazil built on agricultural wealth, there were the interests of established landowners to be reconciled with the demands of a new generation of modernising industrialists who saw a very different way forward to a Brazil of the future. And there were also the conservative but intermittently rebellious demands of the military to be met.

Football will only ever reflect the society of which it is part. Brazilian football in the early 1930s was no different: fragmented, factionalised and still finding its way. The integration of black and mixed-race players such as Arthur Friedenreich was already underway. So too was the game's accessibility to ordinary people outside the narrow urban elite who had introduced football to Brazil. For *futebol* – the people's game – to take advantage of the passion for it that was evident everywhere, clubs and players realised professionalisation was the next great leap forward to be made. Football in São Paulo had been set against itself by the conflict between amateur traditionalists and those in the vanguard of professionalism. Some of the finest moments in Friedenreich's career were in the red and white of Paulistano. The club dug its heels in over paying players, though, and in 1930 Friedenreich was among those who joined the new – and professional – São Paulo FC. Four years later, the same controversy put paid to whatever hopes the *Seleção* might have harboured when they set sail for Italy and the 1934 World Cup.

★ ★ ★

Hypocrisy, like football, knows no geographic boundaries. In 1934, the CBD – the *Confederação Brasileira de Desportos* – found themselves battling the rising tide of professionalism, a development led by the leading clubs in São Paulo and Rio. They were also the body responsible for sending a team to compete in Italy at the World Cup. Brazil had qualified automatically, thanks to withdrawals by several other South American countries. This left the CBD in a fix: Botafogo, in Rio, were the only significant club still committed to the old amateur regime. As a result, nine of their players were selected for duty with the *Seleção*. To flesh out the squad, the CBD swallowed its pride – and, presumably, its principles too – and went cap-in-hand to several leading professional players with huge cash offers, should they agree to board ship for Europe. In a messy, unpopular and last minute compromise, Brazil took a squad of just 17 players. Little wonder, once they reached Italy, the team barely had time to unpack their boots before they were on their way home again.

The trip, aboard an Italian cruise ship, the SS *Conte Biancamano*, took the best part of two weeks. Many of the players had never sailed before and so seasickness was a common complaint and the World Cup party lacked either the personnel or the on-board facilities to ensure they reached Italy in anything like a fit state for top-level international football. They even stopped in Barcelona en route to pick up the Spanish squad who would eventually prove their undoing. The *Seleção* docked in Genoa on Friday, May 25. Two days later, they and Spain ran out at the Stadio Luigi Ferraris for their First Round game. The 1934 tournament had dispensed with Group Stages in favour of a knock-out format from the off, which meant Brazil's tournament was fated to be over almost before it began.

Spanish striker José Iraragorri opened the scoring from the penalty spot and then, minutes later, added a second from open play. With just half an hour on the clock, Isidro Lángara added a third. Brazil roused

themselves after half-time. Leônidas da Silva, warming up for glory in 1938, impressed throughout, scoring and having another goal-bound shot punched away by a Spanish defender out of sight of the referee. Brazil did win a penalty later on, though. Waldemar de Brito is best remembered now as the man who discovered Pelé but, against Spain on May 27 1934, he became the first man to miss from the spot at a World Cup. The *Seleção* climbed aboard the *Biancamano* and slunk home. While at sea, Italy fulfilled the destiny – *Vincere o Morire*, 'Win or Perish' – outlined for them by Benito Mussolini, beating Czechoslovakia in the final.

Luigi Ferraris Stadium, Genoa, 1934

One remarkable Brazilian, it should be said, finished the 1934 World Cup with a winner's medal. Amphilóquio Guarisi Marques was born in São Paulo, to Italian parents, in 1905. Known more manageably as 'Filó', he played up front alongside Arthur Friedenreich for Paulistano, scoring in the seven-goal rout of a France XI on the club's European tour of 1925 and making his debut for Brazil against Paraguay the same year. Denied a place in the *Seleção* for the 1930 World Cup by the same bureaucratic wrangling that kept Friedenreich on the sidelines, Filó was signed by the Italian club Lazio in 1931. He joined a clutch of *Oriundi* – Italian-Brazilians – in Rome as a handsomely paid pro. Dubbed 'Brasilazio' by Italian fans, the squad already included two brothers and a cousin

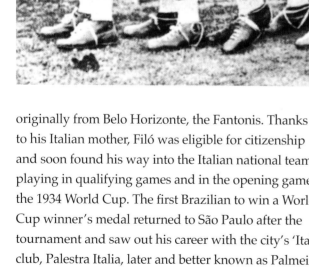

originally from Belo Horizonte, the Fantonis. Thanks to his Italian mother, Filó was eligible for citizenship and soon found his way into the Italian national team, playing in qualifying games and in the opening game of the 1934 World Cup. The first Brazilian to win a World Cup winner's medal returned to São Paulo after the tournament and saw out his career with the city's 'Italian' club, Palestra Italia, later and better known as Palmeiras.

★ ★ ★

Luigi Ferraris Stadium, Genoa 1934

Under the terms of Brazil's constitution, Getúlio Vargas should have been unable to run in the presidential elections of 1938. Here was a man, like the autocrats worldwide who were his contemporaries, who had got used to power and was in no mood to relinquish it, though. A communist plot was invented, dissent from all quarters suppressed and Vargas declared martial law, which was then established for the long term as the *Estado Novo*, the 'New State'. Brazil was now, effectively, a dictatorship and Vargas proved adept as a populist and propagandist. He brought the liberal elite and

OSCAR'S BRAZIL

Brazil's economy to heel, nationalising and centralising as he went. At the same time, he carved out an identity as a man of the people, *O Pai dos Pobres*, the 'Father of the Poor'.

Though he never committed to the Axis cause before or during World War II, Vargas – like Mussolini – was quick to recognise football's effectiveness as a political tool. In the best totalitarian tradition, he regularly used stadiums as arenas for public speaking; in São Paulo, he made sure he was a highly visible presence at the opening of the magnificent new Estádio do Pacaembu; in Rio, his links with Fluminense were so strong that he was named an honorary president of the club. Vargas had taken note of *Il Duce*'s exploitation of the World Cup for propaganda purposes in 1934. The 1938 tournament was held in France, much to the disgust of the South American countries who had expected to take a turn after Italy hosted the previous tournament on Europe's behalf. The likes of Argentina and Uruguay withdrew. Brazil, however, were ready to make the trip and clearly had the President's backing: Vargas' daughter, Alzira, accompanied Brazil's official party when they set sail from Rio at the beginning of May.

1938 is remembered as the tournament that marked Brazil's arrival as a serious force in international football. It was no coincidence that it was also the first World Cup for which the *Seleção* prepared properly. The issues that had previously undermined the team – the inclusion of black and mixed-race players, the balance of power between the leagues of Rio and São Paulo and the amateur status of the old CBD – were in the past. Sport, like everything else in Brazilian life, was controlled and managed from the centre by the Vargas regime. The players gathered in early May to train and integrate as a squad at a facility set aside for them in the spa town of Caxambu in Minas Gerais. Although the boat trip to Europe was still a two-week haul, this time around Brazil arrived with 20 days in which to recover before their first game of the tournament.

LEONIDAS

O maior artilheiro do Brasil
(Copa do Mundo — 1938)

Homenagem do Lab. Leão do Norte — Bahia

Most importantly, the 1934 team included the very best players available to the coach, Adhemar Pimenta: meaning, above all, *O Diamante Negro*: Leônidas.

Leônidas, the man who picked up the baton passed on by Arthur Friedenreich, is one of a handful of players who can be said to have changed the history of world football. Born into a lower middle class, mixed-race family in São Cristóvão, a traditional neighbourhood in the north of the capital, his father kept a bar near the local football ground and, so the story goes, dreamt of his son outgrowing his roots and pursuing a career in medicine or the law. Instead, Leônidas was among a first generation of Brazilian players who learnt their football in the street, chasing a bundle of socks or anything else that would pass muster as a ball, in endless barefoot *peladas*. He joined the junior ranks at his local team, São Cristóvão, as a 16-year old in 1929. Two years later, he moved on to the club where he made his name, Bonsucesso. By the end of his first season there, Leônidas was ready to rise to the most perfect and dramatic of footballing occasions.

During the 1920s and 30s, the Brazilian inter-state championships were as close as the country came to a national club competition. Invariably the Final was dominated by representative teams from Rio and São Paulo. As usual, 1931 pitched *Os Paulistas* up against *Os Cariocas*. The Rio XI, though, were without the services of injured star striker Nilo, of Botafogo, who had been in the Brazil team at the World Cup in Uruguay the previous summer. The São Paulo XI were led by Arthur Friedenreich and were firm favourites but they were undone by Nilo's last-minute replacement, an 18-year-old forward by the name of Leônidas da Silva. The youngster only found out that he was in the team on the morning of the match, to be played in front of a capacity crowd at the Estádio São Januário. If the championship debutant was nervous or unprepared he didn't show it, scoring two second-half goals to settle the game. Among those seen congratulating Rio's hero at full-time was Arthur Friedenreich, the *Paulista* captain and the man Leônidas would succeed as Brazil's brightest-burning international star.

★ ★ ★

In the same year that Leônidas exploded onto the scene with his performance against Arthur Friedenreich's *Paulistas*, a new international cup competition was played for the first time. The rivalry between Brazil and Uruguay goes almost as far back as the history of the game in the two countries and remains as tense as it's ever been: these are neighbours, after all, and represent very different traditions of the game. The idea of turning the derby into a regular tournament had first been suggested back in 1916 but the Rio Branco Cup wasn't played for until 1931, when Brazil won 2–0 in Rio at the Estádio das Laranjeiras. The following year, the game moved south to Montevideo. Uruguay, as World Cup holders, were firm favourites to restore pride and the pecking order. The experts, though, had reckoned without the two new stars of the *Seleção*: a gifted and imposing defender named Domingos Antônio da Guia and Brazil's 19-year-old striker, whose athleticism matched his talent for improvisation: Leônidas.

After Brazil's shock 2–1 victory at the *Estadio Centenario*, the Uruguayan press described Domingos as 'El Divino Maestro' and the best defender in the whole of South America. The undoubted star of the show, however, was Leônidas. As well as scoring both goals for his country, he gave the world a first glimpse of the technique that would make his name: Leônidas didn't invent the bicycle kick but he became synonymous with it. His *bicicleta* was the trademark trick of a true innovator: *O Homem de Borracha*, the 'Rubber Man'. His talents were memorably described in Brian Glanville's obituary, published in the *Manchester Guardian* after Leônidas, suffering from Alzheimer's and diabetes, passed away in 2004 at the age of 90:

Fast as a greyhound, as agile as a cat, and not made of flesh and bones at all, but entirely of rubber. He was tireless in pursuit of the ball, fearless, and constantly on the move. He never conceded defeat. He shot from any angle and any position, and compensated for his small height with exceptionally supple, unbelievable contortions, and impossible acrobatics.

Meinau Stadium, Strasbourg 1938

The Uruguayans, who were a couple of years ahead of their neighbours in respect of the professionalisation of football, didn't need a second look. Domingos was snapped up by Nacional of Montevideo and won the Uruguayan league with them in 1933. Leônidas, meanwhile, signed for Nacional's city rivals, Peñarol, who would finish runners-up. While most of Brazil's leading players would have to wait to be rewarded for playing the game they – and the nation – loved, a clutch of pioneers headed off in search of fortunes to go with their fame. Domingos and Leônidas headed over the border to the Uruguayan capital. Another leading light, dubbed the *Maravilha Negra* – the 'Black Wonder' – after

catching the eye at the 1930 World Cup, midfielder Fausto dos Santos was spotted while on tour in Europe with Vasco and signed, first, for Barcelona and then, the following year, for Swiss club, Young Boys.

This was a new generation of players, from black and mixed-race backgrounds, for whom football was more than a sporting pastime: the game offered a professional career and financial security. In a Brazil struggling to come to terms with the mix of ethnicities and cultures inherited from the post-colonial era, football and footballers seemed unique in that they represented the entire nation. The *Seleção* was Brazil in all its complex glory, a role seized on and exploited by the nationalist presidency of Getúlio Vargas. That it should be Afro-Brazilians, like Domingos, Fausto and Leônidas, who were coveted by clubs across

the world was a source of both pleasure and pride for a community unrepresented and uncelebrated elsewhere in Brazilian society. To be a fan of the national team was to be a fan of a country finding a new and inclusive sense of its own identity. Brazil, so often described as 'the country of the future', seemed almost ready – on the football pitch, at least – to arrive.

★ ★ ★

Leônidas spent just one year in Uruguay before returning to Brazil, where he became the leading light of a golden era for football in Rio de Janeiro. He won the first title of his career, the new and professional *Liga Carioca de Futebol*, with Vasco da Gama, pioneers both in drawing players from across all ethnic and social backgrounds and in paying them salaries comparable to those on offer beyond Brazil's borders. It would be the striker's only season with the club, though: he had to resign as a professional in order to appear as an 'amateur' – albeit a very well-paid one in the event – at the 1934 World Cup. By the time he returned from Italy, having scored Brazil's only goal of the tournament, Leônidas was the most in-demand player in the country and signed for another of Rio's leading lights, Botafogo, just as they joined the ranks of the professional clubs. He picked up another winners' medal with O Glorioso – 'The Glorious' – in his first season and then repeated the trick after joining Domingos da Guia and Fausto dos Santos in a star-studded side at Flamengo.

By the time he got off the train in Strasbourg ahead of Brazil's first game at the 1938 World Cup, already Leônidas felt the weight of expectation on his shoulders. He was, after all, his country's most celebrated player, the iconic figure in a team glittering with talent. From the outset, *O Diamante Negro* showed himself ready to thrive under the pressure. Brazil's first round opponents were World Cup debutants Poland and the game was

Parc Lescure, Bordeaux 1938

one that has gone down in the tournament's history. In wet and windy conditions and in front of a crowd made up mostly of Polish supporters who lived and worked in France, Leônidas scored a hat-trick – his last, the winner, bare-footed after he lost a boot in the mud at the Stade de la Meinau – with further goals from Perácio, Romeu and then Perácio again. It was just enough: Brazil won 6–5 after extra time, the Polish centre forward Ernest Wilimowski scoring four goals but still managing to finish on the losing side.

For their next game, Brazil travelled 600 miles back across France to face Czechoslovakia in what became known as the Battle of Bordeaux. Leônidas gave them the lead before the game turned into a kicking match: the Czech star Nejedlý broke a leg, his team-mate Plánička broke an arm; both Perácio and Leônidas suffered injuries, too; and three players were sent off, Machados and Zezé of Brazil, and Ríha of Czechoslovakia. The scrap ended 1–1 after extra time. Two days later, the tie was re-staged, again in Bordeaux, the last-ever replay at a World Cup finals. This time around, the Parc Lescure was the setting for an altogether more peaceful affair. Although the Czechs scored first, Brazil played some of the best football of the entire tournament: Leônidas equalised before Roberto scored a winner on the hour. Europe's sportswriters were in awe of the *Seleção*, and their leading goalscorer in particular. Raymond Thourmagem declared in *Paris Match:*

> Whether he's on the ground or in the air, this rubber man has a diabolical gift for bringing the ball under control and unleashing thunderous shots when least expected. We saw Leônidas perform scissor kicks, taking crosses and striking the ball with his back to goal. When Leônidas scores, it all feels like a dream. You rub your eyes. Leônidas is black magic!

Stade Vélodrome, Marseille 1938

Sadly for Brazil, the team were about to sleepwalk their way to disappointment. Their semi-final against Italy was played just two days after the defeat of the Czechs. They had to travel again, too, this time to Marseilles. Why coach Adhemar Pimenta chose the starting XI he did is a question still without a definitive answer. Certainly some of his players were carrying injuries, Leônidas among them, but the real problem seems to have been an overweening confidence inspired by the quality of their performance in the replay in Bordeaux. Pimenta was alleged to have said he rested players against holders Italy in anticipation of Brazil's appearance in the Final. Leaving out the leading goalscorer – not just of the *Seleção* but the whole tournament – proved disastrous and Italy ran out comfortable winners, 2–1, at the Stade Vélodrome. Leônidas was back for the Third-Place Playoff against Sweden in Bordeaux, scoring twice in a dazzling second-half comeback to secure a 4–2 victory.

★ ★ ★

Too much travelling, not enough time between matches, mistakes in team selection, tactical naivety … the Brazilian players weren't short of explanations as to why they'd missed out on a genuine shot at glory in France. They had, however, been applauded by a European audience delighted by the technical skills and daring improvisation of their World Cup showing. Furthermore, 1938 was the first time the national team's games had been broadcast live on the radio across the country back at home. Leônidas – the Golden Boot winner and a scorer in every World Cup game he ever played in – returned to Brazil with his team-mates to be met by cheering crowds at every turn. The radio commentaries had done the trick. Getúlio Vargas wrote in his private diary: 'The game of football was everywhere. Brazil's defeat against Italy caused huge disappointment and public sadness, as if it were some sort of national disgrace.' Leônidas, meanwhile, remembered, 'When we passed through

Salvador, the crowd nearly overwhelmed me.' On arrival in Rio de Janeiro, the team inched through the city on a military bus guarded by officers from the Marine Corps, as thousands of fans spilled onto the streets, hoping to catch a glimpse of their heroes.

The real point of Brazil's World Cup experience in 1938, though, lay not in the excitement or the disappointment generated by the country's third-place finish, the pride taken in glorious victories or the anguish felt after the defeat against Italy. Something more – something far more significant – had happened while the players were in France. For the first time, a new medium – radio – had allowed a World Cup to be experienced simultaneously across the country, the whole population investing their hopes and fears in the fortunes of the Brazilian national team. Vargas may have felt the pain of the semi-final loss broadcast live from Marseilles but he knew, too, that football had done what he, as a dictator, dreamt of doing: the *Seleção* had united the whole country in a common cause. And, just as importantly, the team Brazilians had cheered on in bars, restaurants, halls and homes everywhere reflected the new and modern nation Vargas sought to build: this was a working man's team, players and fans alike drawn from across ethnic and social boundaries. The 1938 World Cup gave Brazil – the whole of Brazil – a sense of itself at last.

Leônidas was no fool and proved ready to trade on the new-found cult of celebrity accompanying a World Cup star's national profile. Lacta, one of Brazil's leading food manufacturers, renamed a chocolate bar in his honour. To this day the *Diamante Negro* – 'Black Diamond' – brand remains one of the country's most popular and, it must be said, saw Lacta reap greater rewards than the player who lent the bar his image and nickname ever did. Thanks in part to his unrivalled reputation, Leônidas would later work for 20 years as a radio and television commentator after he retired. Amid all the acclaim

Rio de Janeiro 1938

THE RUBBER MAN

after his return from France, however, Leônidas was quickly back to doing what he did best: scoring goals and winning titles with Flamengo, alongside the man who would eventually succeed him as Brazil's favourite footballing son: Zizinho, soon to emerge as the star of the next World Cup.

Fame proved to have its darker side, too. In 1941, a very public scandal broke. Leônidas was in dispute with Flamengo over a European tour commitment: he claimed he was injured; they knew that, without their biggest star, the proposed money-spinning matches in Europe would be a fiasco. Flamengo suspended his salary; the player took his club to court. Understandably, the row became big news across Brazil. Gossip columnists of the day claimed the club president, the formidable Gustavo Adolpho de Carvalho, had resorted to dirty tricks. It was alleged that Leônidas had forged a certificate of military exemption several years before and an apparently forged signature dating from 1935 was duly found. Instead of summoning Flamengo to court, Brazil's first footballing celebrity found himself in the dock. Leônidas was found guilty and sentenced to eight months in prison.

On his release, Leônidas turned his back on Flamengo and on Rio. Almost 30, he followed the money to São Paulo FC, where thousands turned out to witness his first training session. He made his debut for his new club in May 1942. Over 71,000 crowded into the Estádio do Pacaembu for a derby against Corinthians, the biggest gate in the stadium's history witnessing a 3–3 draw in which – for once – the main attraction failed to score. During the 1940s, though, Leônidas would make the same impact at São Paulo as he had at a succession of clubs in Rio and with the national team. For nearly a decade, the *Tricolor* were pretty much untouchable, winning the *Campeonato Paulista* five times in seven seasons before the great man decided to hang up his boots in 1949. Leônidas had, by then, transformed the fortunes of the last employers of his career. The São Paulo team he joined for a record transfer fee of 200

Contos de Réis (or about £40,000) were traditionally seen as also-rans behind the giants of *Paulista* football, Corinthians and Palmeiras. By the time he left, the club was firmly established as one of the biggest and most successful in the whole of Brazil.

It's impossible to overstate the importance of the place Leônidas occupies in the history of Brazilian football. Here was a boy from the humblest of mixed-race backgrounds who through talent alone rose to the top of the game, his name and achievements celebrated across his homeland and around the world. His style of play was a definitive expression of the freedom, unpredictability and individual trickery which together were supposed to compose the happiest face Brazilian football had to offer. He was the first player to establish himself – and the game he played – at the heart of the nation's life and culture. And, in the process, he became Brazil's first true footballing superstar.

There's something resonant in the nickname given to Leônidas: *O Homem de Borracha*. For 50 years before his birth, Brazil and the nation's burgeoning economy had been synonymous with the exploitation of rubber grown in Amazonia. The career of Leônidas began just as the rubber boom was being punctured. By the time he retired in 1949, though, football had become the single most important element in the cultural life of his country; here was a game, a profession and a passion that could rally a nation, it seemed, bringing its disparate peoples together in joy, anguish and every emotion in between. More than any other, Leônidas was the player who established Brazilian football on the international stage. In 1950, the world would arrive in Brazil for the first post-War World Cup. By then, thanks in large part to the exploits of 'the Rubber Man', what had once been the Kingdom of Rubber was now a country re-invented as the home of *futebol*.

Paris, 1938

I may have seen games before then but my first really strong memory of watching football was Brazil at the World Cup in 1998. I remember us getting to the Final and then watching us lose to France – I was probably about seven years old. Of course I can remember where I watched that game, too. Because it was Brazil, we were all watching together at home in Americana with family and friends. As I was still young, I was right at the front near the screen and I just burst into tears at the end. With lots of other people, I guess, all over the country.

It's an amazing thing to experience for the first time as a child. All the family, watching together – and, you know, everybody: all over Brazil – watching this happen together, experiencing it together. Anywhere you go in the country during a World Cup, wherever there's a space and a big screen showing the game, people will flock together for it. In São Paulo, they put up a big screen on the Avenida Paulista and there are hordes of people there for the games. It's what happens everywhere in Brazil. When I was a kid, though, there wasn't a big screen anywhere near us but someone in our family had quite a big TV set so everybody would gather at their house instead!

I have strong memories of seeing games on TV but the radio was very important too. As a child I was a São Paulo fan and I used to listen to all their games. I think a lot of people in Brazil had that connection with football through the radio, especially if you were a fan of one of the big clubs because they'd have live commentary from those games. People could listen on the radio back before there was football on TV. It's where a lot of our football history happened.

We don't forget the great players from the past – there are so many clubs and every club has its own heroes. At São Paulo, people still talk about Leônidas even though he played for the club 70 years ago. It's the same with a figure like Pelé: he's a legend all over Brazil, all over the world. But, first, he's a hero for Santos. Like Garrincha for Botafogo.

It's funny: it makes it hard for us as players. When we're young, the fans will say: *Oh, you're the new so-and-so, Pelé or Garrincha!* You know, we'll get given a nickname, an -inho. But then we grow up and we don't turn out to be the same as the player we were supposed to be the new version of. And then people say: *Oh, but you're not as good as they were!*

So, at São Paulo, they said I was going to be like a new Kaká. I was supposed to do all the things Kaká had done with the club. But I grew up and I became 'Not-Kaká'! I wanted to say: *No, I'm just me.* Already now, when I go and visit little *escolinhas* like the ones I played at when I was a kid, someone always comes up to me and points out a boy: *This one is going to be the new Oscar!* I just have to shrug my shoulders and say: *OK, then!*

5. *BRASILIDADE*

EVERY COUNTRY HAS an idea of itself. An idea or two, in fact: first, what a nation sees when it looks into a collective mirror; then what others see, the face the nation turns to the outside world. For Brazil, since the 1930s, the reflection that has captured the extremes, the hopes and aspirations of its citizens more dramatically than any other has been football. And it is as the greatest of all footballing nations – five times world champions and with a unique approach to playing the game – that Brazil wants to present itself, not least as 2014's World Cup hosts. The rest of us are almost as proud to celebrate the achievements, the style and chutzpah of the *Seleção* as the Brazilians themselves: this, after all, is the second favourite team of every footballing nation on earth. To understand why we see Brazil the way we do, we perhaps need to see the country – and Brazilian football – in the way Brazilians do.

The writer and academic Gilberto Freyre was born in Recife in 1900 and died there, 87 years later. Even now he is looked on as the man who first invented a sense of Brazil as a unique and independent nation. He is most famous for a trilogy of books: *The Masters and the Slaves, The Mansions and the Shanties* and *Order and Progress.* Together, they add up to a complex and very personal analysis of how Brazil became Brazil; according to Freyre the key to it all was sex, the means by which Europeans,

African slaves and the country's indigenous peoples were mixed into a blend of ethnicities unparalleled anywhere on earth. The word for that intermingling of races, miscegenation, had always come freighted – for the colonial powers – with a sense of weakness, corruption and contamination. Freyre's revolutionary vision was that miscegenation was actually something powerful and precious, offering a free and independent Brazil its own identity as a modern, multi-racial republic.

When the national team returned from the 1938 World Cup, they were welcomed as heroes. The third-place finish in France was Brazil's best so far but it wasn't just that success being celebrated. The style of the team, taking its lead from the quicksilver Leônidas, was something to be proud of, too. Thanks to live radio broadcasts from Europe the whole country had heard about the team's exploits. Gilberto Freyre was as excited as anybody and saw in the 1938 squad an image of the Brazil he believed in. He wrote a landmark piece for his local newspaper, one of South America's oldest and best-respected, the *Diario de Pernambuco*, in which he recognised the national team's multi-racial identity – including white, African and mixed-race players – and connected it to what he saw as a uniquely Brazilian style of play:

Our *Mulatto* football, with its artistic flourishes, its success based more on attacking than defending, was brilliantly demonstrated in the games against the Poles and the Czechs. It is an expression like no other of our social democratic identity. It rebels against excessive internal and external organisation, against excessive uniformity . . . the totalitarianism that takes away individualism and spontaneity. In football, as in politics, the Brazilian Mulatto style makes its mark with a taste for the surprising, with an elegance reminiscent of dance steps and *capoeira*. Especially dance . . . improvisation, diversity, individual spontaneity. While European football is a scientific and socialist sport, in which the player is mechanized and subordinate to the collective, Brazilian football is a form of dance, in which the individual stands out and shines.

Not everyone agreed with Freyre back in 1938, not least because the contrast he set out between Brazilian freedom and European uniformity had obvious political overtones as World War II loomed across Europe. Not everyone agrees with Freyre now, either. What's certain is that his piece in the *Diario de Pernambuco* started a conversation – an argument – that has continued to this day. He was convinced he had located the soul of Brazil in the style – and ethnicity – of the *Seleção*. Since 1938, football has been a stage on which the nation has played out its sense of itself, the twists and turns in the drama sparked by successes and failures at 16 subsequent World Cups.

★ ★ ★

In the wake of the 1938 World Cup in France, Gilberto Freyre rejoiced in the freedom and spontaneity that Brazil's Afro-Brazilian players brought to the national team. In 1950, however, came the shock and disappointment of Brazil's defeat at the hands of Uruguay in the final game of the first World Cup held on home soil, dubbed the *Maracanazo* by the victors after they came from a goal down to win 2–1 at the Maracanã. Suddenly the strengths of the multi-racial team which Freyre had celebrated so memorably were identified as weaknesses: Brazil's black players bore the brunt of the blame for a failure that shook the nation's sense of itself as a modern, soon-to-be superpower. Goalkeeper Barbosa and full-back Bigode, in particular, were marked out as the villains of the piece, both in the immediate aftermath of Uruguay's victory and in decades to come. In 1993, a few years before he died, Barbosa was turned away from Brazil's training camp by coaches convinced he would bring bad luck to their preparations for the 1994 tournament in the US. As he later said to his biographer, Roberto Muylaert: 'Under Brazilian law the maximum sentence is 30 years but my imprisonment has been for 50 years.'

As well as the racial undertone – and despite the fact that Brazil had run in goals almost at will against European opponents during the tournament – the soul-searching after 1950 also turned Freyre's view of European football on its head: physical strength and rigid organisation were no longer seen – by a country transformed under the modernising dictatorship of the *Estado Novo* – as shortcomings. Now, those were exactly the virtues that had been missing in the favourites' ranks. Brazil had been let down by indiscipline and a lack of physical and mental courage. Within the space of a generation, 1938's 'dancers' had become 1950's weak-kneed chokers. In hindsight, the *Maracanazo* was Brazilian football's rock bottom: it remains a trauma even famous victories and inglorious defeats since have failed to completely expunge.

Once the immediate heat of anger, soul-searching and self-hatred had cooled a little, there was a sense of Brazil needing to take a long, hard look at itself. In football – and because of that, in every other aspect of national life – it was as if everything had to start all over again. Beginning, it turned out, with the kit. 1950 was the last

Maracanã Stadium, Rio de Janeiro 1950

time Brazil wore white at a World Cup. Like everything else to do with that tournament, the white shirts with blue trim sent out all the wrong messages, it was claimed. In part, at least, as a way of getting the nation's fans to give the *Seleção* a second chance, the *Confederação Brasileira de Desportos* linked up with a prominent Rio paper, the *Correio da Manhã*, to run a competition to design a new strip for the Brazilian team incorporating the colours of the national flag.

The winning design was the work of one of the more unlikely contestants: a 19-year-old illustrator from the deep south in Rio Grande do Sul, a Brazilian

with a leaning towards Uruguay as far as football was concerned. Aldyr Garcia Schlee was born and raised in Jaguarão, beside the river that gives the town its name. On the day of the 1950 Final, Schlee was across the bridge in Uruguay, watching a Roy Rogers Western at a cinema in Rio Branco. The film was interrupted to proclaim the news from Rio de Janeiro. Impressed by the spontaneous and rousing rendition of the Uruguayan national anthem that greeted the announcement, Schlee cheerfully admits to having been a fan of *La Celeste* ever since. His prize in 1953, though, included the chance to work as a design intern in Rio and to spend time with the Brazilian national team. Schlee wasn't impressed, apparently, by the players' attitude either to life or to

football. 'I was totally disillusioned,' he would later tell Alex Bellos, author of *Futebol: The Brazilian Way of Life*. 'The players were a bunch of scoundrels.' And he wasn't alone in this view. Pelé himself would later recall that, until the mid-1950s, 'there were a few players in the national team who considered themselves far superior to the rest and behaved accordingly. Worse, they were indulged: their going out with women, and drinking, were overlooked.'

Pelé, of course, would go on to be part of a golden generation, altogether more disciplined, humble and bound by sense of common purpose, which would re-write Brazilian football history. Aldyr Garcia Schlee, meanwhile, returned to *gaúcho* country as soon as he could, to the town of Pelotas, where he has lived and worked ever since. But he had made his mark – and indelibly – on what football fans everywhere think when they think of Brazil. Those footballers he and Pelé didn't approve of went off to the 1954 World Cup wearing the iconic yellow and green shirts Schlee designed for them. And, famously, they've worn the same colours ever since.

★ ★ ★

By 1954, Brazil was once more – in name, at least – a democracy. The military deposed Getúlio Vargas in 1945, bringing to an end the *Estado Novo*. Vargas, however, was re-elected as President in 1950. It didn't go well: isolated, politically and personally, he would eventually commit suicide with the economy in crisis and his own credibility destroyed by the *Rua Tonelero* scandal, named after the street where a failed assassination attempt was made on one of the President's leading opponents. By the time of his death, Vargas had already assured himself a place in Brazil's history, though. His social and political influence continued to be felt on the national stage long after his own melodramatic departure.

Vargas had dreamt of a modern, industrialised

Três Corações, MInas Gerais

Brazil: a fledgling aviation industry, based around São Paulo, was one of his pet projects during the 1930s. He was also convinced suppression of the threat posed by Communism was essential to Brazil's future. His government was always ready to use that threat, imagined or otherwise, as an excuse to clamp down on dissent and explain away failure. Those two notions book-ended Brazil's participation at the 1954 World Cup in Switzerland. For the first time ever the team travelled by air rather than boat to Europe in May. Their interest in the tournament was ended five weeks later in spectacular and violent fashion by one of the great national teams of all time, communist Hungary's 'Magnificent Magyars'.

Brazil had had to reach the finals through qualifying for the first time, which proved simple enough. Chile and Paraguay were beaten home and away, although the game in Asunción saw the *Seleção* greeted by a shower of bottles and stones and a Paraguayan player hospitalised during an ugly physical encounter. Once the team touched down in Switzerland, the nationalism fostered by Vargas back at home was put on show at every opportunity. After the humiliation of the *Maracanazo* four years earlier, patriotism had to be the very obvious order of the day. The national anthem was sung before every training session; the Brazilian flag ostentatiously kissed prior to every game.

For a while the populist chest-beating looked as if it might work. Brazil had, after all, taken a very good group of players to Switzerland. Only Bauer, Baltazar and Nílton Santos remained from the team humiliated in Rio four years previously. Tough as it may have been on some of those senior players, leaving them out made room in the squad for new faces of real promise, several of whom would become World Cup winners in years to come. Brazil's standout star of 1954 was Waldyr Pereira, better known as 'Didi'. Indeed, he'd have been a standout star in any era. Didi was the complete midfielder: strong, technically flawless, a great

passer, long or short, and blessed with a supremely calm temperament. He also weighed in with goals, not least from dead balls; Didi invented the *folha seca* or 'dry leaf' free-kick. Swerving and dipping on the way to goal, it's now a technique – thanks to the likes of Rivelino and Roberto Carlos – that has become part of the repertoire expected from Brazilian players.

Didi was one of the scorers in Brazil's opening game against Mexico, a comfortable 5–0 win, and hit the equaliser in a 1–1 draw against Yugoslavia which saw both teams through to the quarter-finals. However, Brazil's luck soon ran out. The curious rules of that year's tournament decreed Group winners would meet Group winners in the last eight. Brazil and Yugoslavia had finished level on points but instead of goal difference being counted, lots were drawn to decide who finished top. Brazil's reward was a game against the favourites, Hungary, unbeaten for four years in international football. With the best team in Europe pitched against the best in South America, the match was eagerly anticipated by a capacity crowd of 60,000 squeezed into the Wankdorf Stadium in Berne. They got a match memorable for all the wrong reasons.

Englishman Arthur Ellis had been a linesman at the Estádio do Maracanã on that fateful day in 1950, a bit-part player as Brazil's World Cup dream unravelled against Uruguay. Now, four years later, he was to find himself very much at the centre of the storm: what should have been the best game of the tournament turned into the 'Battle of Berne'. The first half was a football match: Hungary took a two-goal lead before Brazil grew into the game and got a goal back when Djalma Santos thumped in a penalty. Didi was running the show and right-winger Julinho looked ready to make something happen every time he had the ball at his feet. At the break, the game was perfectly poised. Hungary were missing the 'Galloping Major', Ferenc Puskás –

unavailable because of injury and watching from the bench. Brazil had looked flaky under pressure but now had the wind in their sails.

The second half unravelled in a completely different way. Niggling fouls became wild lunges; arguments turned into running battles. Referee Ellis did his best to keep things under control but 22 players clearly had other ideas. With 20 minutes to go and Hungary leading 3–2, Nílton Santos fouled József Bozsik – a deputy in the Hungarian Parliament at the time – and a stand-up fight ensued. Both were sent off. Didi then hit the bar before Hungary broke away to score a fourth, by which time football was the last thing on anyone's mind. At one point, an angry Djalma Santos was seen chasing Zoltán Czibor round the pitch. Santos evaded punishment but, with a couple of minutes to go, Humberto Tozzi's wild kick at Gyula Lóránt saw him become the second Brazilian to be sent off.

It was at the final whistle that things got completely out of hand. The Brazilian coaching staff and some journalists ran onto the pitch. Uninvolved during the 90 minutes, Ferenc Puskás was at the heart of things afterwards, allegedly throwing a bottle at the Brazilian defender Pinheiro. Fighting continued down the tunnel before several Brazilian players and officials invaded the Hungarian dressing room. Lights were smashed and in the chaos Hungary's coach, Gusztáv Sebes, took a blow to the face needing several stitches. Fighting only finished when military police were called to the scene.

The responsibility for the ugliness of the 'Battle of Berne' has traditionally been laid at the door of the *Seleção*. England's *Daily Mail* of June 28 related its own version of the story, one which said at least as much about the messenger as it did about the message: 'the Brazilians were the main offenders and the Hungarians retaliated only under extreme provocation. The South Americans, many of them Negroes, started heavy

tackling from the kick-off. They got wilder as the game progressed in heavy rain, conditions which rendered it difficult for their players, in their lightweight footwear, to control the ball'.

The 'magisterial' Arthur Ellis, meanwhile, has been portrayed as the hero who at least got the game finished, 'the man who kept his cool' according to the following day's London *Daily Mirror*. Ellis himself later remarked that he was 'convinced that the infamous Battle of Berne was a battle of politics and religion, the politics of the Communist Hungarians and the religion of the Catholic Brazilians.' He may well have been right that something more than a football match was being fought out on the day. Certainly the game's coverage in the media – this was the first World Cup to be widely televised, too – suggested a conflict between Old World and New. Times were changing and one Norwegian newspaper, *Aftenposten*, betrayed European attitudes when summing up the Hungarians as 'more refined than the primitive and hot-blooded Brazilians'.

Back in Brazil, the team – without a hint of irony – was hailed for its fighting spirit; the Hungarians' persistent fouling, which often seemed to go unpunished by the English referee, was seen as evidence of dark forces at work. Brazilian fans took their lead from coach Zezé Moreira, who was quoted in *Aftenposten* as claiming that 'luck and doubtful decisions on behalf of the referee were the reasons why we did not beat the Olympic Champions'. FIFA saw fit to wash its hands of the matter and left the Federations involved to punish their own players; unsurprisingly, neither did. Instead, the *Confederação Brasileira de Desportos* – the Brazilian football federation of the day – made a formal complaint to FIFA, accusing Arthur Ellis of having been part of a Communist plot to ensure continued Hungarian success in the tournament.

Deplored in Europe, the Battle of Berne saw a strange, bitter pride restored in the Brazilian team. The Communist threat, meanwhile, offered a ready

Wankdorf Stadium, Berne 1954

explanation for failure at yet another World Cup. Unlike in 1950, there was little soul-searching and there were no recriminations. The Magical Magyars for their part fell to Germany in the Final, back in Berne a week later and were never the same again, the team breaking up after the Hungarian Revolution of 1956. In Brazil, on the other hand, 1954 would soon be forgotten: glory was waiting in the wings for the *Seleção*.

★ ★ ★

Brazil already boasted two of the world's great cities in Rio de Janeiro and São Paulo. In 1956 the nation resolved to build a third. But the idea of a new capital city at the country's centre rather than on its coast wasn't new: the constitution of the new republic in 1891 included Congress being given the right to re-locate the seat of government. Rio, though, remained the capital – by name and by reputation – until the mid-1950s and the election of a new President, Juscelino Kubitschek. Known then and now simply as 'JK', Kubitschek was an extraordinary individual whose achievements ensured his stature and popularity lasted long past his death, in mysterious circumstances, in 1976. JK had something of the JFK about him and the car accident which took his life – after ten years spent in exile during Brazil's military junta – continues to be the subject of frantic conspiracy theory to this day.

During the election campaign of 1955, Kubitschek promised a new capital city for Brazil. Brasilia was to be the most visible expression of an economic policy aimed at delivering 'fifty years of progress in five'. The JK era was one of social, political and economic optimism, fired by the new President's vision of a modern Brazil. Brasilia was the work of urban planner Lucio Costa and architect Oscar Niemeyer, who were given the responsibility of realising Kubitschek's dream of 'a modern capital, the most beautiful capital in the world'.

The site chosen was out in the middle of nowhere, 750 miles west of Rio on the barren and sparsely inhabited highlands of the state of Goiás. It was an extraordinary undertaking, designed in part to inspire a sense of Brazil as a unified nation as opposed to a collection of states each with its own parochial aspirations. The city, built by predominantly migrant labour shipped in from Brazil's impoverished north eastern states, is a landmark of the Modernist era unmatched anywhere on earth. These were momentous times for the nation and, fittingly, by the time Brasilia opened for business, the Brazilian national football team would be crowned champions of the world for the first time.

★ ★ ★

Juscelino Kubitschek was a new force in Brazilian politics. At the same time, a new force emerged in Brazilian football's corridors of power: a former Olympic swimmer who would go on to become the most powerful man in the world game as President of FIFA, João Havelange. In the wake of the Battle of Berne, Brazil's FA, the *Confederação Brasileira de Desportos* (CBD), decided on a change at the top: Havelange was the king maker behind Sylvio Correa Pacheco's election and succeeded his protégé as CBD President early in 1958. By then, preparations for the World Cup that summer were well underway and Havelange would be in place to take his share of the credit – deserved or otherwise – for the success of the *Seleção* in Sweden.

After a disappointing tour of Europe in 1956 and an underwhelming *Copa América* campaign the following year, expectations in Brazil were at an all-time low. Planning and organisation for the 1958 World Cup, though, mirrored the modern age being celebrated in steel and concrete out on the highlands of Goiás. Brazil's team doctor, Hilton Gosling, was sent to Sweden in 1957 to visit two dozen potential sets of hotel and training facilities before Brazil settled on a base in Hindås, just outside Gothenburg, once the draw for the Group Stages

Catedral Metropolitana Nossa Senhora Aparecida, Brasilia

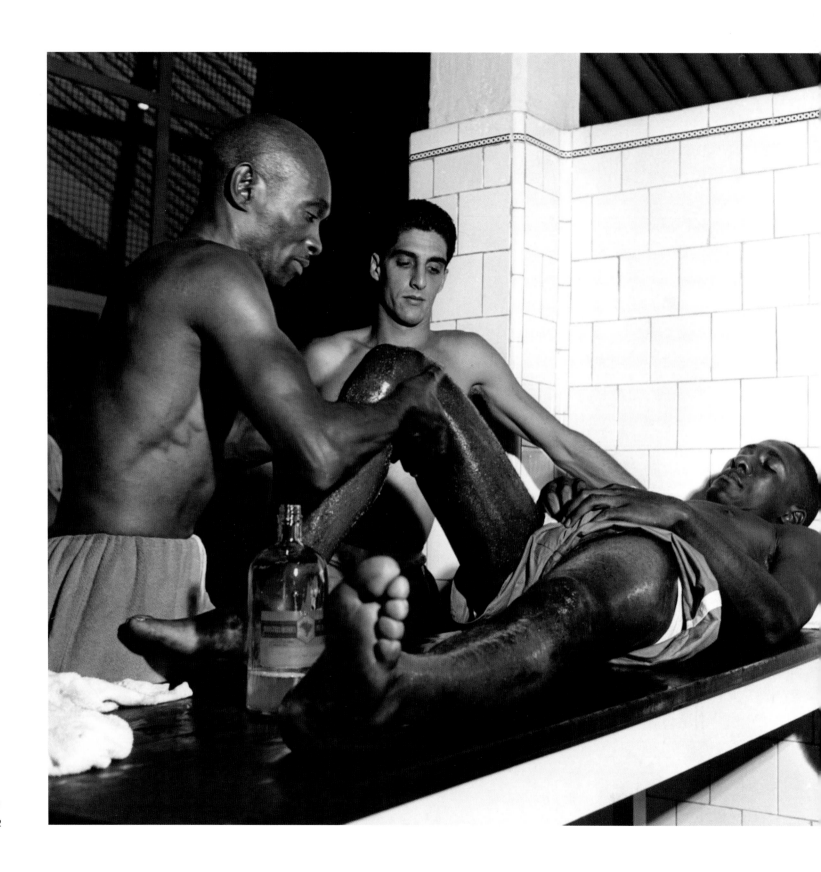

had been made. Likewise, chief scout Ernesto Santos spent most of that year in Europe watching World Cup qualifiers. He returned in 1958 to watch Brazil's first three opponents, Austria, England and the USSR. Gosling and Santos were members of a technical group selected for their expertise in specific areas: they would be joined in Sweden by a technical director, a treasurer, a fitness coach, a dentist, a nutritionist, a physiotherapist and even a psychologist.

Havelange certainly played his part in the forward thinking, not least when appointing his friend Paulo Machado de Carvalho to the key post of head of delegation for the tournament in Sweden. Machado was a wealthy entrepreneur who had made his fortune operating radio stations during the 1930s and 40s. He was also a football man, having served as a director of São Paulo FC during a wildly successful period in the 1940s which established the club as a superpower of the domestic game. Machado had also supervised the Paulista team that proved unbeatable in the early 1950s in the national state championships, the *Campeonato Brasileiro de Seleções Estaduais*. His was a unique combination of talents: here was a charismatic diplomat and natural leader, without ulterior political or financial motives, who knew how to run a business properly and also understood what made a successful dressing room tick.

A 40-day training camp and warm-up games against European club sides were arranged and managed with extraordinary attention to detail. The players were made aware of their responsibilities, having signed a 40-point code of conduct covering everything from dress code to calorific intake. Management by committee hasn't often worked in elite sport but it did for the *Seleção* in 1958. Machado had inherited a dilemma he saw in simplistic terms: 'football which was technically great but an organisational structure which was defective,

Djalma Santos, 1958

especially in the vital matter of selection.' His remedy was equally simple: 'teamwork, from the head of delegation down to the wardrobe attendant; every single person having a job to do, being competent to handle that job, and performing it to the uttermost of his ability and feeling.' The head coach, the genial and experienced Vicente Feola, was therefore just one cog in a bigger wheel.

Without question, one of the secrets of Brazil's ground-breaking success in 1958 was that the management team's focus was entirely on the well-being of the players: Gosling's treatment room was set up as a cross between a retreat and a social club for the players, injured or not; the team dentist performed miracles, rescuing teeth badly damaged during impoverished childhoods and years of poor diet; in Machado's words, 'the players needed and were entitled to maximum support off the field and everybody in the party had to work to that end, not just the coach'. Preparation, then, was thorough and enlightened. The real reason Brazil won their first World Cup in Sweden, though, was because they had assembled a group of players on the brink of greatness. Two significant senior figures from 1954 remained: Nílton Santos, Brazil's first great attacking full-back, and Didi, whose free-kick against Peru had secured qualification for the tournament. More importantly still, Brazil had two young stars waiting to make their own unforgettable marks on the tournament; two players who, in 40 matches playing together for the *Seleção*, would not once finish on the losing side.

★ ★ ★

In 1958, the Brazilian national team was as much a project as the new capital city, Brasilia. The government underwrote the team's pre-tournament expenses and the players' salaries, for example. Like the Machado Plan for the 1958 World Cup, Brasilia was designed by wealthy, urban professionals. Its physical construction, though, was the achievement of poor Brazilians from the back-lands of the North East, the *Sertão Nordestino*. In Sweden, meanwhile, a very good team was transformed into World Cup winners by the contributions of two players who had emerged from desperately poor backgrounds on the fringes of Brazil's great cities further south: Edson Arantes do Nascimento and Manuel Francisco dos Santos. It was the element of the project that could never have been planned: in Pelé and Garrincha, Brazil had uncovered the two best footballers on earth.

In so many ways, the pair could not have been less alike. Even at 17, Pelé was a physically perfect specimen, powerful, lithe and athletic. Garrincha, on the other hand, earned the nickname *O Anjo de Pernas Tortas* – 'the Angel with Bent Legs' – such were the apparently crippling deformities he'd been born with. Pelé grew up in the state of Minas Gerais, in a mining and farming town called Três Corações. His father, João Roams, had played professionally but was forced into early retirement through injury. The son was intent on enjoying the career denied the father and from an early age was professional in outlook and attitude. By the time he was 15, Pelé had left home to join Santos FC and would never look back.

Garrincha, on the other hand, was one of the game's last true amateurs, in spirit at least. He spent his childhood in the back of beyond in a sleepy town outside Rio called Pau Grande. Football was a game he enjoyed along with other available teenage pastimes such as hunting, fishing and girls. He played for the love of it – un-coached and, perhaps, un-coachable – throughout a career as financially and emotionally haphazard as Pelé's was single-minded and purposeful. Pelé remains a significant presence in Brazil and worldwide, successful as a businessman and politician since he finished playing. Garrincha's career was a spectacular

adventure and was followed by equally spectacular decline: he died a penniless alchoholic in 1983.

What both Pelé and Garrincha brought to football, though, was the distinctive Brazilian trait of *jeitinho*, a word that can be roughly translated as 'knack', the capacity to overcome obstacles with cleverness, trickery and originality. Pelé had masterful ball control, raw power and astonishing self-belief: he could score from all angles and all distances. Garrincha had extraordinary balance, mesmerising dribbling skills and a burst of pace: his intentions were difficult to read and, as often as not, impossible to defend against. Both players were able to re-write the script of a game as and when it suited them, finding or inventing solutions to footballing problems in the most unexpected ways. Together they supplied the *jeitinho* which would define the manner of Brazil's victory, at last, at a World Cup.

★ ★ ★

Though they finished the tournament as key members of the team, both Pelé and Garrincha might have missed out in 1958. The former was aged only 17, after all, and travelled to the tournament carrying an injury. His place in the starting line-up for Brazil's first game, against Austria in Uddevalla, went to José Altafini, known as 'Mazzola', who scored twice in a 3–0 win. The team was certainly strong: Brazil played four at the back with the team captained by the imperious centre half, Hilderaldo Bellini, and sparked by attacking full-back Nílton Santos; Didi pulled strings in a two-man midfield and the damage was expected to be done by a four-man attack which included the redoubtable Mário Zagallo on the left, whose boundless energy allowed him to tuck in and make a third midfielder when Brazil had to defend. The 24-year-old Garrincha's absence was altogether more controversial and was determined by a report by the team psychologist describing him as below average intelligence and lacking aggression. His place went to the Flamengo right-winger, Joel. Interestingly,

Nilton Santos, Garrincha, Didi and Gilmar, 1958

Ullevi Stadium, Gothenburg 1958

the same psychologist, a gentleman by the name of João Carvalhaes, suggested Pelé would be too immature to make any significant contribution to the 1958 team.

The 3–0 scoreline against Austria probably flattered the *Seleção* and, despite the inclusion of the imposing and goal-hungry Vavá, Brazil drew a blank against England in their next game, with a man-marker – Wolves' Bill Slater – negating Didi's influence in midfield. Exactly

what happened after the game in Gothenburg has been discussed endlessly since. There have been as many versions as people to tell the tale, the most compelling being that a deputation of senior players approached the technical committee to argue for the inclusion of both Pelé and Garrincha in Brazil's third Group game, against the USSR. However the decision was reached, the pair were in the starting line-up on June 15, back in Gothenburg. What followed is the stuff of fairy tales: the first three minutes of the game are still remembered as the most thrilling three minutes in the history of Brazilian football, the three minutes which have defined *Brasilidade* – Brazilian-ness – in regard to football ever since.

A powerful, experienced and well-drilled Soviet side – like Hungary four years previously, Olympic Champions and proud representatives of the Communist bloc – were quickly reduced to a disorganised rabble struggling to stem the tide. The passage of play after kick-off, which set the tone for much of what followed, was memorably described for English readers by the English football writer and World Cup historian Brian Glanville: 'Garrincha's incomparable swerve left his opponent Kuznetsov helpless. First he beat him to the wide, shot and hit the left-hand post. Next, Pelé hit the right-hand post. Finally, after three minutes, Didi emerged calmly and magisterially from a group of Russian opponents, and with an exquisite pass found Vavá who dashed through to score'. Vavá scored again with quarter of an hour left but, by then, according to Glanville, the Soviets were already utterly demoralised: 'At one late, memorable, instant, Garrincha had and held the ball against five encircling Russians. Genius had overwhelmed mere effort'.

Garrincha had tormented the Soviets. It was Pelé's goalscoring prowess that took Brazil to the Final. His first at a World Cup came against Wales in the quarter-final and was *jeitinho* personified: taking a pass from Didi on his chest, with his back to goal near the penalty spot, a flick over his shoulder took Mel Charles, his closest marker, out of the game. Pelé then turned and volleyed the ball past Jack Kelsey before disappearing under a mêlée of celebrating team-mates in the back of the net. In the semi-final against France – who were inspired by Raymond Kopa but weakened by injury before and during the game – Pelé helped himself to a hat-trick during 25 second-half minutes. Brazil it seemed, had found a perfect and irresistible blend. Five days later they went into the Final against

hosts Sweden at the Råsunda Stadium in Stockholm as firm favourites.

★ ★ ★

At home in Brazil – and at the team's hotel in Solna – the *Maracanazo* continued to cast its long shadow. Nílton Santos had been on the bench at the stadium on that fateful afternoon in 1950. Mário Zagallo had been in the crowd. Even the young Pelé could remember his father listening in tears as Brazil's heartbreaking and utterly unexpected defeat unfolded. Only Garrincha, it seemed, had been left completely untouched by Uruguay's victory, having spent the afternoon fishing rather than listening to the game. Now, eight years on, Brazil were again racing certainties yet there was a deep-seated fear that weakness of spirit and a failure of nerve might again cost the national team dear.

The management did all they could to keep preparations low-key, insisting supporters and journalists be banned from the hotel in the run-up to the Final. No newspapers or magazines were available to the players. The Machado Plan remained single-minded and detailed to the last. Hosts Sweden were to wear yellow in the Final and so Brazil had to choose a change strip. Offered white, green and blue as alternatives, they chose blue, the colour worn by four of the previous five World Cup winners. Blue was also the colour associated with *Nossa Senhora Aparecida*, an image of the Virgin Mary with profoundly patriotic associations and held particularly dear by Afro-Brazilian Catholics. Shirts were duly found in Stockholm. Numbers and CBD crests were carefully cut from the shirts that had got them to the Final and sewed onto the new blue ones overnight.

June 29 1958 dawned anything but a Brazilian day: mid-summer in Sweden was wet, windy and cold. Nonetheless 52,000 fans crammed into the Råsunda, the vast majority of them locals, hoping the conditions and the favourites' suspect mentality would tip the match in their favour. Five minutes in, when the veteran Leidholm picked his way past several half-hearted challenges on the edge of Brazil's box and finished low past Gilmar, it seemed as if ghosts from the past were about to ambush the *Seleção*. This time no one froze as Brazil had at the Maracanã in 1950; no one lost their heads, as in Berne in 1954. Instead, Brazil – and Garrincha, in particular – got on with doing what they'd been doing better than anyone else for the previous three weeks.

On ten minutes, Didi slid the ball wide to the right; Garrincha left his marker, the hapless Axbom, spinning like a top before cutting the ball back from the byeline. The ball sped across the six-yard box and Vavá was on hand to slide it home. Twenty minutes later, the same three players fashioned an almost exact replica to give Brazil a 2–1 lead at half-time. The 1958 World Cup was won in that opening 45 minutes, thanks to Didi's intelligence, Garrincha's unplayable talent and Vavá's coolness in front of goal. In the 45 minutes that followed, the spotlight shifted: Pelé inspired what was to become a founding myth for his country and for the game. This was a Brazilian style – grace, athleticism, power and *jeitinho* – which the whole world could fall in love with. A soggy afternoon on a muddy pitch in Stockholm saw the start of a passionate affair of the footballing heart; one which still burns bright, half a century on.

By the time the second half kicked off, the passionate Swedish crowd were cheering Brazil on as forcefully as they were their own team. Geoffrey Green was watching the game for *The Times*. A veteran chronicler of countless classic contests, Green was well aware that he was witnessing something truly extraordinary: 'They showed football as a different conception; they killed the white skidding ball from all angles as if it was a lump of cottonwool . . . right through the team they were fused in swift, intimate thought and execution at changing tempos. They combined the theatrical with the practical . . . Ten minutes after the change of ends, Pelé with sleight of foot jugglery, flicked up a cross from Zagallo, balanced

Råsunda Stadium Stockholm, 1958

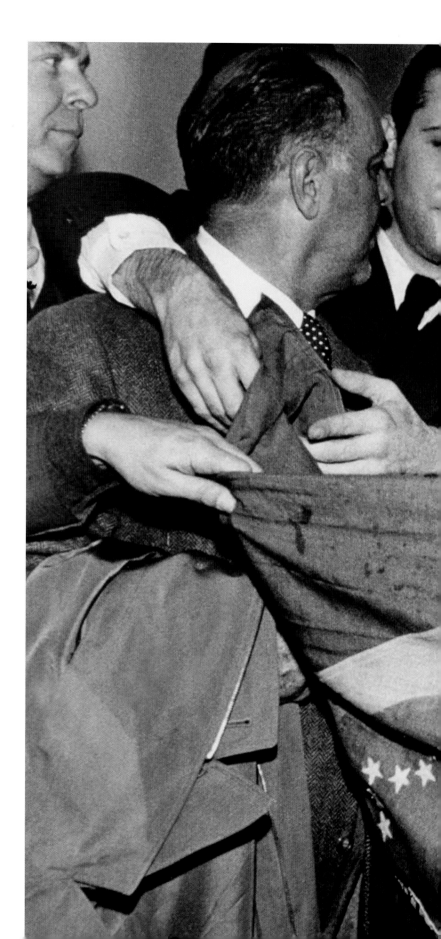

BRASIL CAMPEÃO MUNDIAL DE FUTEBOL DE 1958

CORREIO Cr$ 3,80

CARVALHO

ORLANDO

COPA "JULES RIMET"

BRASIL

CBD

VAVÁ

DIDÍ

MÁRIO AMÉRICO

ZAGALO

PEPE

CAMPEÃO DO

VICENTE FEOLA

CASTILHO

DE SORDI

MAURO

ZÓZIMO

DINO

JOEL

ORÉCO

MOACIR

MAZZOLA

MUNDO

the ball on his instep, chipped it over Gustavsson and leapt round the centre-half to volley home. Who can live with this sort of stuff?'

The diligent Mário Zagallo – who would go on to become the first man to win World Cups as both player and manager – added a fourth. The Swedes pulled a goal back through Simonsson but the closing moments belonged to the 17-year-old Pelé. Right on full-time, he leapt to head in Zagallo's cross from the left and then fell into the net, where he passed out. By the time he came round, the whistle had been blown and Brazil were, for the first time, champions of the world. Pelé hugged Gilmar and burst into tears on the goalkeeper's shoulder before being hoisted aloft by his team-mates. As the Brazilians celebrated, they trotted around the pitch holding a giant Swedish flag in humble and innocent tribute to the reception they'd received. In Geoffrey Green's words: 'The stadium stood to them as if it were the host nation herself who had won, and at the end the King of Sweden himself posed for photographs with the victors, while many of them were openly overcome by their achievement.'

The journey home was a long and circuitous one which took in brief stops for congratulations and speeches in London and Paris. A street parade in Lisbon followed before the World Cup winners flew to Recife where, after the pilot had twice been forced to abort landing due to torrential rain, they disembarked to a reception they could scarcely have dreamt of when they left Brazil six weeks before: here were heroes for the age, their achievements celebrated across every geographic, social and racial divide. Little wonder that, the following day, the players were welcomed to the Presidential Palace by Juscelino Kubitschek himself. For the first time, perhaps, in the country's history, Brazil's disparate peoples had found, in the *Seleção*, a common sense of identity – *Brasilidade* – in which every citizen could rejoice and take pride: this was a Brazil which, for the first time and under the world's gaze, had truly won.

A Special Bond

Everybody has important role models in their life, don't they? Even though I didn't have the chance to really know him, the person I always aspired to be like was my father. He wasn't there but I always felt that connection with him and what he represented. The person who's had the biggest impact on my life, though – the person who if I'd never met them everything would have been different – is Ludmila. I'm a different person because I met her. I was seventeen and it was a very difficult time, off the pitch, for me at the club. Ludy helped me grow and change as a person. And as a player, too. My agent, Juliano, helped, too, but it was Ludy that transformed everything for me.

Growing up as a footballer, I think my style just developed on its own, from playing all the time. So, when I was 19 and moved to Internacional, I went with an idea of my way of playing. But there was a coach in Porto Alegre: Celso Roth. I'd do the things I'd always done and he would say: *No. I want you to do that instead.* It was as if I had to go back and learn everything all over again. He used to tell me off. Almost every day! At the time, I wanted to rebel against it. But later I realised: *Wow! This is what you were saying. This is what you were doing.* Celso Roth hadn't changed my game but he'd added a lot to what I was able to do.

Through a career, other players have a big effect on you. The time between 12 and 16 was so important for me. The group of boys I was with, all of us picked from the *escolinhas* to go to São Paulo, was together all through that time. We all lived together in the same dormitory. We were together all the time. One boy, Mateus, lived just around the corner from me in Americana and we'd travel home together at weekends to see our families.

The group of us played together for the same teams. We became great friends but knowing each other so well gave us great confidence as players as well. We believed in each other and it made it very special when we were out on the pitch as a team. It was like having another kind of family around me and definitely pushed my football forwards through those years. That togetherness is something special, at whatever level.

When I look at the Brazil team of 1970, I can see they were great players: Pelé, Jairzinho, Rivelino, Tostão. But I also see the kind of togetherness we had as a group of young boys at São Paulo. Look at the fourth goal in the Final against Italy: from one end of the field to the other; pass after pass after pass. And Carlos Alberto – the right back – is the one who scores. That kind of goal is only possible when there is a very special bond in a team. The confidence you have in yourself can come from playing with players you trust and who believe in you.

At that same World Cup in Mexico, everyone remembers the goal that should have been but never was: when Pelé ran through and ran one way past the goalkeeper and let the ball run the other way. I think every Brazilian laments that it didn't go in, that it wasn't the beautiful goal it could have been. But we remember it, don't we? I remember some of Pelé's goals that I've seen on TV but the goal that wasn't I remember as well as anything he ever did. What an amazing thing to do: and at a World Cup!

6. IN COLOUR

THE BRAZILIAN TEAM that won the World Cup in 1958 was very different to the one that had kicked the tournament off. Five players in the starting XI against Sweden hadn't featured in the first game against Austria: Pelé, Garrincha, Djalma Santos, Zito and Vavá. Purely in footballing terms, the fresh faces changed everything, bringing qualities plainly lacking in workmanlike displays early on: audacity, pace, power, athleticism and an eye for goal. The freedom and artistry of the display in the Final captivated world football. At the same time, the Brazilian line-up represented a far truer picture of the nation the team represented: against Austria, the only black face had been Didi's. Against Sweden, three Afro-Brazilian and two mixed-race players were included and made key contributions. In 1958, Brazil became the first multi-racial team ever to win a World Cup and, in the process, completely changed how the world judged Brazilian players. It was a watershed: the beginning of Brazil's history as the world's greatest exporter of footballers.

Brazilian talent had occasionally been lured across the Atlantic to European football in the past, of course, by the promise of new horizons and bigger salaries. Júlio Botelho – 'Julinho' – grew up in São Paulo and became a star with one of the city's smaller clubs, Portuguesa. He was Brazil's right-winger at the 1954 World Cup but missed out four years later. By then, he was playing for Fiorentina in Italy, where he is still remembered as perhaps the club's greatest-ever player, winning Serie A with them in 1956 and then reaching the European Cup Final the following season. Playing in Europe meant Julinho was less well-placed to pursue his international career. Vicente Feola, by all accounts, was nonetheless ready to include him in the squad for Sweden. Julinho himself turned down the chance, though, arguing the place should go to a home-based player. Maybe he just didn't fancy what was still a very long haul across the Atlantic to prepare with the rest of the squad.

The player who replaced him turned out to be Garrincha, whose extraordinary talents meant Julinho would be forced to play second fiddle thereafter, despite homesickness bringing him back to São Paulo to play for Palmeiras later that year. But Julinho's real heartbreak was still to come: having passed up his chance in 1958, he missed out again when he suffered a knee injury just days before the *Seleção* left for Chile and the 1962 World Cup. During his time with Fiorentina, the Italian FA had been eager to explore the possibility of Julinho becoming an Italian national and representing his adopted country but the player chose to remain loyal to Brazil. Presented with the same

opportunity, however, another World Cup star – José João Altafini, known to Brazilian fans as 'Mazzola' – decided otherwise.

Altafini was born in Piracicaba, in São Paulo state, and was the son of Italian-Brazilian parents. He came to prominence with Palmeiras as a stylish centre forward, scoring two of Brazil's three goals in the opening game of the 1958 World Cup against Austria. Altafini's World Cup in Brazil colours finished there, however. Already approached by AC Milan, the management team felt those discussions had turned the player's head. Instead his place went to Vavá, who went on to become Brazil's top scorer in Sweden. Altafini, meanwhile, headed for Milan, where he enjoyed huge success, winning two league titles and a European Cup with his new club.

Thanks to his family background, switching nationalities proved no obstacle and he was soon turning out for Italy at international level as well. Having played as Mazzola for Brazil in Sweden in 1958, Altafini represented the *Azzuri* in Chile in 1962.

★ ★ ★

Brazil's success in Sweden was more than enough to open doors for the players who had inspired it. Two of 1958's leading lights headed for the same city in the months that followed. Centre forward Vavá joined Atlético Madrid. The man voted Player of the Tournament, meanwhile, the elegant and intelligent midfielder Didi, was snapped up by the world's most powerful club, Real Madrid. Subsequent World Cups would serve a similar function as shop windows for outstanding Brazilian talent. A move to Europe promised not only better wages but also, in theory at least, the chance to develop as a player. 1958's pioneers, however, soon discovered the process wasn't as simple as they – or the clubs they joined – might have hoped.

Vavá – Edvaldo Izídio Neto – was born in Brazil's North East, in the city of Recife. He began his career with the local club, Sport Recife, whose stadium was the only one north of Rio to be used during the 1950 World Cup. After winning the state championship, the *Campeonato Pernambucano*, in his first season, Vavá proved more than ready to adapt to new surroundings; he moved to Rio to join Vasco da Gama and won further titles there, his powerful physique earning him the nickname *Peito de Aço* – 'Chest of Steel' – along the way. He also got a first taste of European club football when he won the inaugural *Tournoi de Paris* with Vasco in 1957, beating Real Madrid in the Final. The following year, two goals in the World Cup Final – over his career, Vavá scored 15 in 20 appearances for the national team – were enough to secure a lucrative move to Spain.

By his own account, Vavá enjoyed Madrid and La Liga. He spent three seasons with Atlético, the best of them being his first; his goals took them to a European Cup semi-final against Real which they only lost after a replay. Impressed as he was by the professionalism of players at European clubs, though, Vavá claimed he missed the flexibility and sense of freedom at the heart of the Brazilian game:

> European football in general is much more rigid and systematic than our own. When a European coach hands out an idea his players too often take it reverently, as if Moses were handing them the tablets; we take it as an invitation to improvise on a theme. In Brazil, our trainers also have their

theories – but they do not entrap their players with them. They recognise an established player is a man of accomplishment, fond of the game, and having the ability to change the course of a battle by his own initiative when necessary . . . this freedom is Brazil's characteristic tactic!

By 1961, Vavá was concerned that his place in Brazil's World Cup squad might not be guaranteed. He returned home – this time to São Paulo – and joined the rising stars of Brazilian club football, Palmeiras. The following year in Chile he was again a key player for the *Seleção*. The move back to Brazil ensured that, at 28 and at the height of his powers, he would pick up another World Cup winner's medal before seeing out his professional career abroad, first in Mexico with Club América and then in the US with the San Diego Toros.

Vavá proved a happy traveller. His team-mate Waldyr Pereira – Didi – considerably less so. For much of the 1950s, he was the most talked-about man in Brazilian football, starring for two of Rio's great clubs, first at Fluminense and then, alongside Garrincha, at Botafogo. His love affairs were as well-publicised as his unique *folha seca* – 'dry leaf' – free-kicks, not least by the doyen of mid-century Brazilian sportswriters Nelson Rodrigues, who nicknamed him *O Príncipe Etíope*, the 'Ethiopian Prince', and wrote: 'Didi treats the ball lovingly. At his feet, it seems to become a rare and sensitive orchid, which must be looked after with affection and pleasure.'

Didi had been born into poverty north of Rio de Janeiro, and never forgot the privations of his boyhood, working as a peanut-seller to help his parents make ends meet. What others saw as a mercenary streak, Didi regarded as his professional responsibility:

I make no secret of the fact that I am always seeking for the place which will pay me best. In my own eyes, I do not lose grace by this. After all,

is provision for one's future not logical? A man can speak lightly of poverty only if he has never experienced its terrors.

The edge to criticism of Didi – when things went badly for the *Seleção* many would be quick to lay the blame at his door – may well have had something to do with his African roots. His team-mates, however, adored him. He played for Brazil at the 1954 World Cup and then marshalled the team's resources four years later in Sweden. One of the goal-scorers in the 1958 Final, Mário Zagallo, credited Didi as the inspiration for Brazil's recovery from going a goal down early on in that game, calmly walking back to the centre circle with the ball under his arm, reassuring his desperate team-mates that they had nothing to fear.

Didi's performances at that World Cup earned him a contract with Europe's most successful club, Real Madrid. Already Real were a team blessed with exceptional talent from all over the world: Ferenc Puskás, Raymond Kopa, Francisco Gento and Héctor Rial. First among equals at the Bernabéu, however, was the naturalised Argentine Alfredo Di Stéfano. And there lay Didi's first problem: there was only room in the ranks for one general. Didi himself recognised that, if it came down to a popularity contest, his playing style wasn't likely to see him come out on top:

Spanish fans, I got to learn, like those players with lots of physical gusto, running all over the place, falling down, flailing their arms like windmills, assuming pathetic attitudes to make a point and so on.

Here was a player, after all, who would regularly leave the field without a spot of mud on his shirt, his ability to influence a game lying, instead, in his ability to spot the right pass at the right time. There was also the matter of what Didi later described as 'a determined campaign

National Stadium, Santiago 1962

against me, brought about, I am sorry to say, by the attitude of Alfredo Di Stéfano'. Real were astonishingly successful during the two seasons Didi spent at the Bernabéu, twice winning the European Cup. The Brazilian, though, was shunted to the sidelines, playing just 19 times in La Liga and not at all in European competition. By 1960, he was ready to cut his losses and come home.

★ ★ ★

Vavá and Didi were the first of many outstanding Brazilian players whose exploits at World Cups saw them snapped up by Europe's elite clubs. Their very different experiences of life in Madrid foreshadowed some of what lay ahead for subsequent generations, too. Both, of course, were back in Brazil ahead of the 1962 World Cup in Chile and joined up with a national squad which had changed very little since winning the tournament four years previously. Mauro replaced

Bellini at centre half and as captain; injury to Orlando meant a place in defence for Zózimo. Illness caught up with coach Vicente Feola. His replacement was Aymoré Moreira, whose brother, Zezé, had been in charge of the team in Switzerland in 1954.

Brazil took world football by surprise in Sweden. This time around, the rest had had four years to prepare against what was expected to be a team showing signs of its age: Didi, for example, was now 32; full backs Djalma Santos and Nílton Santos were even older, 33 and 37 respectively; all three would be playing at a third consecutive World Cup. But this was a *Seleção* which

Botafogo, Rio de Janiero 1960

made up in canniness for anything it now lacked by way of youthful exuberance. As Didi pointed out at the time: 'It is the ball that needs to run, not the player.' Once again the squad were looked after by a technical team expertly managed by Paulo Machado de Carvalho; only the psychologist who'd advised against the inclusion of Pelé and Garrincha in 1958 had been left behind.

Mexico were dispatched 2–0 in Brazil's opening game of the 1962 World Cup at the little Estadio Sausalito in Viña del Mar, Pelé beating four defenders – and then the goalkeeper from distance – for the second. Now regarded as the world's best player, he looked in the mood to prove it. In the second Group game, against the Czech team Brazil would meet again in the Final, disaster struck: Pelé fired a fierce shot against the post and, trying to reach the rebound, tore a thigh muscle, an injury which kept him out of the rest of the tournament. Before the days of substitutes, Brazil's ten fit men re-grouped and hung on for a 0–0 draw.

Pelé's replacement was Amarildo Tavares da Silveira, a youngster who had been raised, like Didi, in the dour surroundings of Campos dos Goytacazes, north of Rio. Presented with his big chance, Amarildo seized it with both hands. Brazil's final Group game, which they needed to at least draw in order to progress, was against Spain. It was the nearest the team came to failing to defend the World Cup. Normally the calm focus at the heart of the *Seleção*, Didi was anything but that as he took the field against Spain. Injury had deprived the Spanish of the services of Didi's nemesis, Di Stéfano, but his perceived failure in Madrid still rankled:

> I was burning with the idea of winning the match to show them the kind of player I was. It was really a pity Di Stéfano was not on the field of play. He would have had the chance to learn a few things.

Didi was so obviously wound up that coach Moreira considered leaving him out and during the first half Spain had much the better of things. Trailing 1–0, the Brazilian players trooped into the dressing room in silence, although Moreira was convinced 'that they knew what was wrong without my telling them.' The actions of the oldest head on the team and the youngest proved decisive thereafter. Just after half-time Vavá's former team-mate at Atlético Madrid, Enrique Collar, broke into the Brazilian area only to be upended by Nílton Santos. The Brazilian's reaction was a definitive exercise in trickery, the street-wise face of the football – another kind of *jeitinho* – which had so delighted spectators at the 1958 World Cup. Seeing that neither the referee nor his linesman had had a clear view of the incident, Santos stepped outside the area, flung his arms in the air and, feigning affronted innocence, complained that Collar had taken a dive.

Spared the penalty which could have left them trying to claw back a two-goal deficit, Brazil wore down Spain as the game itself wore on. One of the reasons 22-year old Amarildo had been chosen to step into the shoes of the injured Pelé was that he played his club football alongside both Zagallo and Garrincha at Botafogo. The connection plainly worked: first, Amarildo stabbed in Zagallo's cross from the left; minutes later he got his head to a Garrincha cross from the right. Brazil's coaching staff and dozens of photographers swarmed onto the pitch: the *Seleção* had found a new hero when it mattered, in the only match in Chile Brazil ever looked remotely likely to lose.

★ ★ ★

Renowned as a dribbler, Garrincha, it seemed, had learnt new tricks since 1958. Chile 1962 will be forever remembered as his World Cup. In the quarter-final against England, in the words of Nelson Rodrigues, Brazil 'had no Queens, or House of Commons or Lord Nelsons. But we had Garrincha'. The 'Little Bird's' extraordinary spring saw him out-jump giant and statuesque English defenders at a corner to open the scoring. Eventually, his shot – right-footed, bent round

Springett in goal from well outside the area – finished England off. In between times, Garrincha wrought havoc all over the pitch against an England side who'd made plans for containing him wide on the right.

In the semi-final, hosts Chile seemed to have no better idea how to stop Garrincha other than lining defenders up to tackle him. And kick him, if necessary. Garrincha scored twice more and further goals from Vavá secured a 4–2 win. As the clock ran down, however, Garrincha kicked back at Chile's Eladio Rojas after one foul too many. He was sent off by Peruvian referee Arturo Yamasaki, who had missed the incident but took advice from his Uruguayan linesman, Esteban Marino. Yamasaki, under pressure from a passionate home crowd, was doubtless eager to even up the numbers having already sent off Chile's Honorino Landa moments before. As he wandered off towards the dressing rooms, an outraged spectator let fly with a stone which caught Garrincha on the back of the head; eventually he left the stadium with his head bandaged.

At the time a cut head seemed the least of Garrincha's worries. The Final, against Czechoslovakia, was three days away and the idea of Brazil going into it without the tournament's best player seemed unthinkable – unthinkable to Brazilians, anyway. Tancredo Neves, the Brazilian Prime Minister (the country was experimenting with a parliamentary model of government at the time), added his voice to the Brazilian Federation's appeal for leniency on the grounds that Garrincha had been much provoked. More mysteriously, the one official who'd actually witnessed the incident – linesman Esteban Marino – had elected to take the first plane home to Montevideo and was nowhere to be found. In his absence, FIFA cleared Garrincha to play against the Czechs.

On the day – June 17, 1962 – Garrincha probably shouldn't have played anyway: he took to the field dosed up with aspirin and running a high fever. As a result, for once he wasn't the match-winner. The Czechs took the lead in Santiago through Masopust but Brazil fought back thanks, in large part, to the efforts of the youngster, Amarildo. Pelé's stand-in scored the equaliser before setting up the second for Zito. Brazil ran out 3–1 winners and became only the second side in history to defend a World Cup. As for Amarildo, unknown outside Brazil before the tournament, his moment in the Chilean sun saw him become the latest star invited to head off to Europe. He spent the next ten years of his career in Italy, playing for Milan, Fiorentina and AS Roma.

Garrincha, FIFA's Player of the Tournament, returned to a hero's welcome in Rio. The nearest he ever came to crossing the Atlantic was the following year, when Botafogo agreed a world-record fee for his transfer with Inter Milan. A knee injury sustained by *o Anjo de Pernas Tortas* – 'the Angel with Bent Legs' – scuppered the deal. By the time Amarildo returned to Brazil to join Vasco in 1973, Garrincha had already retired. Ten years after that, Brazil's 1962 World Cup winners would join the nation in mourning the passing of *o Alegria do Povo* – 'the Joy of the People' – a player who captured the spirit of his nation, for better and worse, more perfectly than any other ever has. Garrincha died an impoverished alcoholic but Brazil remembers him still, perhaps as the greatest – certainly the best-loved – player of all time. As Nelson Rodrigues observed, 'Everything about Garrincha was Brazilian. He was everything to Brazil.'

★ ★ ★

One of the running debates in Brazilian football over the past 50 years has been over the relative merits of *futebol-arte* as opposed to *futebol-força*. Literally, that's: 'art-football' versus 'power-football'. Depending on the point of view, it's an argument that sets style against substance, the game against the result, improvisation against organisation, pretty football against winning football and – at the extreme – Brazil against the rest.

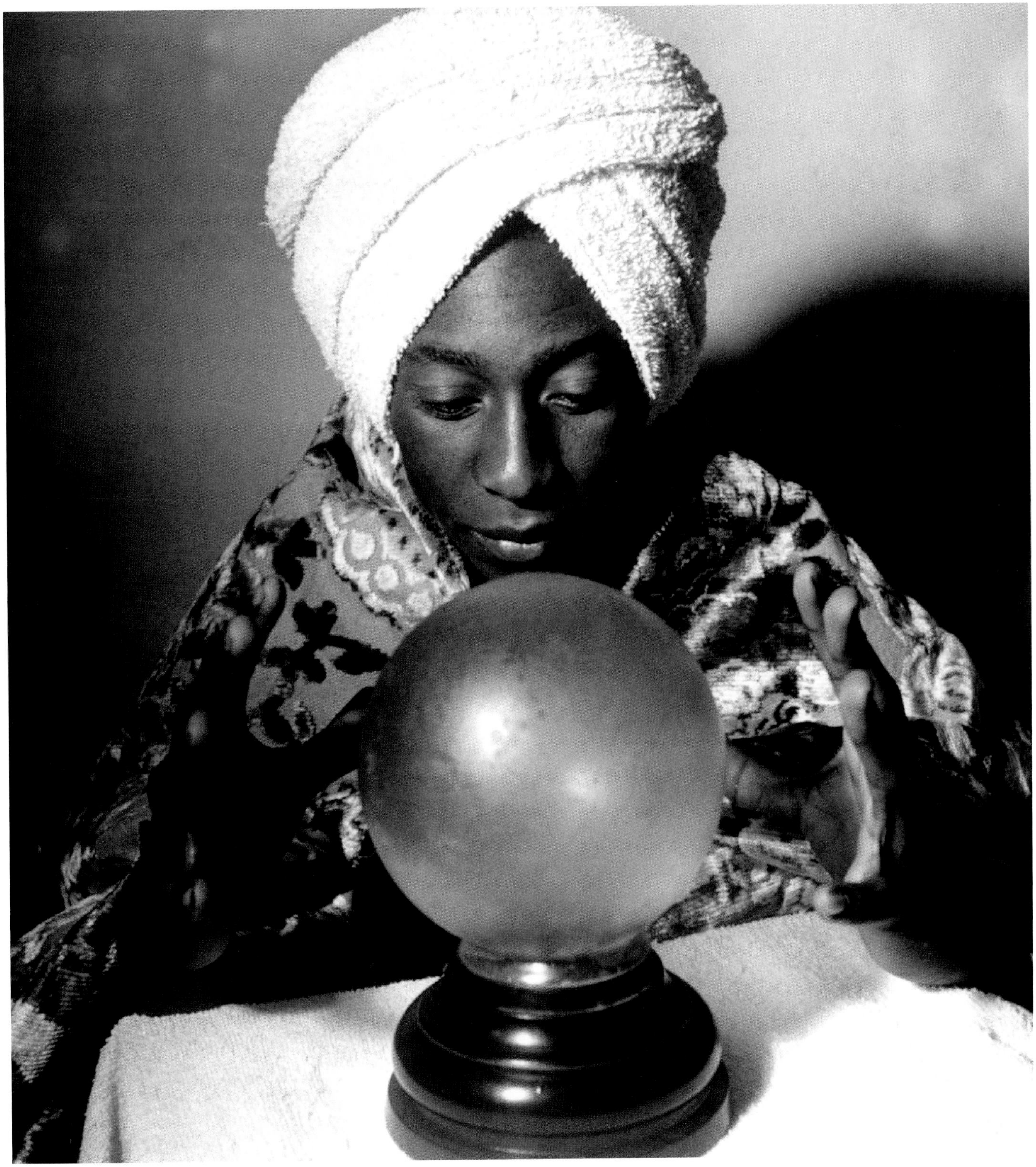

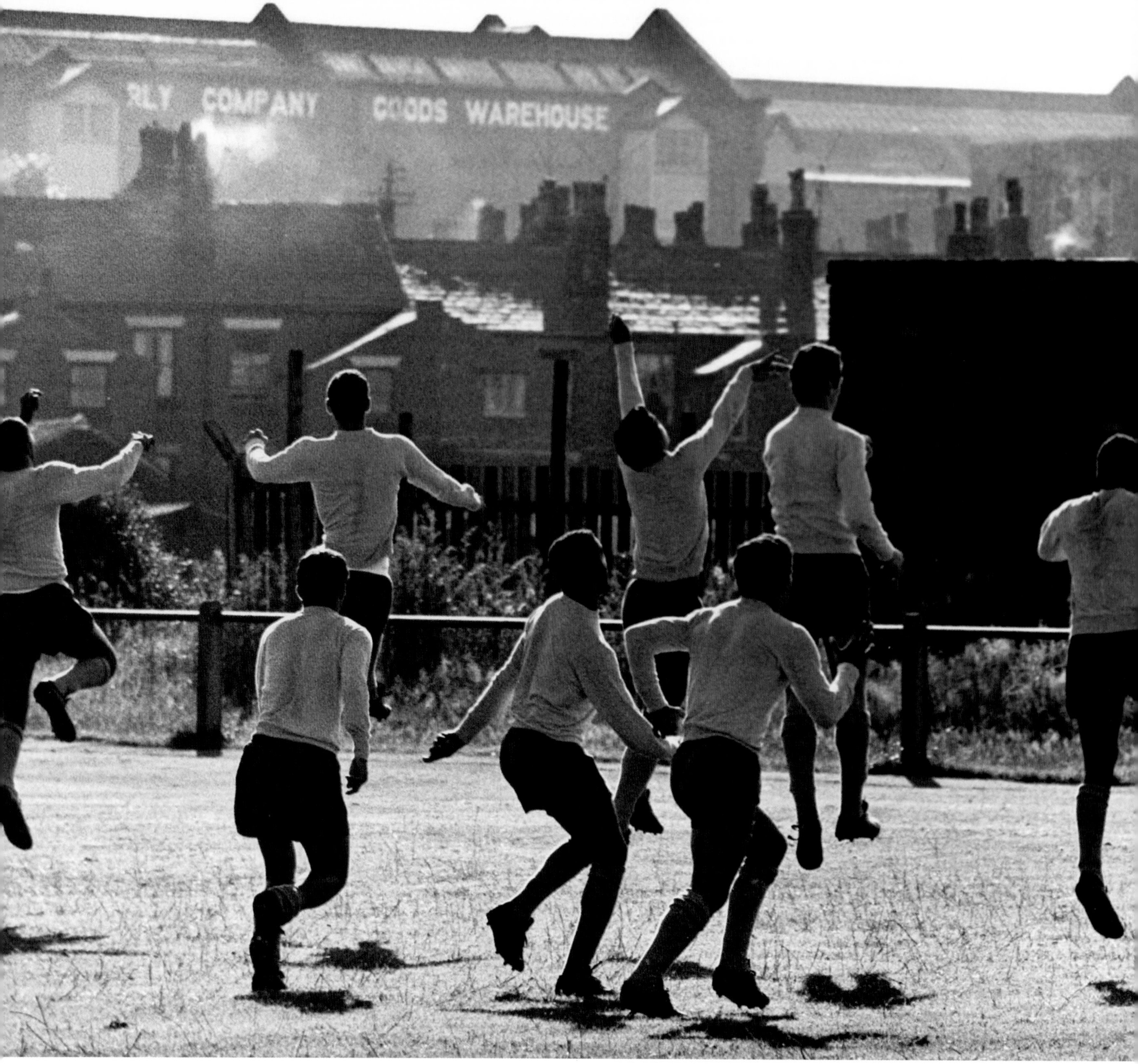
RLY COMPANY GOODS WAREHOUSE

Every head coach of the *Seleção* is defined and judged by where his footballing philosophy fits on the sliding scale between beauty and power, *arte* and *força*. Up until 1962, Brazilian football's identity had been agreed on and little changed since the 1930s. A sense of freedom, of individuality and spontaneity, had been celebrated since Gilberto Freyre's day. The World Cup winners of 1958 and 1962, canny and cynical though they could occasionally be, conformed to the *futebol-arte* ideal. How could they not, with the likes of Pelé and Garrincha in their ranks? The World Cup of 1966, however, would cast that received wisdom – and a lot more besides – into doubt.

For all that the previous two tournaments had been triumphs, the World Cup in England was an almost unmitigated disaster. Much of the responsibility for Brazil's fall from grace can be laid squarely at the door of one man. And, perhaps, be traced back to one single decision. In 1958 and 1962, Brazil had the best players. Their success, though, was facilitated by them also having the best organisation behind the scenes, thanks to the efforts of Paulo Machado de Carvalho, head of delegation in Sweden and Chile. Such was his standing in Brazilian football, Machado was often referred to as *o Marechal da Vitória* – 'the Marshall of Victory' – and, in 1961, São Paulo's Estadio Pacaembu was re-named in his honour. His boss, however, the President of the CBD, João Havelange, had set his sights on a position for himself in world football to match that already achieved by the national team. Already his campaign to succeed the Englishman Stanley Rous as president of FIFA was picking up steam.

It's safe to say that Havelange's decision to dispense with the services of Paulo Machado sprang from a desire to be more intimately associated with Brazilian success, success he was convinced would continue in England in 1966. When Brazil became world

Bolton, 1966

champions for a third time, Havelange wanted it to happen on his watch. He appointed himself as head of delegation and was quick to betray almost total ignorance of the footballing challenge that lay ahead. The coach of the team that had won in Chile, Aymoré Moreira, had begun the painful process of renewing what was an already ageing squad. After the handful of bad results which, inevitably, accompanied untested players being given their chance, Moreira was sacked and replaced by the elderly – and more pliable – coach of the 1958 team, Vicente Feola.

Away from football, the dynamism and focus of Juscelino Kubitschek's presidency had been followed by internecine battles for power, the manoeuvrings of party politics and a swift descent into chaos. By 1966, Brazil was once more living under a military dictatorship. Havelange, for his part, knew very little about football but an awful lot about football politics: he had no qualms about using the national team as a platform for his ambitions, at home and abroad. The preparations for the World Cup were a perfect case in point. Machado had kept life as simple and straightforward as possible for his players with the intention of building a sense of togetherness that could liberate individual talents. Havelange had the squad spend three months traipsing from training camp to training camp around the country, currying favour as he went by insisting on the inclusion of particular players to please the powerful presidents of Brazil's most influential clubs.

Vicente Feola found himself with a squad of 45 players, fewer than half of whom would eventually be able to board the flight to England. The group was unwieldy and riven by cliques, with most of the players unsure as to whether or not they'd be picked when the squad was trimmed to 22 ahead of the tournament. As it was, the chosen few turned out to be not particularly well chosen at all. It was an unbalanced mix of youngsters – some of whom would come good in 1970 – and very old hands who'd already given it their best

shot at the previous two World Cups. Even Garrincha made the trip despite being plagued both by injuries, the most recent of them sustained in a car crash, and the cumulative effects of his taste for cachaça, Brazil's liquor of choice.

But Brazil had Pelé and the belief – both at home and abroad – was that, with the world's greatest player at his best, the *Seleção* would once more be victorious. Opponents in Sweden and Chile had found him unplayable. In England, though, the Europeans – and the exponents of *futebol-força* – would take their revenge. Both Pelé and Garrincha started Brazil's first game of the tournament, against Bulgaria at Goodison Park, and both scored spectacularly in a 2–0 win. It was the last time the pairing which had driven Brazil to the top of world football would ever line up together. Despairing of stopping Pelé by fair means, the Bulgarians resorted to fouls. He was tracked round the pitch and kicked at every opportunity. It was the beginning of the end for his – and Brazil's – hopes in the tournament.

Pelé was unavailable for Brazil's next game against Hungary and, in his absence, Brazil looked ordinary. The senior players – Djalma Santos, Bellini and Garrincha – struggled to keep up, while youngsters of great promise – Jairzinho, Gerson and Tostão – weren't yet ready. Tostão scored but Brazil were well beaten. The 3–1 defeat was Garrincha's last-ever appearance for his country: he was part of a cull ahead of Brazil's final Group game against Portugal, which they would now have to win if they were to progress. Pelé still wasn't fully fit but was pushed into battle anyway and later remembered the chaotic preparations for the game:

The build-up to the Brazil-Portugal game was very strange, with no one having any idea who was going to play, and the whole team being constantly shuffled around until the very last minute. The selectors were in a complete panic.

Gerson, Garrincha and Pelé, 1966

In the end, seven changes were made to the team that had lost to Hungary, including an entirely new defence and goalkeeper. The Portuguese were coached by a Brazilian, Otto Glória, and were only too ready to put the boot into the fading hopes of the *Seleção*. Portugal ran out comfortable winners 3–1, with the magnificent Eusébio scoring twice. The game will be remembered, though, for the brutality of the treatment dished out to Pelé over the course of the afternoon. After two merciless hacks by the Portuguese midfielder João Morais, either of which ought to have seen him sent off, the man who'd been expected to light up the tournament had to be carried off the pitch. It had been an exercise in *futebol-força* at its cynical worst. Pelé hobbled away along the touchline and Brazil's slim hopes went with him.

Back at home, the humiliation in England saw some Brazilians ready to indulge once more what writer Nelson Rodrigues had called, back in 1950, *O Complexo de Vira-lata*: 'the Mongrel Complex'. The team's multiracial identity, so enthusiastically celebrated in the warm glow of victories in Sweden and Chile, was now held up again as evidence of the innate inferiority of a mixed-race people. Journalist and film-maker Igor Natusch has summed up the sense of shame which was re-attached, in some quarters, to the team's efforts: 'We were mutts again. We left the house barking like mad and returned home soaking wet and with our tails between our legs.'

For his part, João Havelange was unwilling to take any responsibility whatsoever for the national team's failings. The fact that European sides had done the kicking – and that the perpetrators had been indulged by English referees who, to their shame, did nothing about it – gave him a ready-made excuse. In 1964, Brazil's military regime had set up the *Serviço Nacional de Informações*, a department of internal intelligence that sought to develop a political and social climate in which any dissent could be ruthlessly stamped out. With paranoia increasingly the order of the day in wider society, Havelange was quick to foster a conspiracy theory which could explain what had happened to the team in England. Into his dotage – and despite his own credibility having long since been compromised in the wake of a trail of corruption scandals – Havelange would continue to insist the 1966 World Cup had been fixed by Europeans desperate to ensure one of their own won the tournament.

However he managed it, the head of delegation stepped away from the wreckage of 1966 and, eight years later, a lifetime of sports politicking was duly rewarded when Havelange was elected President of FIFA. It took him a while to reach the top of his chosen greasy pole. It took the *Seleção* rather less time to find their way back to where they belonged: respected, celebrated and adored, at the very top of the world's favourite game.

★ ★ ★

Since the 1930s, every Brazilian political leader – apart from the academic and intellectual Fernando Henrique Cardoso in the late 1990s – has seen the value of hitching his own reputation to that of Brazilian football and the world's best-loved team. This was certainly true of the military government, which had seized power in 1964, ostensibly to claw the nation back from a descent into communism under the presidency of João Goulart. These were troubled times in Brazil: protests, bombings and kidnappings escalated under an authoritarian regime struggling to bring the economy under control. As a result, at no time in its independent history had Brazil been subject to so much criticism from abroad. By 1969, Emílio Médici – the third military president – instituted new measures to control dissent: torture became widespread and press censorship ever stricter. At the same time, major infrastructure projects were undertaken in an attempt to drive economic growth. Success at the 1970 World Cup wasn't just a sporting ambition for the nation, it had become a political objective for the Médici regime as well.

In the wake of the 1966 World Cup, the successful coach of the 1962 squad, Aymoré Moreira, was reinstated. By the time preparations became serious, however – and this would be the first World Cup for which Brazil had faced qualifying in a decade – he'd been moved on. His replacement was, under the circumstances, an extraordinary choice: a leading Rio sports writer named João Saldanha, who had briefly –

and successfully – managed Botafogo. It's been said that Havelange appointed Saldanha in the hope that having a journalist at the helm would keep the Brazilian press onside. Even more remarkable, though, was that the new coach was also a former member of the now-outlawed Brazilian Communist Party.

Whatever the circumstances surrounding it, Saldanha's appointment worked. Brazil came through their qualifying campaign with a perfect record, winning all six of their games and scoring plenty of goals, thanks to the now-recovered Pelé and the maturing and stylish Tostão. Lessons had been learnt, obviously, since 1966 and by 1969 Saldanha had put together a squad which not only won football matches but did so in style: it seemed the perfect balance had been struck between arte and *força*. And just at that point, less than a year before the tournament in Mexico, it all started to unravel – for Saldanha, at least.

It's hard to tell exactly when the trouble started. Already Saldanha had a reputation for being outspoken and confrontational. By late 1969, he seemed to be picking fights for the sake of it: dropping established members of the squad for no reason; suggesting Tostão and Pelé were too alike in style to play together and that the latter might be the one to miss out. The world's greatest player, according to the manager, was myopic. In fact it was Tostão who almost missed the World Cup after detaching a retina in a training ground accident. A disappointing defeat in a friendly against Argentina – who'd been knocked out in the Qualifiers by a Peru side managed by the great Didi – soon followed. As did an argument with Emílio Médici. The President was a fan of the Atlético Mineiro striker, Dario, an out-and-out goalscorer who, by his own admission, 'was too busy scoring goals to learn how to play football'. The face-to-face exchange between general and head coach has gone down in Brazilian football history. Médici, the story goes, told Saldanha that Dario should be brought into the team. Saldanha replied: 'I'll tell you what, Mr President.

Let's make a deal. I won't tell you who to select for your government and you won't tell me who to select for my team.'

João Havelange was ordered to immediately sack Saldanha and did so, installing one of the heroes of 1958

Azteca Stadium, Mexico City 1970

and 1962, Mário Zagallo, in his place. Much credit, quite rightly, has gone to his predecessor, who had assembled an impressive squad. Zagallo, though, proved as wily and dogged a coach as he had been as a player and it was he who put the final pieces in place. 1970 was his victory and saw him become the first man to win a World Cup in both roles. He accommodated both Tostão and Pelé by identifying the former as his centre forward and giving the latter the Number 10 shirt and a more flexible role in behind. Rivelino was moved left and urged to attack, leaving the experienced and astute Gérson to conduct matters from central midfield with his *canhotinha de ouro*, the 'golden left foot' which was his calling card. Finally, centre half Clodoaldo was moved forward to play alongside Gérson and, from there, protect the back four which many considered the team's weakest link.

Preparations for the tournament were run with military precision. Unsurprisingly, the head of delegation was a brigadier, Jeronimo Bastos, installed by the junta to ensure their considerable investment in the *Seleção* would bear suitably well-publicised fruit. Football and the World Cup in Mexico, after all, were expected to serve as a trump card for the otherwise unpopular regime, rather as the 1978 tournament would for Argentina's even more brutal junta eight years later. Brazil's players conducted a charm offensive on arrival in Mexico before retreating to the fortress of their training camp to prepare. Changes to the rules ahead of the tournament were expected to help: the introduction of red and yellow cards was designed specifically to eradicate the vicious fouling which had blighted Brazil's appearances in England in 1966; substitutes, too, were allowed for the first time at a World Cup, allowing Zagallo to rotate his squad, fostering team spirit by keeping fringe players involved.

Nevertheless, Brazil arrived in Mexico with a very definite first-choice XI. The same team lined up for Brazil's first game against Czechoslovakia as started the Final, three weeks later against Italy. It's not only Brazilians who can run off the names: Félix, Carlos Alberto, Brito, Piazza and Everaldo; Clodoaldo, Gérson and Rivelino; Jairzinho, Tostão and Pelé. 1970 was the first World Cup to be broadcast live and in colour on television. Kick-off times, controversially, were even changed to accommodate European TV schedules, meaning many games were played in the punishing heat of mid-afternoon. Brazil's breathtaking and irresistible

march to a third triumph was witnessed everywhere: the dazzling yellow of the players' shirts, the shimmering green of the pitches, the clear blue of the skies above; all picked out on camera in the thin air and bright sunshine of Mexico. No one who witnessed it will ever forget it. The team of 1958 is still revered at home: after all, they were the first to win a World Cup for Brazil. In 1970, though – and for the first time – the whole planet was able to watch on in wonder as they won for the third time.

Matches played at altitude and in soaring temperatures helped make 1970 the most open of all World Cups: this wasn't a tournament for chasing the ball or your opponents for 90 minutes at a time. The conditions favoured technicians and visionaries, the proponents of *futebol-arte*. Brazil won all six of their games, scoring 19 goals in the process, including four in a complete dismantling of Italy in the Final at the Estadio Azteca in Mexico City. The last of those, scored by the captain, Carlos Alberto – who is still known as o *Capitão* in Brazil to this day – summed up everything that made this a team of which every Brazilian remains fiercely proud: nine players involved in the passing move which took the ball from one end of the pitch to the other before the right back arrived – an express train – to smash his bullet-shot across and beyond Albertosi in the Italians' goal. The celebrations at the end of the game were as joyful and unconfined as the football that inspired them had been. A third World Cup for the *Seleção* meant the trophy would return to Brazil, and this time for good.

Pelé's reputation as the best football player of all time owes much to his performances at the 1970 World Cup: at the very height of his powers, he led an outstanding team by example. He himself scored four memorable goals in the course of the three-week tournament and laid on several of the seven which saw the dashing Jairzinho – *O Furacão*, 'The Hurricane' – become the only player in history to score in every game at a Finals. The goals and the victories, though, were only part of the

story: two of the best-remembered moments in Mexico were might-have-beens, breathtaking adventures in *jeitinho*. Against Czechoslovakia, on the way to Brazil's 4–1 win in their opening game of the tournament, Pelé spotted Ivo Viktor off his line; his shot from ten yards inside his own half missed by no more than a foot as the Czech keeper scurried to make up ground. Then, towards the end of Brazil's 3–1 victory over Uruguay in the semi-final, Pelé raced onto a through ball. As the goalkeeper advanced on him, he let the ball continue on its course while he ran diagonally away from it. Mazurkiewicz bought the dummy and followed Pelé, who then cut back onto the rolling ball only to slide his shot inches wide of the far post.

This latest triumph delighted Brazil and delighted the country's military rulers, too, who were quick to connect the World Cup victory to their own 'economic miracle' at home. *Pra Frente Brasil*, 'Forward Brazil', the team's official song, was adopted as its own anthem by the regime. That political manoeuvre was even easier to finesse because so many Brazilians had been watching events in Mexico unfold: easy access to credit had enabled 40 per cent of Brazil's urban homes to acquire television sets by 1970, representing a four-fold increase in less than a decade. What's more, the tournament in general – and, of course, Brazil in particular – delighted the rest of the world. The 1970 World Cup – played in glorious sunshine and with such élan by its winners – rekindled a global love of the game. Football had seemed, for a decade and more, to be in danger of becoming trapped in the defensive tactics and cynicism of European *futebol-força*. In Mexico, Brazil threw off those shackles, playing breathtaking football; playing football for fun. The *Seleção* returned to be fêted by politicians and public alike. A national holiday was declared. Brazil had won three World Cups in 12 years. No one could have imagined it would be twice as long before they'd win one again.

Carnival is the most incredible experience. It's a huge part of life for all of us in Brazil. I love it and used to go every year to the little Carnival we would have in Americana while I was growing up. Of course, I watch the big carnivals on TV and the thing that always amazes me is how different the celebrations are in the different parts of the country: you know, in Rio you have the big processions with the samba schools along the walkways in the Sambódromo; in Bahia, it's another kind of festival, with the trucks driving around town, and the singers and the sound systems.

When I was a kid, in our neighbourhood we didn't have *blocos*, the samba groups that take part in the big parades. It was more a case of everybody getting together for a party. In a park or somewhere open, they'd put up a big tent; everyone would come, there'd be music and we'd celebrate together. Now, there's a *bloco* in Americana but not one that goes into São Paulo. It just goes round and round Americana, with everybody in fancy dress. I must admit I've never got so far as to put a costume on – I watch other people in their outfits. But I don't watch the dancing: I do that myself!

There's no real way to explain Carnival to someone who's never experienced it. I think I'd have to pick the person up and put them down in the middle of it all, in the middle of a samba school in Rio, and then let them come up with their own explanation! It's not even something you can understand watching it. You have to be there: meeting new people, feeling the happiness all around you. It's not like in England where you might have the chance to look and decide whether you want to be involved. In Brazil, people are just going to grab you, hug you: *Come on. Come and dance! We'll show you how!*

More than anything, Carnival is a party, a chance for people to get together and have fun. But there's something about it as well that's very important for the culture of our country: it's a time when things get all mixed up together. The social divisions that we have in Brazil disappear for a while. You know: it's hot and it's crowded; everyone's dancing; T-shirts and shorts, people wearing as little as possible. You can't dress up as you normally would so there's no way of telling the difference between a rich person and a poor person. Everyone is in the Carnival together and the differences between us stop mattering; you can't tell who anyone is. Carnival turns the world upside down!

7. CARNAVAL!

'IT'S BETTER TO DO CARNIVAL than to define it.'

At least that's the advice of one of the characters in *João Ternura*, a story by one of Brazil's greatest authors of the mid-twentieth century, Anibal Machado. How, after all, to pin down something so sensual, so complex and so full of contradictions? Carnival is lived in the physical moment – a feast of the senses and for the senses – and, as soon as you reach out to try and capture it, it's gone: lost in laughter and the beat of the drum as the party moves on. Roberto DaMatta is a Brazilian anthropologist and intellectual who has tried, for most of his professional life, to get to grips with what Carnival means to his country. He's probably been the only one; certainly his book, *Carnavais, Malandros e Heróis* – 'Carnivals, Rogues and Heroes' – is the closest anybody's come to an academic interpretation of Brazil's great popular festival.

DaMatta recognises Carnival as being – alongside football – fundamental to his country's idea of itself as 'great, creative and generous, having a glorious future'. The communal sense of celebration and abandon opens the door to a 'kingdom of equality and social justice.' DaMatta attempts to describe Carnival's effects but he knows better than to try and fix in words what Carnival

actually is, beyond saying that, as a celebration in which all society, all rules – all life – can be turned upside down, 'Carnival is an absolutely wondrous enigma that Brazil poses to itself and to the world.'

★ ★ ★

Like football, Carnival is not Brazilian by origin. Football was brought across the Atlantic from England and transformed from a game into something like an art. Certainly, Brazilian football is truly unique and has found its way into every corner of Brazilian life as an expression of the country's heart and soul. So too Carnival: an import from Europe that has realised its true potential only in its adopted home. Carnival is a party – and much more. It gives Brazil carte blanche to celebrate its own existence in a form as tangled, elaborate and intricate as the nation itself. It's joyful, passionate, abandoned, seductive, erotic, generous and still tinged with sadness and nostalgia. Every barrier is broken down, every hierarchy challenged. Carnival laughs at the rich and powerful; men become women, adults plunge back into childhood. The rules are set by the clowns – harlequins, pierrots, columbines – and by the rascals: Brazil's favourite anti-heroes, the *malandros*. For four or five days, Brazil gives itself over to the madness and for the rest of the year looks forward: stitching costumes,

rehearsing songs and making plans. Maybe even more than *futebol*, *Carnaval* is the heartbeat of Brazil.

The history of Carnival goes back as far as you want to track it: the experience of wild celebration is fundamental to the human spirit. Certainly the Dionysian festivals of the Ancient Greeks featured recognisably carnivalesque elements: processions led by figures in outlandish costumes, competitions featuring poets and musicians and, last but not least, rowdy behaviour in the streets after the formal proceedings were complete. Later, the Romans celebrated *Saturnalia* and *Lupercalia*, both of them festivals that a modern-day carnival-goer might recognise bits of: during Saturnalia, parties were held everywhere and social norms overturned with masters – reportedly – serving food at their slaves' tables. Throughout *Lupercalia*, a fertility rite which included animal sacrifice and priests dressed as beasts, young men would run through the city streets slapping young women with thongs made of goatskin in the belief that it would help them bear healthy children.

Some of those pagan festivals were inevitably taken up and transformed to suit the demands of early Christian beliefs and practices. The customs we now recognise as Carnival became closely linked to the period immediately before the fast, which marks Christ's 40 days in the wilderness. Before giving up meat – and whatever else besides! – there would be days of celebration, of feast before the fast. The word 'Carnival' comes from Latin: either *carne vale* – 'farewell to the flesh' – or *carne levare*, meaning 'to remove meat'. Once Holy Week was instituted, a key staging post in the Roman Catholic calendar, Lent became of equal importance: the 40 days of fasting and self-sacrifice between Ash Wednesday and Easter Sunday. Carnival, therefore, falls seven Sundays before Easter Sunday, any time between early February and mid-March. The dates change from year to year, but whenever it's celebrated – and wherever, across Brazil – the party stands as a farewell to sensual pleasures, a communal 'one for the

road' before the days of reflection and seclusion that follow: a celebration of the profane and the earthly before concentration on the spiritual and sacred begins.

Across Medieval Europe, and especially in Italy, the Lent festivities developed into a tradition, with costumed processions and masked balls. Theatrical productions celebrated the struggle for the human soul fought between 'Mr Carnival' and 'Mrs Lent'. The celebrations were embraced at all levels of society, albeit in different ways. Ordinary people took to the streets and to the bottle, while the Venetian nobility created elaborate masquerades and their French counterparts threw spectacular parties in the royal salons of Paris. Slowly but surely, Carnival began to blur the distinction between social classes and became an occasion to upset the traditional hierarchies of rich and poor. Servants pretended to be masters, while masters indulged their carnal selves as servants. This was the Carnival culture that arrived in Brazil with the European colonisers and would eventually be transformed – made uniquely Brazilian – by the collision with rituals and traditions that crossed the Atlantic in the holds of slave ships arriving from Africa.

The Portuguese called it *Entrudo*, 'Shrovetide': whatever else, it was an excuse for street mischief like splashing water or perfume, throwing eggs, sand and even stones and waste at unsuspecting passers-by. In its wildness and lack of respect for the usual social boundaries, it was a key element of the pre-Lent festivities brought to Brazil by the Portuguese. First noted as happening in Rio in 1600, the first attempt to ban *Entrudo* was set down in a statute book of 1604. It was the first prohibition of many. Forty years later, to celebrate the coronation of a new king in Lisbon, D. João IV, organised musical processions – *préstitos* – took to the streets of Rio. Some claim that 1641 was therefore the date Carnival was born in Brazil. Of course this was only the start; the *Entrudo* continued to delight and frighten in equal measure: occasional outbursts of violence, like the murder of a particularly unpopular magistrate during the festivities of 1720, would be countered by banning orders that outlawed masks or hoods from being worn in the street as well as forbidding the pelting of passers-by.

More importantly, in the North East, on the coast around Salvador, African music, dance and costume flourished, expressed in traditions such as the ritual coronations of black, African 'kings' such as the *Folia Negra da Coroação dos Reis do Congo*, crowning a king of the Congo. It was a culture underpinned by the religion of *Candomblé*, a synthesis of belief systems developed by the millions of slaves transported across the Atlantic to work on Brazilian sugar plantations. The sounds, the costumes and the elaborate planning of the African traditions soon spread across the country, especially to Rio, which succeeded Salvador in 1763 as the capital of Brazil when the colonial administration recognised its supremacy as a port.

The first parades to take place specifically in the pre-Lent period of Carnival were known as the *Serração da Velha*, 'Sawing the Old Lady', and involved the sawing up of giant wooden dolls to symbolise renewal and rejuvenation. By the mid-nineteenth century the parties and balls of the Rio elite had become sufficiently popular that around the city shops began to open, selling Carnival masks and costumes. In the street festivities, meanwhile, African music started to define the sound of Carnival parades: *Jongo*, the precursor of Samba, had originated in Angola and developed in Bahia. Like *Samba*, Jongo was fostered by clubs and semi-secret societies and soon became a street parade soundtrack around Rio as well.

As Brazil moved towards independence, Abolition and urbanisation in the mid-nineteenth century, the traditions of Carnival developed a uniquely Brazilian character. Carnival societies, precursors of the samba schools, were organised, beginning with the *Congresso de Sumidades Carnavalescas*, the 'Congress of Carnival Characters'. They were soon followed by the *Ranchos*

Carnevalescos, processions bringing distinctly African elements south from Bahia, such as flag-bearers and *mestre-salas*, the masters of ceremonies, the marching leaders who have transmuted into the samba hosts of today. The *Ranchos* also introduced a fierce spirit of competition to proceedings. Often the *mestre-sala* was a master of the Afro-Brazilian martial art of *capoiera*, part of his job being to protect the flag of his band from attack by other groups.

By the time the twentieth century dawned, Brazil had broken from Portugal and slavery was formally abolished. Carnival processions and street bands – known as *cordões* (literally, 'strings') – had become hugely popular: in February 1902, 200 licences were issued to *cordões* by the Rio police. The first organised Carnival costumes contest took place a few years

Salvador

later and then, in 1910, Rio's first *Rei Momo* – 'King of Carnival' – appeared: the famous black singer, actor, writer and clown, Benjamin de Oliveira. In 1911, the biggest Carnival societies arranged to parade together on 'Fat Tuesday', the evening before Ash Wednesday and the beginning of Lent. Fifty thousand lamps were hung along the city's Central Avenue to illuminate the occasion.

Brazilian Carnival had found its way to an identity we would recognise in all its glory today: music, costumes, dancing and the processions – the neighbourhood-based and intricately-themed *blocos* – which emerged to replace the *cordões* and became the pulse of street carnival. Rich and poor; black, white and mulatto; the powerful and the powerless; the haughty and the humble; men, women and children … all of Rio took to the city streets for the greatest party on earth. And they've been doing it ever since. From its beginnings in *carioca* high society, Carnival has reached out across the whole of Brazil, flowering in its own colours, dancing to its own beat, wherever the celebration has put down roots. Each corner of the country has its own way of celebrating but the same spirit – tumultuous, daring, beautiful and profane – is alive and well everywhere: these are the days to let loose all shackles and celebrate what it means to be Brazil; days of miracle and fascination, nights of golden fantasy and sweet illusion in Carnival's enchanted world.

So, zip yourself into your costume, paint your bare flesh, put on a mask, sip the evening's first *Caipirinha*, tap your toe to the beat and get ready to let yourself go. Come celebrate with Brazil …

★ ★ ★

It's the middle of a bright Friday morning before Carnival. In the *Cidade Maravilhosa* – Rio de Janeiro, 'City of Wonders' – already the temperature is

Rio de Janeiro

beginning to rise. The sun shines brightly and colours of the rainbow spill across the curves of the city. The business executive, tie tight around his collar, glances impatiently at his watch again; the baker is distracted, thinking he can hear a distant drum-beat, before the first trail of smoke from the oven warns that his loaves are about to burn. Out in the street, the garbage man, alone in a world all his own, dances between the bins, swinging his broom and imagining he's a *mestre-sala*. The taxi driver has already festooned his car with decorations and switches his radio to the samba mode, singing along at the top of his voice. Up on the hillside, where the *favela* has long since been bristling with excitement, a young lady carefully sews the last hem on her costume and, in her mind's eye, sees herself as the most beautiful princess in the fairytale. *Cariocas* everywhere are feverish in anticipation, their city crackling with the thrill of the Carnival to come.

The air carries a certain fragrance, everything feels somehow weightless; sensuality wraps itself around the city, cloaking Rio in an atmosphere that's mysterious, different, intoxicating. Eyes shine brightly, smiles are breaking out on faces everywhere: people just can't wait, like children on Christmas morning before the presents are unwrapped. An African beat, a *batuque*, comes to life somewhere: first, the drumming of the *batukaderas*, then the voices of the singers, the *kantaderas*. And then, a wisp of song, drifting from an open window somewhere down the avenue, an anthem in celebration of the *Cidade Maravilhosa*. High above the city of Rio, the birthplace of *Carnaval*, the statue of Christ the Redeemer looks down on one and all. His benign gaze seems almost to be blessing us, blessing the revelry that's about to begin.

Early on in the afternoon it's just not possible to work anymore. It's not even possible to pretend we can. The executive kicks back, loosens the knot on his tie. Tapping

his fingers to a familiar rhythm on his desk, he looks out through the office window. On the streets already the samba groups are tuning up their instruments: bass drums (*surdos*), tambourines (*pandeiros*), little guitars (*cavaquinhos*), snare drums (*caixas de guerra*), beaded gourds (*afoxés*), cowbells (*agogos*) … And many more. The *Rei Momo* is about to be crowned.

Nowadays, there are nearly 500 street groups – *blocos de rua* – in Rio de Janeiro. It's they who are responsible for getting Carnival underway. Two weeks earlier, they begin to come out around the neighbourhoods to warm up the atmosphere of celebration in time for the real thing. The *Cordão do Bola Preta* group – the 'Polka Dot Bloco' – is one of the oldest and perhaps the most famous of them all. Founded in 1918, it attracts over two million people onto the streets of downtown Rio. *Bola Preta* shows up every Carnival Saturday, samba drummers leading the way and chanting the 'little marching songs' – the *marchinhas* – which are their anthems. The parade is closed with 'Cidade Maravilhosa', perhaps the most famous of all *marchinhas* since it was composed in 1935 – a song that has to be part of every Carnival celebration.

The *blocos* and their songs are the essence of Rio's Carnival. The first *marchinha* was composed in 1899. *Ó Abre Alas* – 'The Open Wings' – was written for the Rose Gold group, the *Cordão Carnavalesco Rosa de Ouro*, by a 52-year-old grandmother named Chiquinha Gonzaga and it is still sung throughout Brazil during Carnival, especially by the *blocos* in Rio. There are other old *marchinhas* that have survived to be remembered and re-sung year after year, too: *Allah-La Ô, Aurora, Máscara Negra, Jardineira, Saca Rolha, O Teu Cabelo Não Nega Mulata, Me Dá Um Dinheiro Aí* and hundreds more.

Carnival on the streets is an experience like no other. The sense of freedom, the happy abandonment rippling through the crowds, even the simple press of bodies around us, means we're all at the same level – literally. The harassed executive now has his tie in his back pocket and is face-to-face with the garbage collector, dancing

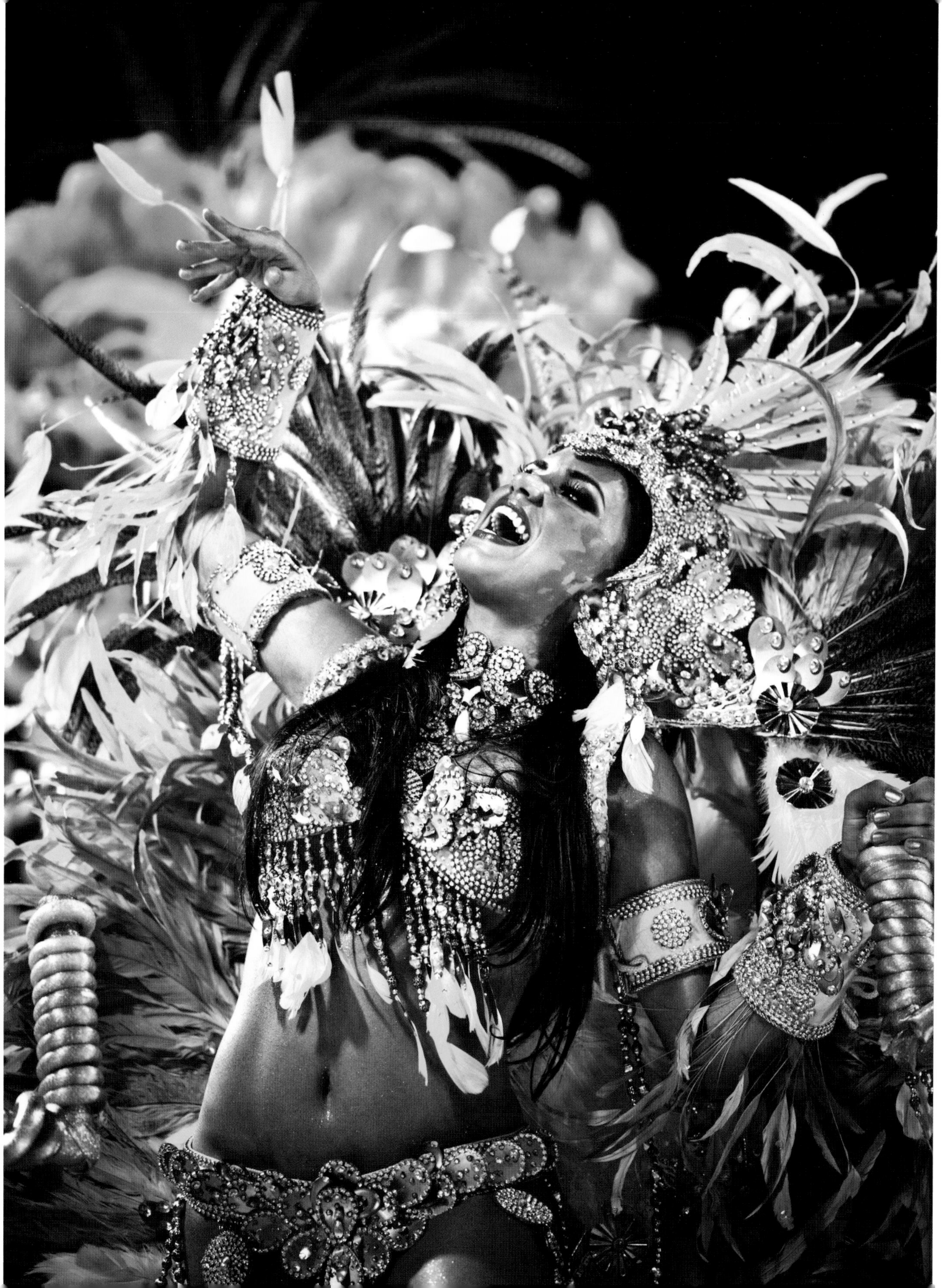

a samba with his new friend's broom. The baker who forgot to watch his bread has now forgotten everything – he's making eyes at the young seamstress from the south of the city. There's an emotional democracy at work in the *bloco de rua*. Everybody's singing; everybody's dancing, laughing, flirting. The world's a happy place where, for now at least, anything seems possible. Anything at all.

★ ★ ★

It was the *blocos* and their sense of fun, combined with a desire to put on the very best show in town, which gave rise to the *Escolas de Samba*, Rio's famous samba schools and the parades at the *Sambadrome Marquês de Sapucaí*, the purpose-built stadium with its 'samba runway' which is the international face Rio turns to the world at Carnival. Back in the 1920s, poor *Cariocas* – who didn't join the big parade in downtown Rio where the wealthy organised processions on vehicles, the *corsos*, and costumed troupes, the *ranchos* – began to create their own carnival groups. It was from them that the samba schools would eventually grow.

The neighbourhood of Estácio, not far from the city centre, is reputed to have been the cradle of the *Escolas de Samba*. It was there that *União Faz a Força*, a group founded by important samba personalities of the era, such as Ismael Silva and Mano Rubem, was born. The group was wound up in 1927, when Rubem died, but soon reappeared under the name *Deixa Falar*, 'Let's Talk'. From that group, which eventually grew to become the *União do Estácio de Sá*, emerged the samba school, the *Estácio de Sá*. They still wear the red and white first chosen in homage to the district's local football heroes in Três Rios, América Futebol Clube.

Meanwhile, in the Mangueira neighbourhood, Angenor de Oliveira – known as *Cartola*, meaning 'Top Hat' in Portuguese, and one of the grandfathers of samba – created a *bloco* named *Arengueiros*, which would soon emerge as the *Estação Primeira de Mangueira*. *Mangueira* eventually grew into one of Brazil's favourite samba schools. In other districts of Rio, other *blocos* were being created at almost the same time, like the Oswaldo Cruz group, which became the *Portela* samba school, and *Unidos da Tijuca*, a school which grew out of the fusion of several *blocos* based around the *favela* of Morro do Borel.

Until well into the 1930s, the carnival parades were enormous fun for all concerned but pretty much haphazard as far as their organisation was concerned. They happened when they happened, from year to year, with no fixed calendar or schedule. It was only in the early 1940s that dates and times started to be set and the samba schools would always appear on the Sunday of Carnival. The venue for the riot of colour, costume, music and dance was changed many times before finding a permanent home in 1984. The Sambadrome Marquês de Sapucaí was designed by Oscar Niemeyer, who had long since left his mark on the Brazilian landscape by building the new capital, Brasilia. The Sambadrome is a 700 metre-long stretch of road, painted fresh white each year, with grandstands along each side that can accommodate up to 90,000 spectators.

The samba schools have always been the product of local neighbourhood groups who would come together each year to plan, write, design, make and practise. They emerged from the grassroots of *carioca* culture, the show an expression and affirmation of local identity within the framework of a festival representing the whole city's idea of itself. More recently, thanks to tourism, television coverage and the exploitation of Carnival's commercial potential, the parade of the *Escolas de Samba* has seen marketing, sponsorship and prize money become increasingly important. Alongside the schools' traditional members, celebrities and television personalities have begun to use the event as a way of linking themselves to a mass audience, climbing aboard the floats and making

sure they are very obviously connected with Carnival on the big day.

As Brazil has found its way towards becoming a sophisticated consumer society, Carnival has had to surrender some of its credibility to the logic of the market. Even so, as with the World Cup, the event itself is so captivating that a sense of wonderment survives. Even amid the celebrity glitz of the *Sapucaí*, the magic still captivates those taking part and those watching on. The continued creative involvement of ordinary people and the local neighbourhood groups in every aspect of Carnival has preserved the pure and essential beauty of the Parade: the joyful expression on the face of the old lady in the *Ala das Baianas* – the women's wing of the school – who has saved all year for her costume and earned her place on the runway; the breath-taking accuracy and grace of the *mestre-sala*, tall and elegant, his fancy footwork setting the standard for everyone who follows behind; the unaffected delight of the girl chosen this year as the school's flag-bearer, the *Porta-Bandeira*, the 'flag bearer' girl.

It is impossible not to feel intoxicated by the blur of vibrant colours, the wildly extravagant costumes, the heart-stoppingly beautiful women and the insistent rhythm of the samba percussion band, the *bateria*. The musicians are unique, essential: rhythm selectors whose efforts combine and interweave with each other and with the dancers, like a star-studded football team at its best. The band master beating out the first step on his double-sided drum, the *repinique*, is samba's equivalent of the playmaker in the number 10 shirt. He conducts proceedings with his whistle, with gestures or just with facial expressions and eye movements. A picture of absolute concentration, he is in total command of the music. The main singers, meanwhile – known as 'samba pullers', *puxadores* – are marathon men. They belt out the school's *samba-enredo*, its theme song, and other samba compositions for hours at a time, power and eloquence never flagging for a moment.

And alongside the formal proceedings Carnival comes to life in other ways all over the city. Street parties led by informal groups – the *bandas* – will break out at every corner. No need to dress up or observe any traditions. All you need to join in is a sense of rhythm and a readiness to let yourself go. At the same time, too, Rio de Janeiro still holds old-style Carnival balls hosted at venues all across the city and across every social level, from local community-based clubs through to smart hotels such as the Copacabana Palace. A tradition dating all the way back to the colonial era, the balls still attract dancers and revellers by the thousand: they're an excuse to dress up to the nines, party and recall the spirit of the old European carnivals, with their masks and fancy-dress parades.

From high above the city streets, on Mount Corcovado, *Cristo Redentor* looks down on the blessed inhabitants of Rio as they dance and sing into the night. Is it too much to imagine that the overwhelming samba beat is the sound of Christ the Redeemer's monumental stone toe-tapping? The *Cariocas* are his people, after all. Is He not tempted to join the party, stepping down to take His place among the poor, the humble and the joyful celebrating Carnival?

★ ★ ★

Several hundreds of miles to the north, meanwhile, a light in the distance captures our gaze, offering up an invitation of its own. It is the *Farol da Barra*, the lighthouse of the city of Salvador, still guiding vessels from its commanding position on a tip of land where the Atlantic gives way to the shoreline reefs of the *Baía de Todos os Santos*, 'All Saints Bay'. The lighthouse guides us, too, towards a spectacular welcome at the heart of the most energetic of all Carnival celebrations in Brazil,

the Carnival of Bahia in Salvador. Perhaps the world's biggest outdoor party, Bahia dances to an African and Afro-Brazilian beat, with more than two million people each year taking to the city streets.

Above all else, Bahia's Carnival is about the *trios*. The party that Salvador rocks to today began in 1951. Two local musicians, Dodô and Osmar, piled into the back of an old 1929 Ford, driven – so the story goes – by a character known just as *Muriçoca*, 'Mosquito'. They wound their way through the city's narrow streets, playing their electrified instruments and inviting bystanders to follow along. Soon they had upgraded to a pick-up truck and cranked up the amplification. They had been joined by other musicians but there would only ever be three of them playing at a time: the *trio eléctrico* was born. It remains the musical heartbeat of the Carnival as trucks laden with massive sound systems creep through Salvador, luring party-goers and revellers along in their wake, some of whom pay good money to be on the truck or at least within a cordon maintained by stewards and security teams.

A flurry of *trios* emerged during the 1960s, then groups began to appear. The evolution has been less about a change in spirit and much more about a simple ramping up of voltage. Carnival in Bahia is big business: it brings at least a quarter of a billion pounds into the local economy each year. The original and wayward circuit followed by Dodô and Osmar has now been replaced by three more formal parade routes: the one from Barra to Ondina carries Dodô's name in his honour, the Campo Grande to Avenida Sete route is named for Osmar and the quieter, family-friendly circuit of the old City Centre is called *Batatinha* in tribute to a famous local composer and *sambista*, Oscar da Penha. As in Rio, local groups have always made sure there are alternative parades to join in other neighbourhoods around Salvador, too.

Carnaval Baiano has its own distinctive look and feel, thanks to the *Blocos Afros* and the *Afoxés*. The

music, costumes and traditions of the Afro groups all pay tribute to Salvador's African heritage. Three of the best known are Olodum, Ilê Aiyê and Ara Ketu, all established in the 1970s. The groups grew as a movement away from Salvador's samba schools, adding a reggae backbeat to the samba songs by then so closely associated with Carnival in Rio. It was in Salvador that traditional *frevo* music from the state of Pernambuco was electrified and amplified to create *guitarra baiana* and then *axé*, a genre happy to cannibalise influences from anywhere and everywhere and then transform the sound into something unique to Bahian Carnival. Over the last 20 years, it has crossed over into the mainstream and some of Brazil's biggest pop-stars – like Ivete Sangalo and Claudia Leitte – are *Axé* artists who first broke through at Carnival.

The *Afoxé* groups have a cultural connection to the Afro-Brazilian religion of *Candomblé*, which had to be observed more or less in secret by successive generations of the descendants of African slaves. *Embaixada Africana* – 'African Embassy' – was the first *Afoxé*, parading in the Carnival of 1895. The groups proliferated and soon became so popular that they broke out of the city's traditional black neighbourhoods and began to rub shoulders with the more European traditions on display downtown. As ever, Carnival was about breaking down barriers – for the few days it lasted, at least. The most famous of all the *Afoxés* was established by the city's dockworkers in 1949 in tribute to Mahatma Gandhi, who had been assassinated the previous year. The *Filhos de Gandhy* – 'Sons of Gandhi' – now have 10,000 members who parade in white and blue, their costumes inspired by India. They dance to the sound of *agogô*, bells used in Yoruba music from West Africa which are also the distinctive sound of the martial art of *capoeira*.

Experiencing Carnival means crowding into the city streets with hundreds of thousands of others and surrendering to the overpowering sounds of the *trios* and *axé* as their trucks inch along, surrounded by party-

goers, the volume turned up to 11 and pounding in your chest. It took a while to happen but, by the 1980s, high society and the desperately poor had found a way to come together at Bahia Carnival in a truly African melting pot of an occasion. Loud, passionate and wild, this is after all a place the writer Gilberto Freyre described as the *Bahia de Todos Santos e de quase todos os pecados*: the 'Bay of All Saints and nearly all sins'. To really take your place here, you'll need the energy of an athlete as you will be straining every muscle, jumping, springing and dancing. And you'll need stamina, too. In Bahia no one ever really knows when Carnival begins and ends. This year's Carnival and the next one seem to beat out a never-ending pulse, looping one celebration into the next; there's a bit of *Carnaval* in every single day that dawns in Salvador.

★ ★ ★

Recife

As the sounds of *axé* fade into the distance and we travel north up the coast, we start to pick up a new beat, the stamp of a different culture. Listen: *frevo* and *maracatu* tell us we're in Pernambuco state and its capital, Recife. The word *frevo* gives us a clue: it describes both a music – fast-tempo and loaded with brass – and a dance – based on the jumps and spins of *capoeira* – and comes from the Portuguese verb *ferver*, meaning 'to boil'. *Maracatu de nação*, too, describes both a music and a show. The sounds are percussive, up to 100 drummers leading a troupe of singers and dancers dressed up to parody the Portuguese court of colonial times. As Roberto DaMatta says, Carnival is a 'fundamental way of making fun out of the rich, the superior and the powerful'. Each troupe carries its own *calunga*, a giant doll representing their favoured deity. The spirit of Recife Carnival dates back to the crownings of the *Reis do Congo*, the 'Kings of Congo', ceremonies that helped slaves in Brazil's North East keep their African traditions alive.

In Recife, the famous *Galo da Madrugada* – the 'Rooster of the Dawn' – is the morning parade on the Saturday of Carnival and it is claimed to be the biggest anywhere in Brazil, even bigger than the *Cordão do Bola Preta* in Rio. Over two million people follow an apartment-block-sized and dazzlingly colourful rooster doll through the streets of São José, a neighbourhood next to downtown Recife. Boats out on the adjacent Capibaribe River follow the procession on shore. The old songs – and some new ones each year – are on every reveller's lips.

As if Carnival in Recife wasn't enough for residents of Pernambuco state to be going on with, there's another carnival – as famous and popular as any – just a few miles north of the capital in Olinda. The parties in Rio, Recife and Salvador tend to follow specific routes and are dominated by the samba schools, the *trios* and the *Galo da Madrugada* respectively. Olinda is something else again: Carnival takes over every street and every corner of the old town. There are no competitions and there's no sense of hierarchy. Everything is free and open to all – it's genuinely a Carnival for the masses. And by the masses, too: 500 different groups crowd the cobbled alleyways and winding lanes. Music, costume, dance … the sounds of *frevo* and *maracatu* are everywhere. It's a party alright, but one without a price tag and which goes on for days on end.

The famous giant puppets have dominated Olinda Carnival since the 1930s: anything up to 15 feet tall and made of papier mâché. They represent everything from figures inspired by local folklore and native tradition through others based on caricatures of modern-day politicians and celebrities. The best-loved of them all has been around since 1932: the *Homem da Meia-Noite* – the 'Midnight Man' – whose appearance on the Saturday at the appointed hour gets *Carnaval* underway. As with every Carnival in Brazil, Olinda's brings every level of society under its spell. It's a party for the whole

family, too: every age takes to the streets. Children learn to celebrate with their parents while Grandpa and Grandma reminisce about the old days, good and bad.

From the cobblestones of Olinda, south and inland we follow the parade into the state of Minas Gerais and another of Brazil's famous carnivals in *Ouro Preto*. Unlike the parties on the coastal flats, here it's all about the hills. The city, nestled in the spectacular Espinhaço

Mountains, is a tourist attraction all year round and packed for Carnival. What was once a wealthy colonial mining town – ouro preto means 'black gold' – still looks, with its narrow lanes and pastel-coloured buildings, as it did in its eighteenth-century heyday. Some of Brazil's most beautiful baroque churches dating back to that period are in Ouro Preto and give its Carnival a unique dimension: the sacred stands as host to the profane, the revels exploding against a backdrop soaked in spirituality.

The claim is that the oldest of all carnival groups was formed in Ouro Preto in 1867: the *Bloco Zé Pereira Clube dos Lacaios*. Its founder worked in the government offices of what was then the capital of Minas Gerais and to this day 'Zé Pereira's Footmen' still parade in top hats and tails while carrying their giant puppets around the streets. Today Ouro Preto is a thriving university town, which means new student *blocos* emerge every year to join the traditional groups as one and all make their way through winding lanes and narrow alleys before the climb uphill to Tiradentes Square, the highest point and the heartbeat of Carnival.

Carnival in Ouro Preto, in keeping with the serenity of its place in the landscape and the gentility of its architecture, is warm, hospitable and carefree. Families, students, the elderly and the very young, Carnival wraps them all in smiles. Here, the days of *festas* unroll without the commercial edge evident elsewhere. This fun is all for free: the joyful rhythms, the *cachaça* – sugarcane spirit – and the warm welcome from the people of Minas Gerais. Why would you want it to end? It's only tired legs that ever cut the evening short, aching after a day climbing up – and skittering down – the maze of cobbled hills criss-crossing the city, each cresting for just long enough to catch another vista: church, mountain and parade.

★ ★ ★

While Brazil's great cities put on their spectacular shows, towns and villages across the country celebrate Carnival in their own ways. Families gather, for example, in the little villages – *aldeias* – dotting the countryside around São Paulo: a grandmother paints her grand-daughter's face while Auntie makes last-minute adjustments to the little girl's handmade harlequin costume. Grandfather, grinning away behind his pirate's eye patch, plays with his grandson, who already looks the part, dressed as a little sailor. During the day, it's a street party: no pecking order and only the loosest organisation as the party spills through the streets: fancy dress, music, food and

a celebration to be enjoyed by all the generations. At night, the *festa* moves indoors: in clubs, town halls and community centres, brass bands swing to the samba; everybody joins in, singing favourite carnival songs; lines of dancers, confetti, masks and the elaborate costumes the grown-ups have been looking forward to climbing into all year.

São Paulo is a restless city: its own inhabitants complain they never stop work. Even in the nation's biggest city, though, Carnival turns the routine grind of the everyday joyfully on its head. The streets of *Sampa*, as *Paulistanos* call their city, usually so devoted to the relentless business of getting and spending, cut loose. The party first started towards the end of the nineteenth century: rural populations moved to South America's fastest-growing city in search of work and a future, bringing music and the spirit of the *festa* with them. Samba infected São Paulo just as it did Rio, even if the beat had a rough edge that captured the character of a city dedicated to profit and to toil. In the downtown clubs, high society gathered for carnival balls and masquerades. On the city's outskirts, meanwhile, the party happened on the streets, where migrants from across Brazil banded together to sing, dance and dress up, competing to outshine rivals from the next neighbourhood or factory.

During the 1950s, São Paulo's first samba schools were born: *Unidos do Peruche, Nenê de Vila Matilde, Vai-Vai* – the city's oldest – and a dozen more. In 1968, the first-ever parade of the *Escolas* rolled out along the city centre's Avenida São João. From there, the parade migrated first to Avenida Tiradentes and then, in the early 1990s, to the Sambódromo Anhembi, designed by Oscar Niemeyer and now home to a carnival show some 25,000 performers strong, including samba schools dedicated to the city's football clubs, such as the *Gaviões da Fiel* of Corinthians and the *Mancha Verde* of Palmeiras. In São Paulo, Carnival retains a street presence too, in the *blocos* drawn from across every neighbourhood, although the physical and structural deterioration of the city during the last years of the twentieth century saw the decline of street parades.

The *blocos* haven't disappeared altogether, though. The tradition remains particularly strong out in communities on the city's fringes, where local *festas* continue to thrive. Some of the traditional groups have lit up street Carnival now for 50 years and more: the city centre's *Banda Redonda*, for example, the *Vai Quem Qué*, from the neighbourhood of Pinheiros, and the all-female Afro-Brazilian *Ilú Obá De Min*. And, in recent years, the citizens of São Paulo have begun to reclaim the streets in earnest, thanks to the emergence, particularly on the west side of the city, of new *blocos* in neighbourhoods such as Vila Madalena, Vila Mariana and Butantã. The new groups have made it their business to ensure Carnival starts early in São Paulo: *Pré-Carnaval* is becoming the new and distinctly *Paulistano* tradition, thanks to *Bloco Unidos da Maria Antônia*, *Bloco da Ressaca*, *Bloco do Ó* and *Cordão Carnavalesco Confraria do Pasmado*, among others – and is growing in popularity at least as quickly as its glitzier downtown cousin, which dances through the Sambadrome.

Carnival holds sway from Rio to Recife, from Bahia to Belo Horizonte. Even Sampa – São Paulo, the city that claims it never stops working – downs tools and takes its place in the *cordão* at the sound of the *Samba-Enredo*. Year after year the sense of anticipation is the same, building to a feverish pitch before the party kicks off up and down the country.

It is Carnival that, more than any other national institution, assures us of the continuity of Brazil.

Perhaps Roberto DaMatta managed to resolve the enigma, after all: Carnival is Brazil – and Brazil is *Carnaval*.

Between Myself and God

I was raised as a Catholic and I'm still a Catholic today. In Brazil, perhaps, people would say I wasn't a practising Catholic because I don't go to Mass every afternoon. But my faith is something very important to me and I pray every day; I pray before every game. It helps me find focus and calmness, both as a person and as a player. I believe in God and I have my own way of connecting that with football. I have my own way of celebrating a goal, for example: I might point towards heaven if I score. I've never had messages written on T-shirts under my kit – I think that way of testifying is more of an Evangelical thing. My feeling is not that I want to show everybody what I'm doing; it's a quieter, more personal thing: between myself and God, perhaps.

Catholicism was my father's religion and, even though my mum is an Evangelical Protestant, I was brought up in the Catholic faith. I think that, in Brazil, people are aware of religious differences; we're aware of whether a person is a Catholic or an Evangelical or something else. But the feeling is almost that religion's not a subject worth arguing about: one person believes one thing, another something else. It goes beyond something you can debate or argue over: it's deeper, it's about faith. Religion will always be a personal thing in that way. And certainly there is no conflict, no aggression, as a result of those differences between people's faiths.

People have come from all over the world to live in Brazil and they have brought their own religions with them. In Brazil, we have the African religions from the slaves, of course. When people came from the Middle East, they brought Islam. The Germans brought Lutheranism. People from India have brought Hinduism. Jewish people, Japanese people, Italian Catholics

... everybody has brought their own faith. There is a freedom here: most people are Catholic or Evangelical but, even within Evangelicism, they will be part of different churches, each of the churches having its own slightly different beliefs.

I think you can see something true about Brazil if you look at religion in our country. There are all sorts of different people in Brazil; we are a very diverse people. And that is in our attitude to religion as well. Each person has his own faith and his own way of expressing it. Religion is as diverse as everything else in Brazilian life. We have a respect for each other's beliefs. There's a tolerance in us: I know that from my own experience and from within my own family, where we have both Catholicism and Evangelical Christianity living side by side, one family under one roof!

8. *TENHA FÉ*: BELIEF IN BRAZIL

ONE OF THE MORE FAMILIAR comparisons is describing football as a religion. And it's true – these two global phenomena both appeal to our need for a sense of community, for the reassurance of ritual and the certitude of shared belief. The football supporter has something in common with the member of a religious congregation: there's joy there and the feeling you're letting go, the idea that you're part of something bigger than yourself. In some cultures, indeed, where the secular has overtaken the spiritual, where the worldly has shaken off its connection with the divine, football can be the nearest we get to those experiences that have comforted and thrilled believers almost since the beginning of time.

In some countries football is almost a replacement for religion; for the certainties, privileges and responsibilities religion used to offer, but not in Brazil. Brazilian football supporters are as passionate as any but football is a faith that doesn't stand in place of religion; rather alongside, in what is still overwhelmingly a religious nation. For all but a few, to be Brazilian – now as much as ever – is to believe. Faith in God – or gods – is still a powerful charge running through everyday life, a fundamental part of how the nation collectively understands its identity. That

said, there is a religious diversity here to match the racial diversity so fundamental to the bigger Brazilian story.

The religious life of this nation of believers is in the midst of profound change and has been so for nearly 30 years. Almost 500 years after the arrival of the first Portuguese Catholics on its shores, Brazil is undergoing a fundamental change of heart, witnessing an overwhelming shift across the landscape of belief. Historically, in terms of sheer numbers, Brazil is the most Catholic country on earth but, right now, the nation is at the vanguard of an explosion in the rise worldwide of Evangelical Protestantism. Today, there are some 123 million Catholics in Brazil, roughly 65 per cent of the population, but over the last ten years the number of people identifying themselves as Protestants has grown from 27 million to over 42 million, 22 per cent of the population. Should the current rate of conversion continue, by 2040 Evangelical Protestantism will become Brazil's most prominent religion. The Catholic Church, which counted 90 per cent of Brazil's believers in its flock as recently as 1980, is watching its influence decline, as elsewhere around the world.

The dizzying rise of the Evangelical movement has, of course, been witnessed in the context of football just

Basílica de Nossa Senhora Aparecida do Norte

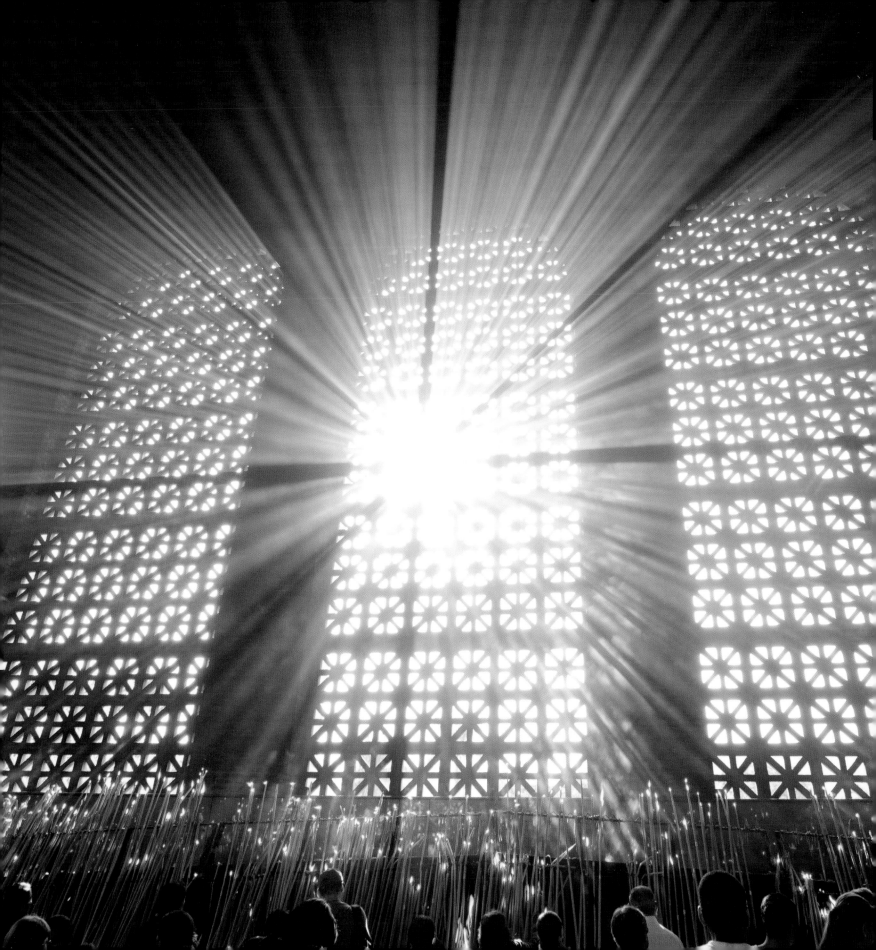

as in every other walk of life. Over the past two decades the football stadium has become a highly visible setting for testimony and for declaration of faith. Across the country – and wherever in the world Brazilians are playing football – entering the field of play, leaving it and, especially, the moment when a goal is scored have become opportunities for a player to express his faith. Especially an Evangelical player: arms reach to the sky in thankfulness and in prayer. Underneath team shirts, vests carry messages like 'Jesus Loves You', 'I Love Jesus' and 'Only Jesus Saves'. In interviews after games, players are quick – and sincere – in expressing gratitude to Jesus for the blessings received over the course of the preceding 90 minutes. They may be committed to the team they play for, but first and foremost, they are footballers for God.

As in so many aspects of our shared cultures, football reflects what happens in the wider world, capturing the same transforming waves as in the rest of our lives. Nowadays, whether in the sprawling cities of the South and East, such as São Paulo, Rio de Janeiro and Belo Horizonte, or in small, half-forgotten inland towns across Brazil, the Evangelical presence is manifest: huge churches, plain and unprepossessing as often as not, are everywhere, welcoming the faithful and the converts they bring. As many as 14,000 new buildings are inaugurated every year. Evangelical Protestantism, as elsewhere, is a single movement but one that is also fragmented into different sects: *Assembleia de Deus, Evangélica Batista, Congregação Cristã no Brasil, Universal do Reino de Deus* and *Evangelho Quadrangular*.

Each sect is comfortable using twenty-first century means to reach believers and those they are committed to converting through the powers of television, radio and social media. The Evangelical Churches preach and fundraise via their own TV and radio stations to reach millions in every corner of Brazil. Many have their own

Sao Paulo

newspapers, too: *Folha Universal*, a weekly periodical of Igreja Universal do Reino de Deus (IURD), for example, distributes over 2.5 million copies. *IURD* was, in fact, the first of the Evangelical Churches to establish a national prominence. It was founded in 1977 by 'Bishop' – a self-assigned title – Edir Macedo, whose profile leapt during the early 1990s after he acquired the TV broadcaster *Rede Record*, which is currently the second largest TV channel in Brazil, just behind *Rede Globo*.

The numbers may demonstrate the significance of the Evangelical movement in Brazil today. However, they don't explain the country's 'religious revolution'. The Churches carry an undoubted and captivating spiritual charge: the ministers – 'on stage', as it were – are charismatic leaders of their flocks. Crowds in the hundreds and, in some cases, thousands are swept along by scripture, music, song, ritual and moments of collective epiphany. The Churches offer a radically different experience to the formality and hierarchical tradition of the Catholic Mass. There are important political, social and cultural cross-currents at work but part of the falling-off of numbers declaring themselves Catholics – in Brazil and worldwide – may be explained in part by the very different context in which they express their faith: the Mass feels stringent, old-fashioned, elitist even, in comparison to the heady and all-encompassing emotionality of the Evangelical Church service.

For now, Catholicism continues to be the predominant religion in Brazil after being introduced by Portuguese Jesuits, who accompanied the early settlers and whose missionary agenda played a distinctive and defining role in Brazilian history during the colonial era. The Jesuit missions spread the faith throughout the country and once established, the Catholic Church exercised a profound social, political and cultural influence on all levels of Brazilian life. With the advent of the Republic at the end of the nineteenth century, State and Church were separated. The ending of its place as the 'official religion', however, did nothing to stem the rising numbers of those eager to commit their souls to the Catholic faith.

If nowadays the Evangelicals have become increasingly prominent in Brazil's big cities, thanks to their ever-widening media reach, in smaller towns, despite the Protestant presence, Catholicism survives – endures – resilient and strong. Pope Francis conducting a Mass for over three million Catholics on Copacabana Beach in the summer of 2013 is proof of that. Every village, be it perched above the coast or clinging to a dusty hillside in the interior, has a church at its physical and spiritual heart that welcomes practising Catholics every day, without fail, to late afternoon Mass. Catholicism plays a particularly important role in the impoverished states of Brazil's North East. It also retains its pre-eminence inland, where there are areas of the countryside still relatively untouched by the impact of the national mass media. There, the faithful remain loyal to their saints, such as *Nossa Senhora Aparecida*, 'Our Lady of Aparecida', a figure of the Virgin Mary who is revered, in the words of Pope Pius XI, as 'Queen and Principal Patroness of Brazil'. The pilgrimage tradition to the city of Aparecida do Norte, located north east of São Paulo and south of Rio de Janeiro, attracts some seven million visitors a year to its Basilica, built in 1955 to hold a congregation of up to 45,000 people.

★ ★ ★

So, Brazil remains, overwhelmingly at least for now, a Catholic nation. It's a free nation, too: free from the colonisers, free from slavery, free from military dictatorship. For every Brazilian, those hard-won freedoms also encompass freedom of religion. Here, awareness of differing belief systems doesn't mean conflict. Catholicism doesn't exploit its prominence to undermine other faiths: tolerance and diversity run deep through the culture of the nation, nowhere more

so than across Brazil's spiritual landscape. Syncretism – the reconciliation of differing beliefs – is pretty much all-encompassing: mosques, synagogues, temples and shrines of every denomination have their place in every major Brazilian urban area, often standing a few doors or a couple of streets away from each other. Brazil's Catholic tradition has been sufficiently enlightened to allow other faiths to prosper, resulting in an extraordinary melting pot of ritual, heritage and belief.

According to the census figures of 2010, there are almost 600,000 followers of a range of Afro-Brazilian religions in Brazil. Indeed, 400 years and more of

Umbanda shrine, Rio de Janiero

OSCAR'S BRAZIL

cross-currents at work, especially in the North East, have blurred the lines between manifestations of ancient African belief systems – which arrived with the millions of slaves brought to Brazil to work on the sugar plantations – and the Catholicism practised by their masters. *Umbanda* is the clearest example of that admixture of beliefs known as syncretism. Precepts, deities and ritual practice have all been plucked from Catholicism, spiritualism and African and indigenous

religions then mixed into a uniquely Brazilian whole. The religion originated around Rio de Janeiro in the early years of the last century, with services among poor Afro-Brazilians held in rooms, tents and even backyards, often in secret. Even now, *Umbanda* temples often look like ordinary houses from the outside and double as premises for community organisations. Services are led by a priest or priestess, a *pai-de-santo* or *mãe-de-santo*, and involve making connection with a spirit world of powerful deities and the worship of a single Supreme Being and creator.

Jacarepaguá Forest

Umbanda is widely practised across southern Brazil. *Candomblé*, on the other hand, centres on the North and East and is a more singular and distinctive belief system, its basic tenets brought to Brazil by African slaves. *Candomblé*'s roots lie in African animist faiths and found fertile ground among Afro-Brazilians, who had been brought up in the religious traditions of different tribal peoples, such as the Yoruba, the Fon, the Ewe and the Bantu. Today it is practised by the *povo de santo*, the 'people of the saint', and is based around the worship of a creator, *Olodumare*, and other deities, *orixás*. Those deities are paid tribute in the shape of animal, vegetable and mineral sacrifice; worship involves sometimes spectacular dance, song and costume elements. As with *Umbanda*, there are priests of both sexes. Many *Candomblé* practices have developed in secret but there are two great and very public festivals: *Lemanjá*, which is held along the entire Brazilian coast on February 2 and celebrates *Lemanjá* or *Yanaína*, goddess of the sea. The festival features baskets of flowers, jewellery and perfumes, among other offerings, being taken out to sea by fishermen. The *Festa do Bonfim* in Salvador, Bahia, is an example of the merging of Afro-Brazilian faiths with Catholicism. Its date coincides with a Christian observance – the second Thursday following the Kings' Day on January 6 – and rejoices in both Catholic and *Candomblé* ritual practice.

In terms of numbers claiming it as their faith, the third most significant Brazilian religious group is the Spiritists, also known as Kardecists. Almost four million people – 7 per cent of the population – subscribe to a religion that recognises a Supreme Intelligence (as opposed to the Holy Trinity) but finds much common ground with Christian scripture, while also incorporating belief in a world of spirits, reincarnation, communication between the living and the dead and the existence of other inhabited planets. Across Brazil spiritism was disseminated by ministers including Chico Xavier and Bezerra de Menezes but it was first formalised by a Frenchman, Allan Kardec, in the mid-nineteenth century. Kardec's precepts quickly took root in Catholic Brazil, appearing first in Bahia and then developing in Rio de Janeiro before becoming widespread across the country today.

Of course, hundreds of indigenous tribal cultures celebrated their own powerful and sophisticated religions long before the Jesuits arrived in Brazil to win the new colony for Catholicism. Many of those faiths and their ritual traditions have become absorbed into Christian practice over the centuries: again, the syncretic nature of belief in Brazil has had a definitive impact on the nation's religious identity. However, some indigenous belief systems continue to stand separate and unique, lived with the same fervour and humility as they have been for generations, particularly in Amazonia. The creation myth of the Guaraní people, for example, centres on a supreme being named *Tupã*, a god of thunder, who came down to earth and with the help of *Jaci*, the moon goddess, created everything that exists in the world.

Catholics, Evangelicals, Kardecists, Umbandists, Candomblers, Jehovah's Witnesses, Mormons, Jews, Muslims, Buddhists, Hindus, pagans and atheists, too … over the centuries and still today, there have been tensions between the different faiths, even occasional outbreaks of violence or vandalism. However, Brazil is committed to religious belief, its practices defined by an admixture and blending of faiths. In Brazil, there is space for all religions; no country on earth is more diverse. And that's as true of religion as it is of every other domain of Brazilian life. Here, in an enormous country that can admit and celebrate the widest possible variety of cultures under a single nation's flag, there's room to move. There's room to pray and to believe.

Passion, Pressure, Pride

Before I came to England, I played first for São Paulo and then for Internacional. I played in state championships but also the *Campeonato Brasileiro*. So I experienced football all over the country and I can tell you that every club – every city – has its own history, its own football culture. In São Paulo there are four big teams and there are lots of other clubs, too. The supporters are great, very passionate, but São Paulo has supporters all over Brazil: it's a big club in the city and a big club all over the country.

Porto Alegre is completely different. There are really just two teams in the city so everybody supports either Gremio or Internacional. You're either a *Gremista* or a *Colorado*, it's as simple as that. When I was at Internacional, I had to get used to the fact that, if I went out to a restaurant, the waiter was either going to love me or he would hate me! Because it's such a clear-cut division, I have the feeling that the supporters of the two clubs in Porto Alegre are the most fanatical and committed in the whole of Brazil. They take football very seriously down there; maybe that's why the city has produced so many coaches and managers: Celso Roth, Dunga, Luiz Felipe Scolari.

In São Paulo or in Rio, on TV and on the radio, they talk about all the different teams in Brazil because there are fans from all over the country living in those cities. In Porto Alegre, they only ever talk about two teams: Gremio and Internacional. Nobody in the city cares about any other team! It was a great place to play football because there was so much passion – the two sets of supporters absolutely love their clubs, two very big clubs. But that brought pressure too: when I had to play against Gremio in the *Grenal* derby, the atmosphere and the tension were like nothing I've ever experienced, before or since. The only other game I remember even coming close to the *clássico* in Porto Alegre was when we played against Flamengo

at the Maracanã. My first time there, I was a substitute and so I was sitting on the bench: watching and listening to 70,000 of their fans – all singing their songs together – was pretty incredible.

You have four big clubs in Rio, four big clubs in São Paulo, two in Porto Alegre and two – Coritiba and Atlético Paranaense – in Curitiba. And in Belo Horizonte, there are Atlético Mineiro and Cruzeiro. All those cities are towards the south of Brazil. It only looks like there aren't big clubs elsewhere, though: at Paysandu, up in Belém, you can get crowds of 70,000 and the same in Recife, with Santa Cruz. But, on the pitch, those clubs are playing in the lower divisions. There are financial reasons for that. Playing in the state league is one thing, but to play in the top divisions, against teams from all over the country, is expensive. There are lots of good players being produced at those northern clubs but, as soon as they start doing well, one of the bigger teams with more money comes in and takes them. And that happens with even the youngest players. Maybe the World Cup will help, bringing investment into those clubs, especially up in the North and North East.

9. CLUB, COUNTRY, *FUTEBOL!*

MILLIONS OF BRAZILIANS, even those who aren't passionate football fans most of the time, become completely caught up in the drama of World Cups – and even more so when the World Cup is being staged on home soil. It may come as a surprise to the rest of us that, most of the time, die-hard Brazilian supporters can seem relatively indifferent to the fortunes of the national team, the *Seleção*. Focus is firmly fixed on the clubs they follow: the passion of a lifelong commitment and the year-round routine of teasing work colleagues or school mates on a Monday morning after their team has secured a glorious victory over local rivals. Even that love of a lifetime, it's worth pointing out, isn't always enough to get fans out in numbers in support of a struggling team: the emotions involved, however fierce, can also be remarkably fickle.

The nation's distinctive take on the game was made obvious when the Spanish sports newspaper *Marca* tried to start a Brazilian version of their title. It didn't succeed thanks, in large part, to the Europeans failing to understand key features of the Brazilian football landscape. Despite the advice of local journalists, the Spanish publishers assumed Brazilian club football – like that in Europe – would be centred on rivalries between cities. Certainly there's an element of that rivalry in Brazil but the most powerful driver of club culture in the country actually springs from rivalries contested within the cities themselves. The local football bibles, like *Lance!* and *Placar*, recognise this and devote page after page to those contests, the *clássicos*.

As with so many aspects of Brazilian life, the character of football culture has developed because of the sheer size of the country. For a start, that's the main reason why it wasn't until 1971 that Brazil launched a genuine national championship, the *Campeonato Brasileiro*. The foundations of football in Brazil are local rather than national, with the country divided into 27 states, each holding its own – and, in most cases, long-established – regional championship. All over the country crowds still turn out for the big games in those competitions, which deliver significant television audiences to the big broadcasters, too.

The state leagues, the *Campeonatos Estaduais*, have been the subject of much controversy in recent years. Some judge them obsolete: they clutter up the football calendar and leave it out of step with the rest of the world's domestic schedules. What's more, they're plainly not in the best interests of Brazil's biggest clubs: nowhere else would those clubs be expected to spend months on end playing local minnows in a league

Palmeiras at Pacaembu Stadium,São Paulo

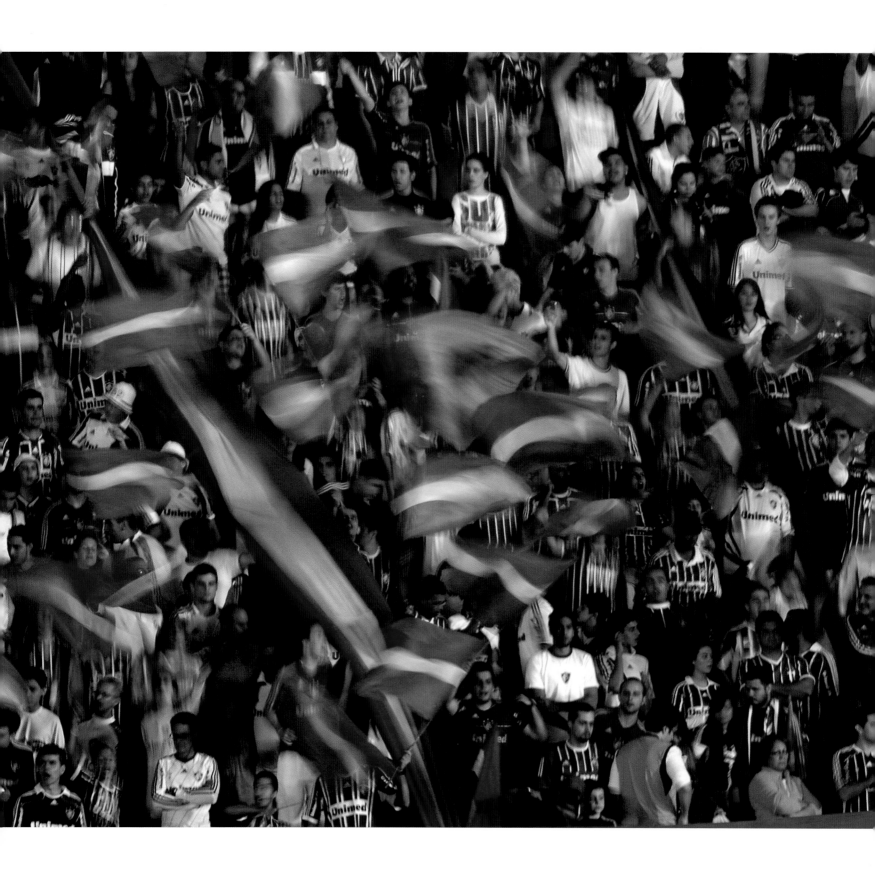

format. Certainly they hamper the giants of Brazilian football competing on a global basis – on and off the pitch – with the European clubs, like Barcelona, Bayern Munich and Manchester United, which they see as their peers. The less well-appointed clubs from smaller states, for their part, argue they lack the financial muscle to compete on the national stage.

The State Championships, in any event, retain disproportionate importance along Brazilian football's corridors of power. Within the *Confederação Brasileira de Futebol*, Brazil's FA, the state federations have more votes than the first division clubs. Given that the *Campeonatos Estaduais* are the key source of income for those federations, it's obvious they won't be agreeing to end – or even rationalise – them any time soon. There is, however, more or less open conflict on the issue and the will to change has been spearheaded by the players themselves. *Bom Senso FC* – 'Common Sense FC' – has united some of Brazil's biggest names. Experienced players from every major club made their feelings known in a series of demonstrations at games during the closing months of 2013.

It may be that modernisation is inevitable, that sooner or later the *Campeonatos Estaduais* will be scrapped or have their format changed. Nonetheless, the huge importance of their contribution to the development of football in Brazil is undeniable. Just as significant is the fact that, over the past 100 years, they have set the agenda for the nation's football supporters. Football culture has grown up in the context of the regional competitions and, therefore local rivalries will continue to be right at the heart of the Brazilian game as far as the fans are concerned. Each major city has its own, very clear footballing identity, nourished by the passion of historic rivalries and played out in the heat of each season's *clássico* clashes.

★ ★ ★

Fluminense at Maracana Stadium, Rio de Janiero

Ah-ha, Oo-hoo, o Maraca e' nosso: 'the Maracanã is ours!' It's one of the favourite chants for supporters of all four of Rio de Janeiro's big clubs. Fans of Flamengo, Vasco da Gama, Fluminense and Botafogo vie for ownership – in spirit, at least – of one of the most iconic of all football arenas, the proud host stadium of the 2014 World Cup Final. There's an irony about the chant, though. Over a century and more, the histories of all four clubs have seen them forge individual identities very much in the context of playing at venues they could actually call home.

In 1902, when Fluminense FC were founded, Rio was the Brazilian capital and the regional championship, the *Campeonato Carioca*, reflected that pre-eminence. Unlike rivals who emerged from clubs devoted to rowing – the popular upper-class sport of the day – 'Flu' were a football club right from the start. What's more, elite connections put them ahead of the crowd early on, thanks to founder Oscar Cox, born in Brazil but from an English background, who had been educated in Switzerland, where he had long nurtured the idea of introducing football back home in Rio.

The club Cox founded built a stadium in the plush Laranjeiras neighbourhood, next door to the stunning Guanabara Palace, once the residence of the President of Brazil and now used by the Governor of Rio. The Estádio das Laranjeiras, with its English-style cricket pavilion and graceful function room complete with beautiful stained-glass windows, made absolutely plain the social milieu from which the Brazilian game had sprung. However, Fluminense soon made it their business to acquire a popular touch, too. They had to in light of the success of a club on the rise just a few miles across Rio.

The city's other leading teams – Fluminense, Flamengo and Botafogo – were all associated with Rio's wealthy, white elite. They were all based in the south of the city, too. Then Vasco da Gama arrived like a rocket from Rio's working-class northern zone, winning the Rio championship in 1923, their debut season in the first division of the *Campeonato Carioca*. Part of the shock

Vasco delivered to the established order was the fact that their team included both poor white and black players. A backlash was inevitable. New rules were invented in an attempt to force Vasco back outside the gates. Players had to fill out a form before taking to the field, a task beyond most of Brazil's illiterate poor at the time. Vasco responded by sending their players to school.

The Establishment's final gambit was to insist all top clubs had their own stadiums. The stadium Vasco built in response is still to be found amid the kind of cramped, dusty, utilitarian streets so typical of traditional working-class Rio. Vasco were – and still are – the club of the city's Portuguese immigrant community, among them – then as now – the owners of countless small businesses. In the mid-1920s, those businessmen clubbed together to build the Estádio São Januário which, when it opened in 1927, was the biggest stadium in Latin America. It's still their home today although derbies and other big games are sometimes moved to the Maracanã.

Vasco's claim as sole representatives of Rio's poor and multi-racial community, though, was short-lived: they were outflanked in the 1930s by Flamengo, a club founded in 1912 by disaffected players from Fluminense looking for a new home. Businessman José Bastos Padilha was elected president of Flamengo in 1933 and had the vision to take in the changing landscape of Brazilian football and, indeed, of the country at large. *Futebol* had become a wildly popular game played by professional players. Brazil's new president Getúlio Vargas, meanwhile, was experimenting with a very local brand of fascism, attempting to forge alliances across social classes in the name of national unity. Black Brazilians found themselves a part of Brazil's idea of itself as never before.

Bastos Padilha was canny enough to see the benefits of applying the same principles at his own football club. Previously an elite association, the club culture at

Vasco de Gama at São Januário Stadium, Rio de Janeiro

'Fla' was changed almost overnight with the signings of a clutch of the leading black players of the day including, crucially, the gifted and charismatic superstar of Brazilian football, Leônidas da Silva. The new faces transformed Flamengo's fortunes and at the same time revolutionised the club's fan base. Suddenly, 'Fla' was a club for the masses, on its way to becoming the most popular in Brazil, with an estimated 35 million supporters. And grassroots appeal still defines Flamengo: when they concede a goal, rival fans will sing, 'It's all gone quiet in the slums'. Although they eventually built their own stadium and named it in honour of Bastos Padilha, Flamengo's colossal support in Rio means the Maracanã is now, to all intents and purposes, their home ground.

Flamengo's cornering of the 'popular' market also undermined other clubs which might otherwise have become football giants in working-class Rio: Bangu, the first Brazilian club ever to select black players; São Cristóvão, where both Leônidas and the star of a later generation, Ronaldo, began their careers; and America FC, a club with elite connections but based in the working-class north of the city. All three were hugely successful – and well-supported – until Flamengo's effective re-branding in the mid-1930s. Instead, Rio had to wait for another giant to emerge in *carioca* football during a golden age for the Brazilian game in the 1950s and 60s.

The city's fourth big club, Botafogo, carries some of the romance of the Juscelino Kubitschek presidential era, when Oscar Niemeyer was building Brasilia and Rio swayed to the sound of bossa nova, the new musical craze of the 1950s and 60s. Today, their smaller but very passionate fan-base still hark back to the club's best days, when half the *Seleção*, including Garrincha and other multiple World Cup winners, were drawn from their ranks. By the 1970s, rising debt led to Botafogo losing

Botafogo, Rio de Janiero

their home ground of 50 years, the Estádio General Severiano. They were condemned to a nomadic existence until they eventually took over the Engenhão, a stadium built for the 2007 Pan-American Games and slated as the 2016 Olympics athletics venue. The problem wasn't resolved, though: after less than six years, the stadium's roof was declared unsafe and work shut it down over the World Cup summer. Botafogo, then, have returned to the Maracanã, which is more popular among supporters anyway, the Engenhão being regarded by many as an uncomfortable trip into Rio's north zone. Botafogo fans, even if they don't fill it, can still sing about the Maracanã being 'ours'.

Since the 1930s, those four clubs – Flu, Fla, Vasco and Botafogo – have dominated football in Rio. And, of course, as the nation's capital at the time, what was happening in football in the *Cidade Maravilhosa* was reflected across the rest of the country as well. Rio, in the 1930s, was the centre for a glamorous, new and increasingly influential medium: radio. Games involving Rio teams were broadcast live all over Brazil. The impact was huge: to this days *carioca* clubs have national followings unrivalled by even the biggest names from other regions: Flamengo claim to be the single, best-supported club in 24 of Brazil's 27 states.

Within Rio, it often feels as if it's Flamengo versus the rest. The 'Fla-Flu', Flamengo against Fluminense, is the city's most celebrated *clássico*. Over the years the fixture took on a new dimension as a result of a literary rivalry that became entwined with the sporting rivalry between the two clubs. Nelson Rodrigues, the country's foremost playwright and a hugely influential football columnist, was a passionate 'Flu' supporter. His brother, the no less influential journalist Mario Filho – after whom the Maracanã is formally named – was equally committed to Flamengo. The argument between famous brothers added spice, gravitas and credibility to Rio's biggest derby.

However the most fiery clash between Rio rivals – and the one that most concerns the football and metropolitan authorities from a security perspective – is Flamengo versus Vasco da Gama, the *Clássico dos Milhões*, the 'derby of the multitudes'. *There's* some history attached: this was a fierce rivalry between rowing clubs even before the football clubs were founded. Today, Flamengo are by some distance Rio's – and Brazil's – most popular team. Vasco are the second best-supported club in the city. And the edge to proceedings? Games between the two have often carried huge significance, in sporting terms, on both regional and national stages. And off the pitch both clubs are followed by huge, sometimes brutally violent, fan groups, the *torcidas organizadas*. The passion – the hatred, even – dates back at least to the 1930s: Vasco have almost certainly never forgiven their rivals for stealing their thunder as the 'team of the people' eight decades ago.

★ ★ ★

Visits by touring British teams did much to spread the popularity of football in South America in the early years of the twentieth century. One such visit, by the legendary Corinthians in 1910, inspired the foundation of what grew to become the biggest club in the South American continent's biggest city. Taking their cue from the renowned English amateurs, a group of São Paulo factory workers got together to found the Sport Club Corinthians Paulista: Corinthians, or simply *Timão* – 'the Big Team' – to their legions of fans, whose passionate support has been rewarded with the nickname *Fiel*, meaning 'Faithful'.

Corinthians quickly wrested domination of the São Paulo football scene from the older, elite clubs. By 1914 they were champions of the state, winning the first of their 27 *Campeonatos Paulistas*. And, as the city itself grew, transformed from a provincial backwater into an enormous and sprawling twentieth-century metropolis, so Corinthians grew with it. With slavery abolished and

trade and industry developing at an uncontrollable rate, immigrants flooded into São Paulo to take up the slack: from Brazil's dusty and impoverished north-eastern interior, from Japan, from the Middle East and all over Europe. The Europeans, particularly, brought with them a passion for football: the Portuguese community, for example, founded their own club, Portuguesa. Most numerous, though, were the Italians, who occupied entire neighbourhoods and have also left their lasting influence on the city's local dialect. They, too, formed a club of their own: Palestra Itália.

By the early 1930s Corinthians and Palestra were firmly established as São Paulo's biggest clubs. Games between them were dubbed the 'Paulista Derby', taking the English usage. The two were clubs with radically different philosophies. Corinthians boasted a working-class culture, all toil, sweat and sacrifice. In keeping with that tradition, their legendary 1980s midfielder, Sócrates, and his Corinthians team-mates were key to the struggle for democracy both within football and in the wider context of the country at large, as Brazil shrugged off years of military dictatorship. Back in the early part of the twentieth century, meanwhile, Palestra were catering to sporting tastes as delicate and refined as the olive oil found on every Italian table. Gentlemen and scholars, they were fashioning themselves as the '*Academia de Futebol*'.

Toss a coin, they used to say: if it lands on one side, then Corinthians would be champions; on the other, and it would be Palestra; for anyone else to prevail, the coin would have to come to rest on its edge. Soon enough, though, the unlikely and unprecedented started to happen. In 1935, São Paulo FC were founded. The new club represented an acceptance by the São Paulo elite that the future of football was as a professional game. São Paulo adapted quickly and well to the new environment. While the city's two longest-established clubs seemed passionate to the point of hysteria, São Paulo came across as calm, rational and well ordered.

Corinthians at Pacaembu Stadium, São Paulo

At first, São Paulo's strategy for establishing themselves as a major force was simple enough: sign big-name veterans. The first, and probably the most significant, of those was Leônidas da Silva, who had been in prison, accused of forging military exemption papers, subsequently falling out with his club in Rio, Flamengo. When Leônidas first arrived in 1942 he was branded a has-been, 'an expensive piece of junk', by São Paulo's rivals. In one of his first games, played at the impressive and recently inaugurated Estádio do Pacaembu, he scored one of the goals that had become his trademark. The radio commentator could hardly contain himself: 'The expensive piece of junk has scored with a bicycle kick!' he shouted over and over again. It was a landmark moment. The following year, with Leônidas leading the charge, São Paulo won their first *Campeonato Paulista*.

From then on, three clubs were in serious contention: São Paulo, Corinthians and Palestra Itália, recently re-named Palmeiras. International tension during the early 1940s, which eventually led to Brazil entering the Second World War on the side of the Allies, made an obvious connection with Italy politically undesirable. The club's new name – meaning 'Palm Trees' – was entirely Brazilian but, to this day, Palmeiras remains a very Italian institution. Indeed, their dizzying run of success in the 1990s was underwritten by sponsorship from the Italian dairy conglomerate Parmalat, who, for their part, exploited the arrangement to make commercial inroads into the expanding Brazilian market.

In the 1950s, the familiar three-horse race of the *Campeonato Paulista* was jolted by the appearance of a fourth thoroughbred. One of the happy accidents of football history – for the player, for the club and for the rest of us – is that Pelé joined Santos in 1956. Already a wonderful team – state champions the previous year – this group of accomplished and experienced players gave Brazilian football's rising star the platform to

Santos

become perhaps the game's greatest-ever footballer. And Santos, for a while, became the world's greatest team – a remarkable achievement for what was, effectively, a small-town provincial outfit.

Santos is the port of São Paulo, about an hour's winding drive down through the hills from the crush of the metropolis. It has a very different feel; even a different climate. If anything, its lush greenery and long, curving beaches give it an atmosphere something like a Rio in miniature. It was from here – and from the rickety confines of their little stadium, the Vila Belmiro – that Pelé and his supporting cast set out to conquer football. For nearly 20 years, Santos – *Os Santásticos* – were so good the entire nation took the team to their hearts. Given their home ground could hold fewer than 15,000 people, some of Santos' biggest games – such as the home leg of the Intercontinental Cup against Benfica in 1962 – were staged in Rio, at the Maracanã, Pelé's favourite stadium. Others were taken into São Paulo and played at the Estádio do Pacaembu, developing a support for the club within the city. After the golden age inspired by Pelé, Santos sank back towards provincial mediocrity but in recent years, they have regained a place at the forefront of Brazilian football, thanks to teams inspired, first, by Robinho and Diego and then, subsequently, by Neymar. Once again Santos have been heading up the hillside to São Paulo to play big games at the Pacaembu.

The Pacaembu – or, to give it its full name, the Estádio Municipal Paulo Machado de Carvalho, after the man who organised Brazil's successful World Cup campaigns in 1958 and 1962 – is owned by the city but has always served as a home ground for Corinthians, who have been endlessly frustrated in their attempts to build a stadium of their own. Palmeiras have long had a home of their own, pokey and small, which is currently undergoing a major – though much delayed – rebuild: the old Parque Antárctica will eventually be re-born as Allianz Parque.

In keeping with their rational approach to the business of football, meanwhile, São Paulo FC decided almost from the outset that building a big stadium of their own was the way forward. The enormous, cavernous bowl of the Estádio do Morumbi opened in 1960 but was only fully completed a decade later. Typically, São Paulo took the long view and were prepared to underperform on the field while funds were ploughed into securing the club's future.

It had long been envisaged that the Morumbi would serve as the city of São Paulo's 2014 World Cup stadium. Among insiders, though, there had always been a degree of scepticism: the structure is now outdated and its surroundings – in one of the city's smartest neighbourhoods – would make rebuilding expensive. There was also a political context. São Paulo FC have always looked upon themselves as an exception, a club in stark contrast to the ineptitude of those who are supposed to run Brazilian football. That self-satisfied stance guarantees the club enemies in the corridors of power. What's more, there was also the small matter of a President of Brazil.

The hugely influential and charismatic Luiz Inácio Lula da Silva, 'Lula', who governed the country between 2002 and 2010, is a self-confessed Corinthians fanatic: as a poor immigrant from the North East, he fits the club's supporter profile to a tee. His presidency, therefore, changed everything: Corinthians had always been the team of the outsiders; now they were represented at the heart of the new establishment. The outcome was Corinthians finally getting a stadium to call their own: the new 2014 World Cup stadium in Itaquera, a neighbourhood way out in the city's eastern zone. Enormous expenditure was justified as a means to transform one of São Paulo's more neglected districts.

A new stadium for Corinthians should certainly be viable long-term. Many of the Fiel – including a very popular former President – are confident that, for a club with a huge fan-base and equally huge football

Santos at Pacaembu Stadium, São Paulo

revenues, the Arena Corinthians will put the club on a footing which allows it to compete with the best in the world and be honoured as hosts of the opening match of the 2014 World Cup. Costs, however, spiralled way beyond the initial projected budget and the site also suffered a devastating accident when its roof collapsed in late 2013. Time will tell whether the popular passion – and best intentions – that have always surrounded Sport Club Corinthians Paulista will be matched by best business practice this time around.

★ ★ ★

The state of Minas Gerais is dotted with beautiful and historic towns, full of ornate Baroque churches and graceful colonial architecture. Ouro Preto and Congonhas, for example, are both UNESCO World Heritage Sites. The state capital Belo Horizonte, though, is very different: a city planned in the late nineteenth century, built in the early twentieth century and still growing, exponentially, in the twenty-first. Construction actually began in the 1890s, just after Brazil had become a republic, at a time when the country was in search of a new identity. Belo Horizonte was to be the proving ground for the partnership behind Brasilia, the new capital for the nation purpose-built in the late 1950s. Future president Juscelino Kubitschek was elected mayor of Belo Horizonte in 1940 and invited architectural prodigy Oscar Niemeyer to design buildings for a new suburb, Pampulha. Fifteen years later, 'JK' having been elected President, turned to Niemeyer once more, commissioning him to design Brasilia.

The city of Belo Horizonte, meanwhile, has made an impact of its own on the architecture of Brazilian football. Two landmarks stand out: in 1966, Cruzeiro overwhelmed Santos – Pelé and all – in the final of the 1966 *Taça Brasil*, the national cup competition which preceded the formation of a Brazilian league. A clearly

embarrassed Tostão, Cruzeiro's sensational young star, was photographed afterwards wearing a crown, hailed as Pelé's successor as the king of football. Then, in 1971, Cruzeiro's city rivals, Atlético Mineiro, were winners of the inaugural national championship, the *Campeonato Brasileiro*. In the space of five years Belo Horizonte's two biggest clubs had served notice that the city was ready to take on Brazilian football's traditional powerhouses in Rio de Janeiro and São Paulo.

The early trail-blazers, though, on Belo Horizonte's domestic scene were a third club, América, who won the local title, the *Campeonato Mineiro*, nine times in a row between 1916 and 1925. The introduction of professionalism in the following decade, however, threw a club with conservative and elite roots off-balance. It never really recovered and now plays in the second division of the Brazilian league. That said, cannier local politicians often announce themselves as América supporters, thus ensuring they don't alienate either of the much bigger fan-bases attached to Cruzeiro and Atlético.

America's place of prominence was first hijacked by Atlético, another upper-class club albeit one that reacted more effectively to changing times and thus built up a following across social classes. Local writer Roberto Drummond captured exactly the intense commitment displayed by that support: 'If you hang a black and white shirt out on the line in the middle of a storm, then Atlético fans will cheer it on against the wind.' For a club that has always imagined itself to be battling heroically against the elements, often without much success, the metaphor is a perfect fit.

From the late 1920s onwards, Atlético's main rivals were a club set up by the city's Italian community: another Palestra Itália. Just as with Palmeiras in São Paulo, the political climate of the 1940s forced the change to a more Brazilian name: thus, Cruzeiro were born. Cultural adaptation in Belo Horizonte proved much more straightforward than in São Paulo: the immigrant community was much smaller and the Italian identity of

Palmeiras at Pacaembu Stadium, São Paulo

the club already much diluted to a degree it has never been at Palmeiras.

The kind of storms Roberto Drummond perhaps had in mind, meanwhile, blew through in 2011 and proved particularly damaging for both Cruzeiro and Atlético. The Estádio Independência, built for the 1950 World Cup, was closed for rebuilding, as was the giant Estádio Mineirão – a copy of the Maracanã – which opened in the mid-1960s. With no viable stadium in the city, both clubs were obliged to play home matches outside Belo Horizonte. Each came close to relegation from the top division because of it. The importance of bricks and mortar has been proved further by how much there has been to celebrate in the bars – for which the city is famous! – since the two traditional home grounds re-opened.

The Independência, in the neighbourhood of Horto, is technically owned by América. Atlético, though, have made it their stronghold. So impressive has been the club's home record that a chant has been invented to strike fear into the hearts of visiting teams: *Caiu no Horto, tá morto*, 'Come to Horto and you've had it!' In 2013, Atlético ended a 42-year wait for a senior title in winning the *Copa Libertadores*, South America's equivalent of the Champions League. It was only with great reluctance that the club staged the second leg of the final away from the Independência at the much bigger Mineirão, newly inaugurated for the Confederations Cup and a key stadium at the 2014 World Cup. It might be a home and a fortress but the Independência's 20,000 capacity simply wasn't enough for a game of such magnitude. It turned out not to matter: Atlético turned over a 2–0 deficit to beat Olimpia of Paraguay on penalties.

Within Belo Horizonte, Atlético's success was seen almost as a challenge by their most bitter rivals. Cruzeiro responded by occupying the Mineirão themselves: excellent home form was fundamental to their convincing march to the 2013 *Campeonato Brasileiro* title. Atlético,

meanwhile, unable to agree terms with the consortium managing the re-vamped and reconfigured World Cup venue, are left playing their home games back in Horto. The restrictions on capacity – and therefore revenues – at the Independência may yet come back to haunt them. Cruzeiro, for their part, have taken full advantage, on and off the pitch, by making the Mineirão feel like their own.

The southern state of Rio Grande do Sul is *gaúcho* country: the inhabitants of Porto Alegre, the capital, don't actually live like cowboys any more but people from this part of Brazil still have a longstanding reputation for taking pride in their traditions, for plain speaking and for a certain bloody-mindedness. They are, if you like, Brazil's Yorkshiremen. The state as a whole is a singular place, distinctive thanks to the strong influence of European immigrant communities, particularly those from Italy and Germany. It's also close to the frontier with Uruguay. And the locals throw themselves into football with a Uruguayan fervour.

There's a strong argument for picking out the big derby in Porto Alegre as the most fiercely contested in all of Brazil: perhaps the most bitter rivalries are always fostered in cities large enough to support two major teams though not large enough to sustain three. On the one hand are Grêmio, who began life as a club restricted to Germans: the wealthy and the white. And on the other: Internacional, whose doors – from the club's inception in 1909 – were open, as their name implies, to players of all nationalities.

Internacional were also ahead of their rivals in fielding black players. Indeed, the story – the myth – has been passed down the years by the club's rivals that Grêmio's original pitch was donated by local German businessmen on condition that the team did not select black players. Whatever the truth of that tale, there remains to this day an undercurrent of racism in the rivalry between two teams, most obviously manifested in terrace chanting. The

OSCAR'S BRAZIL

difference in the social classes from which the two clubs' support is drawn, however, is no longer evident. Over the years Grêmio have re-invented themselves, long since dispensing with the elite associations they had when they were founded. That's clear from even a cursory glance at the respective squads: World Cup winner Ronaldinho – or *Ronaldinho Gaúcho*, as he's known all over Brazil – might be thought to conform to an Internacional demographic. In fact, he came through the ranks at Grêmio.

Rivals they might have been – and still are in the local *Campeonato Gaúcho* – but together the two Porto Alegre giants transformed Brazilian football when the national league system began in 1971. Previously the region had been dismissed as a provincial backwater and so it was a shock when Grêmio and Internacional proved themselves ready to take on all comers. Internacional, in many respects, defined Brazilian club football in the 1970s. It's often argued that, during this period, Brazilian football began imitating its European counterpart, with *futebol-força* getting the better of *futebol-arte*, substance winning out over style. What's not often noted is that this was very much an internal development, the most important contribution being made by Brazil's own European descendants, particularly those from Porto Alegre and the surrounding area.

Styles of football vary from country to country. In a country as big as Brazil, they can vary from region to region. The school of football that emerged in Rio Grande do Sul was physically tough and imposing. Internacional's team of the 1970s was built around the sublime midfield talents of Falcao but they were also very difficult to play against, the club's coaches ensuring the whole team were six-foot-plus and fearsome athletes. A T-shirt still popular with Grêmio fans, meanwhile, proclaims: 'Our number 10 is the number 5', meaning the rock at the back is more important than the gifted playmaker in their dressing room.

Grêmio at Grêmio Arena, Porto Alegre

The Rio Grande do Sul model has made huge inroads across the country, some people suggesting – and not always happily – that *gaúcho* football has conquered Brazil. It's striking how many coaches from the region have gone on to carve out impressive careers in the game. Luiz Felipe Scolari is the third consecutive *gaúcho* coach of the national team. What's more, the coach expected to succeed Scolari after the 2014 World Cup, Adenor Leonardo Bacchi, known as 'Tite', also hails from Rio Grande do Sul and managed both Grêmio and Internacional before leading Corinthians to national, continental and world titles.

Given the importance of Porto Alegre to the Brazilian game, the city was probably under-represented in the scheduling for the 2014 World Cup, selected to stage just five matches, all of them before the quarter-finals. The reason for this is the *Gaúcho* capital's location: down in Brazil's South, June and July are mid-winter months and can be genuinely cold. The tournament will leave an impact on football in the region nonetheless. Internacional's re-vamped and re-developed Estádio Beira-Rio is Porto Alegre's World Cup venue. It's one of Brazil's very few privately-owned stadia and the club should derive considerable benefit from the upgrade to their traditional home.

Grêmio, meanwhile, have invested in a brand new stadium although they won't own it outright. The Arena do Grêmio, inaugurated in December 2012, was built in partnership with a construction company. Changing home has also meant a change of culture for home fans, however: for years a spectacular feature of games at the old Estádio Olímpico Monumental was the 'Avalanche', supporters rushing to the front of the stands in celebration of a Grêmio goal. In the first competitive game at the new Arena, however, an Avalanche caused several injuries and the tradition has had to be banned. The gradient in the new stadium is much steeper: fans are closer to the pitch but the rush forward is now too dangerous. Modern comforts at a new home have cost

Grêmio supporters some of the thrills that were so much a part of life at the old.

The big four cities of the Brazilian game account for the country's leading 12 clubs: four each from Rio and São Paulo, two apiece from Belo Horizonte and Porto Alegre. Anxious – and, apparently, ready – to crash into that elite group, however, are Atlético Paranaense, an ambitious club as forward-thinking as the city they represent: Curitiba, capital of the southern state of Paraná. Curitiba is often held up as an example of an organised, functional Brazil, thanks to its enlightened urban development and sustainability policies. There's a strong European influence, with sizeable immigrant communities from Poland, Ukraine, Germany and Italy, as well as from Japan and the Middle East.

The oldest club in the city – and the one with the most regional titles to its name – is Coritiba. A German businessman by the name of Frederico 'Fritz' Essenfelder is the man who did for Paraná what Charles Miller did for the rest of Brazil in turning up with a football. Essenfelder and a group of his compatriots founded Coritiba in 1909: the team are still known as *Coxa-Branca*, 'White Thighs', in celebration of their German heritage. Coritiba became the first team from the state to win the national championship, back in 1985. Another competitor at regional level is Paraná Clube, borne out of a merger of two older clubs – Pinheiros and Colorado – 25 years ago. Atlético Paranaense pitch their ambitions altogether higher than their two local rivals, however: their sights are set on becoming a continental power and they are convinced the World Cup can help.

Atlético's Arena da Baixada is one of very few privately owned stadiums scheduled for use during the summer of 2014. It was inaugurated in 1999 and planned World Cup investments were supposed to allow the stadium's reconstruction to be completed and its capacity significantly increased. The pitfalls of relying on private

investment, however, have made for a rocky road: as late as January 2014, work had still not been finished and discussions continued as to who would eventually be footing the bills. On the pitch, meanwhile, the club won its first *Campeonato Brasileiro* in 2001. Revenues from a bigger stadium will be essential in taking Atlético's national prominence up to international level.

★ ★ ★

Of all Brazil's regions, it may well be the North East that stands to gain most from the country hosting its second World Cup. These are states with big cities and passionate football cultures but they are also impoverished, in relative terms, which helps explain why the region's clubs, for all that they are supported in

great numbers, have rarely made any lasting impression at the national level of the game. Investment put in place for the 2014 tournament will hopefully change all that.

Salvador, for example, the capital of Bahia and Brazil's most 'African' city, is now home to one of the most impressive stadiums in the country. The Arena Fonte Nova has been built on the site of an older stadium, which was simply dynamited to make way for the new one. The Fonte Nova includes a concert hall, hotel, restaurants and even a football museum, the grandeur of its design is matched by its setting on the shores of the Dique do Tororo, a lake in the heart of the city: an architectural star of the 2014 World Cup.

The Arena is also once more home to EC Bahia, one of the city's two biggest clubs. Despite huge popular

support as the club of the people in Salvador, the team has endured a disastrous first decade of the twenty-first century, slipping at one point into the third tier of the *Campeonato*. They have been back in the top-flight since 2010, however, and are once more face to face with their fiercest rivals, EC Vitória, who are the club associated with Brazilian football's elitist roots but also famous for their incredible success in developing young players. Vitória play home games at their own ground, the Barradão. The Salvador derby, though – the *Ba–Vi* – will get the setting it deserves, in front of nearly 60,000 fans at the Fonte Nova from now on.

Up the coast in Recife, the capital of the state of Pernambuco, football support is split three ways as far as the city's clubs are concerned. Santa Cruz draw huge crowds – an average of nearly 40,000 even when they plummeted into the fourth tier of the *Campeonato Brasileiro* in 2008 – from a fan-base strongest in Recife's poorer outlying neighbourhoods. Sport, meanwhile, are a club with supporters from across the city's social classes and Nautico are the club most strongly associated with origins in Recife's wealthier neighbourhoods. Between them, the three have won the regional league, the *Campeonato Pernambucano*, every year without fail since the mid-1940s and their traditional homes stand close together, near the low-lying centre of the old town.

The lack of available land in cramped downtown Recife inspired the controversial idea of building a new World Cup stadium outside the city, some ten miles away in the neighbourhood of São Lourenço da Mata. The best-laid plans envisaged the 46,000-seater Arena Pernambuco driving the development of a new urban pole for Recife, out towards the airport. In 2014, however, the impressive new stadium was standing, somewhat eerily, in the middle of nowhere. Only Nautico – sensing the long-term benefits of a move – had agreed terms at the new Arena, and with mixed results. In 2012, strong home form at their old ground, the Estádio Aflitos, ensured the club's survival in the top flight but after

the new Arena had been hurriedly opened in time for the 2013 Confederations Cup, Nautico moved in and performed so badly they were relegated. The Arena's anchor tenants, therefore, were consigned to spending Brazil's World Cup year playing in the second tier of the national league.

On Brazil's northeastern coast sits the state of Ceará and its capital, Fortaleza. As a tourist destination, Fortaleza has plenty going for it: 20 miles of perfect beaches, a colourful colonial history and more. It's also grown into a significant economic and industrial hub and is now the fifth biggest city in the country. As popular as the game is in Fortaleza, however, and despite the fact that the state league – the *Campeonato Cearense* – has been fiercely contested since 1915, the region's clubs have struggled to make a serious or sustained impression at a national level.

Ceará, a century old, are known as *Vozão*, 'Big Grandpa'. They have won the local title 42 times and got to the semi-finals of the *Copa do Brasil* a couple of years ago, knocking out mighty Flamengo – Ronaldinho and all – along the way. They were subsequently relegated to the second division of the *Campeonato Brasileiro*, though. Ceará's identity is as the club of the masses. Their biggest rivals are Fortaleza EC who, despite a vestige of traditional upper-class pretensions, play their football a further division below. Big games can still draw huge crowds in Fortaleza and the hope is that renovation of the city's main stadium, the Castelão, for the World Cup can inspire a revival in the fortunes of two of the North East's traditional giants as well.

The other 2014 host city in the North East is Natal. Local rivalry between ABC Futebol Clube and América RN is very much alive in the national second division, and in the Rio Grande do Norte state league, the *Campeonato Potiguar*, which the pair have traditionally dominated between them. You'll see pick-up games, *peladas*, going on everywhere you turn around Natal, too. But the city lacks the truly passionate fan culture that's part of football life elsewhere across most of Brazil: poor infrastructure, lack of funds and only very occasional visits from the super-clubs from the South have all played a part in that. Although Natal has the World Cup legacy of a newly-built stadium – the Arena das Dunas – to look forward to, it's a matter of some doubt whether that will be enough to ensure a better long-term future for the city's clubs or help develop the game elsewhere in Rio Grande do Norte.

Some of the same misgivings apply to three other hosts during the summer of 2014. Of all the new venues across Brazil, the Estádio Nacional Mané Garrincha in the capital, Brasilia, is perhaps the most striking and certainly the most expensive. Yet it's been built in a city with only one club competing in the *Campeonato Brasileiro* and Brasilia FC were playing in the fourth tier in World Cup year. Built by workers from the North East, when the nation's new capital was inaugurated in 1960, thousands of government workers were relocated from Rio de Janeiro to Brasilia. As a result, supporters in the city have retained links to the teams they and their families left behind almost half a century ago. To this day Brasilia's club culture feels much like an offshoot of *carioca* club culture.

Likewise, Manaus in Amazonia and Cuiabá in the Pantanal wetlands were both chosen as World Cup host cities on the basis that impressively designed and costly new venues would be built. In the absence of any deep-seated commitment to club football in either region, however, it's hard to see the Arena da Amazônia or the Arena Pantanal proving, over the long term, to have been money well spent. If, in future years, those new stadiums, against all expectations, can provide a filip for the game at grassroots level in the corners of Brazil yet to be swept up in the national obsession, the World Cup will have done the job the tournament's organisers promised it would. Culturally and economically everywhere else, after all, Brazil is a country that lives and breathes the game.

unity

I played for the Brazilian teams at the younger age groups. I missed out at 17 but otherwise through from under-16. I went to the Olympics. And here we are now: a World Cup in Brazil! At every stage, it's been an exciting experience because, at every different age, it was a first time for something. When I was 16, I represented my country for the first time. At 18, we went away for the first time, to play in Japan. At 20, it was a first junior World Cup. And that feeling has carried on with the senior team: getting called into the *Seleção*, then a first game against Argentina or playing Italy for the first time.

Even the way we're called up for a squad is exciting. There's an announcement to say that there will be a squad for such-and-such a game or tournament and it will be revealed on TV and radio at such-and-such a time tomorrow. The players just have to tune in along with everyone else in the country to find out if they've made the *seleção*. The first time you hear anything official, if you've been picked, is when they e-mail with the details of your flights! No-one ever knows in advance. That's just how it's always been done in Brazil.

We've known that we were going to be hosting the World Cup for quite a long time so, in a way, we've been preparing for it. But a lot has changed with the team over the last few years. At first, we had a slightly older generation: Ronaldo, Ronaldinho, Kaká. Then Mano Menezes came in as coach and it was a mix of the older players and a younger generation: he was trying to find the right blend for his team. But then we changed again and *Felipão* has had to try and create the team he wants for the World Cup. We had a great Confederations Cup last year and that helped. It gave everyone more confidence in the younger players like Neymar, Lucas and Bernard.

What we all realise, though, is that we'll only be as good as past generations if we're able to win like past generations did. Maybe people were surprised how the team came together at the Confederations Cup. We weren't as surprised as the fans, though. We'd been working hard, trying to be united as a team and wanting very much to do well. And that's what we're working towards now. We know the whole of Brazil will be behind us, willing us to succeed. We perhaps don't have the star players that previous generations have had but we have unity. It's a new face for the Brazil team and people recognised that – maybe began to believe in it -- when they watched us win the Confederations Cup. We're at home and, for anyone to beat us at the World Cup, they're going to need to play really, really well! We're all together.

As you grow up, you dream about playing for a big club or playing in Europe. But the first dream? The first one and the one that lasts? That's to play for Brazil. I'd say that's true for every Brazilian boy. I know that to play for the *seleção* was always my dream. Our first game at the World Cup is against Croatia, at the new Arena de São Paulo. Brazil's first game at a World Cup in Brazil, and it's in my home town. I dream about that, too! With everyone there: my mum, my family, my friends, the whole of the country looking on. I don't know who's going to be the most excited: the players? The fans? I think everyone will be together, feeling the same: big emotions, excitement, euphoria, pride. And, we hope: joy.

10. A BRAZILIAN PLANET: 2014

1970 WAS PERHAPS A HIGH watermark for Brazilian football; for world football, indeed. Not only did Pelé and company win the World Cup for the third time, thus claiming the original Jules Rimet trophy as their own in perpetuity, they did so in style. The victory in Mexico, with respect to those who argue the case for the team of 1958, was achieved with a breathtaking blend of collective and individual brilliance and had an impact around the world as no other World Cup triumph has, before or since. Football was helped on its way to becoming the global game we take as read today: since the Second World War, by 1970 membership of FIFA had already more than doubled, from 54 to well over 100 countries. By the time the next World Cup rolled round in 1974, that number had grown to 140.

The 1970 Final was watched by a television audience estimated at 800 million, worldwide and in colour: representatives of the New World dismantled those of the Old – Italy – in brilliant sunshine at the Estadio Azteca; and the multi-racial complexion of the *Seleção* was an inspiration for teams from outside the cabal of European powers who had governed the game for so long. The profound impression made by his country's players afforded one particular Brazilian the opportunity to change football – and its most important tournament – forever. João Havelange had been waiting for his

moment and it was soon to arrive. His fervent lobbying of FIFA's new members, particularly those from Asia and Africa – who had joined the Federation as they won independence from colonial masters, would see him succeed the Englishman, Sir Stanley Rous, as the world governing body's president in 1974.

In the early 1970s, Havelange was off around the world, cultivating friendships in football's high places. At home, darker forces were trying to exploit Brazil's pre-eminence on the field to achieve their own ends off it. Victory at the 1970 World Cup happened against the backdrop of the most repressive period of Brazil's 20 years under military dictatorship. The economy was growing at 10 per cent – the so-called 'Brazilian miracle' – but the country's poor and working class were becoming increasingly less well off. Guerrilla activity – most notably the kidnapping of the US ambassador, Charles Elbrick in 1969 – and anti-government protests were the cue for President Emílio Médici to institute new measures curtailing press and political freedoms. Arrests, torture and assassinations became commonplace even as huge, ill-advised and ultimately disastrous national infrastructure projects were begun as a means to keep the economy on course.

Azteca Stadium, Mexico City 1970

As has always been the way under dictatorships, success in sport was presented as vindication: a populist end to justify profoundly unpopular means. And the military had plenty of good news besides the World Cup winners to be going on with: the charismatic Emerson Fittipaldi won Formula One World Championships in 1972 and 1974; the extraordinary Eder Jofre, having been World Champion at Bantamweight in the 1960s, came out of retirement and, at 37, won the World Featherweight title amid scenes of wild jubilation in Brasilia in 1973. In the run-up to the 1974 World Cup in Germany, the Brazilian public were drip-fed a steady television and radio diet extolling the supremacy of the country's sportsmen, assuring the nation that the team would return with a new World Cup to sit alongside the old.

The original Jules Rimet trophy was actually stolen and melted down by opportunist thieves in 1983. In regards to the new one, as things turned out, the optimism of the dictatorship – and, indeed of coach Mário Zagallo – proved misplaced. Although a handful of the stars of 1970, such as Jairzinho and Rivelino, were still available, Pelé's decision – at 33 – not to play cost the *Seleção* dear. The team sorely missed Brito, Gérson and Tostão, too. Brazil, struggling for goals against defensive opponents, stumbled through the opening round of games before apparently coming good with victories over East Germany and the old enemy, Argentina. However, in the last of those second-round games – effectively, a semi-final – they were comprehensively outplayed by a Dutch team inspired by Johan Cruyff and a new philosophy of 'Total Football'. Beforehand Zagallo had claimed: 'We shouldn't worry about the Dutch, the Dutch should be worried about us.' In fact, Holland's 2–0 victory was so dispiriting that Brazil weren't even able to rouse themselves for the third/fourth place game and lost 1–0 to Poland. Pride had come before the world champions' fall, as it would for the Dutch, who were

Victory parade, Brasilia 1970; Aztec Stadium

losing 2–1 to West Germany in the Final even as the Brazilians boarded their plane to fly home.

Zagallo and his players were pilloried on their return: the freedom and expressiveness of the 1970 vintage had been replaced, it seemed, by something altogether more prosaic. The Dutch, although they had only finished as runners-up, temporarily replaced Brazil as the football romantic's team of choice. Centre half Luís Pereira's sending off for a waist-high, pub player's challenge on the dashing Johan Neeskens was seen as symptomatic of Zagallo's preference for the physical over the technical, for *futebol-força* over *futebol-arte*. The coach would return as assistant manager in 1994 to enjoy a last laugh, his reputation restored. In 1974, however, he and his team had done almost everything they could, it seemed, to undo the impression they had made on the world just four years before.

Above: José Maria Minella Stadium, Mar de Plata 1978

Right: Benito Villamarin Stadium, Seville 1982

Defeat in Germany cost Mário Zagallo his job. As it happened, 1974 signalled the end for Emílio Médici as well, as Brazil began inching back towards democracy. However, the process of détente – *distensão* – would not be complete until 1985. The country's fortunes had been jolted by the 1973 Arab Oil Crisis and the new President, Ernesto Geisel, entered office promising 'the maximum of development possible with the minimum of indispensable security'. Meanwhile, a military regime further south was tightening its grip. Argentina's Generals were intent on using a World Cup on home soil in 1978 for their own propaganda purposes and to detract attention worldwide from the activities of a government far more brutal and murderous than Brazil's had ever been. The junta controlled the tournament, by fair means and foul, and FIFA – now led by João Havelange – pretty much let them get on with it.

Only the Dutch kicked up any sort of fuss about the conditions under which Argentina's World Cup was being played out: Johan Cruyff didn't make the trip

although Holland nonetheless reached the Final again. There was something inevitable about their opponents – and the eventual winners – being the host nation. Under a new and untried manager, an artillery captain named Cláudio Coutinho, Brazil for their part fielded a completely renovated team that included newcomers destined for great things, not least Arthur Antunes Coimbra: the peerless 'Zico'. Inspiration came, too, in the shape of an explosive striker, Roberto Dinamite, Vasco da Gama's all-time leading goalscorer, who later became the club's president and then a state senator in Rio. The team remained undefeated and went out of the tournament only in exceptional and controversial circumstances at the penultimate stage.

The second group round of matches saw a renewal of the longstanding rivalry between Brazil and Argentina. It was a game that would all but have ensured the winners a place in the Final and from the start Argentina appeared to settle for not being beaten. Coutinho, for his part, allowed conservatism to get the better of him too, selecting the powerful but defensively-minded Chicão in place of Brazil's most creative player, Zico. The goalless draw meant qualification for the Final would come down

Sarrià Stadium, Barcelona 1992

to the last set of matches. Brazil duly dispatched Poland 3–1. Argentina, therefore, went into their later kick-off against Peru knowing they needed to win by four goals to go through. They ran in six without reply: a result achieved, many have suggested, thanks to the Peruvian players being bribed or physically threatened – or both – to ensure the Generals got the climax they had planned all along for their tournament.

Brazil came from behind to beat Italy 2–1 in the third / fourth place playoff and returned home with

Cláudio Coutinho insisting they had been 1978's 'moral champions' on the basis that, unlike Argentina, they hadn't lost a game. The Brazilian public wasn't impressed. Neither, it's safe to assume, were their masters: Coutinhno's services were duly dispensed with. It was the first of many changes to the landscape which would combine to ensure that the next tournament – for Brazil and for the rest of us – would be one quite unlike any previous World Cup.

★ ★ ★

The *Seleção Brasileira* has left its mark on a century of world football. So, too, one Brazilian: Jean-Marie Faustin Godefroid 'João' de Havelange. A businessman and entrepreneur already steeped in the politics of sport after spells on the International Olympic Committee and the CBF – the Brazilian FA – Havelange succeeded the cautious and euro-centric Englishman Sir Stanley Rous as FIFA president. He then made it his business to drive football into a new, global and ambitiously commercial era. The Asian and African federations which had helped him win the election of 1974 were amply rewarded: the 1982 World Cup saw the number of teams increased from 16 to 24. Havelange sought out the Adidas executive Horst Dassler and the British sports marketing consultant Patrick Nally to help him exploit the tournament commercially on a grand scale. For the first time, major multi-national brands paid handsomely for the privilege of exclusive association with the World Cup, similarly broadcasters worldwide for the right to show it. Havelange created the World Cup we know today, eventually expanding it again to 32 teams and attracting television audiences in the hundreds of millions, thus creating a sports sponsorship property with which only the Olympic Games can compete.

Havelange, without question, was a man with a vision and so, too, the coach who led Brazil into the first World Cup of the new era. Unlike FIFA's new president, however, he was a man of scrupulous principles, an unapologetic football romantic. Telê Santana was born in Minas Gerais in 1931 and made his reputation as a manager when, 40 years later, he guided a local team, Atlético Mineiro of Belo Horizonte, past the traditional Rio- and São Paulo-based giants to victory in Brazil's first-ever national championship. His commitment to honest, open and attacking football meant a return to the principles enshrined in the philosophy of *futebol-arte*. Santana's appointment as national coach in 1980 promised to re-connect the *Seleção* with the idea of *o Joga Bonito*, 'the Beautiful Game'.

Although Santana's teams, both in 1982 and 1986, failed to win a World Cup, they made a huge impression on the two tournaments, delighting supporters at home in Brazil with their fearlessness, inventiveness and a shared sense of joy. These were teams to be proud of, even as the experts chided the coach for his naivety and bemoaned the inability of the players to match their talents with trophies. Santana's inspiration had been the 'Total Football' of the Dutch team in Germany in 1974: like them, the Brazil team of 1982, which included truly stellar talents like Falcão, Zico, Cerezzo and Sócrates, are remembered as the best team to have played at a World Cup without winning it. Like the Dutch, Brazil were also undone by a combination of over-confidence and an absolute refusal to compromise on footballing principles.

Having won every qualifying game and then beaten England, Germany and France on a pre-tournament European tour, Brazil arrived in Spain as favourites to win a fourth World Cup. From day one they lit up the tournament, attacking with style and at every opportunity. Needing only a draw against Italy to qualify for the semi-finals, though, the most dazzling midfield players in the world came up against the best – and most cynical – defence of the age. Santana's steadfast unwillingness to prioritise the result over his team's performance cost Brazil dear, albeit the game is remembered as one of the best ever seen at a World Cup, a thrilling clash of styles and footballing philosophies.

Claudio Gentile masterminded his team's rearguard and twice Italy led, thanks to Brazilian lapses. Twice, magnificent equalisers from Sócrates and then Falcão seemed to have ensured safe passage for the *Seleção*. Eventually, the match was decided by the predatory instincts of Paolo Rossi – just returned from a two-year ban imposed after a betting scandal – who completed his hat-trick as Santana's team streamed forward in search of a win they didn't actually need.

The coach was inconsolable: Sanatana hugged each player as they left the field in Barcelona having lost 3–2 and missed out on their chance of glory. Minutes later he emerged at a press conference with the Brazilian media and was welcomed by a standing ovation. Little wonder that Santana was brought back out of club management in Saudi Arabia to lead Brazil into another tournament, four years later. Again in 1986, the World Cup was to end in disappointment. It ended, indeed, as another glorious failure. The best players taken to Mexico were those who had starred in Spain. Yet all were four years older and temperature and altitude counted against the senior players. Around them, apart from the striker Careca, the supporting cast were nothing like as inspiring as the 1982 vintage. As a result, expectations were not high ahead of the '86 World Cup and Santana, managing the fitness of his leading players as best he could, wasn't able to send his team out to attack in the same carefree way. Again, though, Brazil's elimination was in a game that, by a distance, proved to be the best of the tournament.

The Brazilian football argument between *arte* and *força* has its counterpart south of the border in Argentina, where it is framed as *Menottismo* versus *Bilardismo*, the opposing styles named after the country's two World Cup-winning managers. In Mexico, the wily and utilitarian Carlos Bilardo was fortunate to have the world's greatest player around to drive a well-organised but workmanlike team on to victory in 1986.

Diego Maradona dominated the tournament in a way no player had since Garrincha in Chile in 1962. The game best remembered from 1986, though, was the quarter-final between Brazil and France, which took place in Guadalajara. In Spain, Brazil had fallen to Italy, a team built on defence; in Mexico, they lost out to a side built very much in their own image.

France had already knocked out the holders, Italy, and boasted a clutch of attacking players who would have fitted comfortably into the ranks of the *Seleção*: Giresse, Platini and Tigana. Coaches worldwide have been watching the game on DVD ever since, the midfield battle perhaps the most enthralling and technically accomplished ever to be caught on camera. Brazil could have been out of sight early on and they took the lead through Careca. The French, however, found a way back into the game and equalised at the end of the first half through Michel Platini, arguably the greatest footballer his country had ever produced. Thereafter the game turned on missed penalties. Unaccountably, Zico, on as a substitute, missed one during the second half and then, in the shootout – another novelty introduced by Havelange with half an eye to the TV audience – the otherwise immaculate Sócrates missed Brazil's first spot-kick, as did Júlio César their last. Hopes were dashed once more around the Estadio Jalisco – where, since 1970, every Mexican fan had cheered on Brazil – and for the millions watching the drama unfold on television at home.

A Brazilian generation that had been marvellous in 1982 – and had then defied the advancing age of the squad's best players to compete in 1986 – finished with nothing to show for their efforts. As did a coach, Telê Santana, still held in the highest regard among Brazilians of a certain age who have always been happy to forgive his shortcomings in light of his passion and commitment to a distinctly – and joyously – Brazilian game. Much of the romance disappeared from *futebol* in the midday heat of that afternoon in Guadalajara. But defeat to France

Sarrià Stadium, Barcelona 1992

didn't signal an end to success for the nation's players and teams at the very top of their game; instead, it would prove to have been a new kind of beginning.

★ ★ ★

Rose Bowl, Pusadena 1994

Brazilian players themselves have a word for it: *rodar*. Depending on context, this can be translated as 'to roll', 'to tour', 'to wander', 'to revolve'; even 'to fail'. Some analysts suggest there may be as many as 5,000 Brazilian players currently earning a living from football outside Brazil. They may be superstars earning millions in the major European leagues; they may just be getting by in obscure circumstances in emerging football nations. For every star in London or Madrid, there are a dozen journeymen toiling in far-flung corners: the Faroe Islands, Azerbaijan or Indonesia. Anywhere football is played professionally, Brazilians will be there playing it.

The circular motion implied by *rodar*, though, tells its own story. Brazilian players tend to be what the Germans call *Gastarbeiters*, 'guest workers' who migrate in search of a decent contract rather than with a view to finding a new home. Most are youngest siblings from low-income family backgrounds; many are churchgoers and evangelical protestants. They travel in search of experience and economic security. And the chance to make their own reputations, even as they trade on their nation's reputation as the world's greatest exporter of footballing talent.

The first Brazilian players were already off to try their luck in the 1920s and 30s, lured by leagues such as those in Uruguay and Italy, which had embraced professionalism at the earliest opportunity. A steady trickle continued to leave Brazil for Europe thereafter, often on the basis of impressive performances at World Cups or because of family ties to a particular country. In the wake of the 1986 World Cup, however, the floodgates apparently opened. Only two of the squad in Mexico played their club football outside Brazil. Four years later, over half were doing so, at clubs in Italy and Uruguay – traditional and historic destinations – but also now in France, Germany, Holland and Portugal. Coaches were looking to import the flair, technical excellence and improvisational ability for so long associated with Brazilian football. The willingness of players such as Jorginho, Romário and Dunga – and those who followed them – to adapt to the physical and tactical demands of the European leagues only served to make the imports an even more attractive proposition.

The stream of players leaving Brazil has continued ever since: even players who might previously have pitched their ambitions at ordinary careers in the lower reaches of the *Campeonato Brasileiro* suddenly found there were teams across the world ready to pay handsomely for their services. The chance to move abroad became the new horizon for players at almost every level of the domestic game. This, however, had its own knock-on effect: athleticism and power, it might be argued, became more highly-prized when recruiting and developing players, especially as Brazilian clubs themselves – under the spell of a rising generation of coaches from the 'European' football environment of states in the South of the country, notably Rio Grande do Sul – were successfully adopting a more hard-headed approach to the game in domestic and continental competition.

Brazil, of course, continues to produce players of the highest quality and, apparently, in greater numbers than any other nation. Part of the reason for this, obviously, is the sheer size of the country, its population now touching 200 million. Since the return to democratic government in 1985, millions of Brazilians – particularly under the presidency of the wildly popular Luiz Inácio 'Lula' da Silva – have been lifted out of extreme poverty to join the growing ranks of the middle classes as the country inches towards a sophisticated consumer culture at home and global significance as a stable and developing economy. All over the country, however, in *favelas* and remote inland towns alike, millions more live on less than very little. Football is a way out for a youngster with talent, not just for the boy himself but for his whole family and, indeed, for his *bairro*, the neighbourhood in which he grew up.

There are other reasons too, practical and cultural, which continue to foster the development of Brazilian footballers on such a scale. The game remains hugely popular across the country, both as a spectator sport and one in which participation is open across every barrier of age, ethnicity, social background and, indeed, gender. The success of the Brazilian women's national team and the emergence of stars such as multiple World Player of the Year Marta Vieira da Silva have less to do with effective or enlightened policy on the part of administrators than with football's accessibility to girls and young women at street and grassroots level.

If anything, for both men and women, *futsal – futebol de salão*, the small-sided game, played indoors and with a smaller, heavier ball – is even more popular in Brazil as an organised participation sport than the 11-a-side game. Certainly, *futsal* promotes the close control, short passing and ability to invent under pressure that have, historically, been so highly prized as elements of the skillset defining the way the country plays the game.

Other than in the far South, Brazil's climate allows *futebol*-mad kids to chase a ball out in the streets, playgrounds or fields and across beaches at all hours and all year round. Crucially, these youngsters will grow up playing in scratch games – *peladas* – against boys older, stronger and more experienced than themselves: those 20-a-side scrambles are universities of hard knocks in which kids learn the trickery, speed of thought and breadth of vision necessary to ensure they survive and prosper even in the most unpromising and unforgiving of environments. Some of those skills are less readily acquired and developed in the more rarefied setting of junior football or club academy teams. They are, though, definitively Brazilian traits, part of a football brand that continues to attract attention – and, indeed, hard cash – from professional clubs all over the rest of the world.

There's little sign of the global appetite for Brazilian players diminishing any time soon, although the strength of the Brazilian economy in general and the increasing levels of sponsorship being attracted to the country's bigger clubs have combined to allow the likes of Santos to hold onto a rising talent such as Neymar for longer than they might have been able a decade ago. Furthermore, they have been able to secure higher transfer fees as a result. The movement of Brazilian footballers has always had a cyclical element, players returning home for economic, cultural or family reasons,

or simply because age has made the slower pace of South American football attractive once more. Significantly, such is the fresh and rising tide of economic confidence at home that even highly-paid stars like Pato, Fred and Ronaldinho have, in recent years, become affordable propositions for the likes of Corinthians, Fluminense and Atlético Mineiro, Brazilian football's big guns. *Rodar* continues to seem both a current and very much the appropriate word.

★ ★ ★

Into the 1990s, Brazil continued to produce gifted attacking footballers, not least the supremely self-confident Romário, who once explained an impressive goal-scoring performance for Barcelona by saying: 'When I was born, the Man in the sky pointed to me and said "That's the guy."' His was a stellar career, book-ended by distinguished spells as a hometown hero with Vasco da Gama and taking in spectacular success in European club football along the way. Romário's humble upbringing and recent forays into politics make his a somehow very Brazilian tale: he is recognised and celebrated as a classic example of a *malandro*, a 'rascal' as skilful, street-wise and manipulative as he needs to be in order to better an opponent. Despite the presence of an outstanding striker in the ranks of the *Seleção*, however, the period isn't one remembered fondly in Brazil, where it is referred to – in casually disparaging terms – as the *Era Dunga*.

Carlos Caetano Bledorn Verri was born in Ijuí, a provincial town in Rio Grande do Sul, and was given the boyhood nickname *Dunga*, 'Dopey' from *Snow White and the Seven Dwarves*. Dunga's family background lay in Italian and German ancestry. As Brazilian football reacted to disappointments in Spain and Mexico by experimenting with a results-driven 'European' style of play, he became the definitive figure in a re-made *Seleção*. By 1990, it seemed, all the flamboyance and sense of adventure associated with the losing teams of 1982 and 1986 had been consigned to the history books.

Instead, a team dominated by players, like Dunga, who were playing club football in Europe squabbled with each other about star billing, with sponsors about bonus packages and with the press about practically everything. Dunga, a supremely effective defensive midfield player, was taken to characterise the utilitarian identity of this Brazilian team. Nicknamed 'The Destroyer' in Europe, Dunga often found the media at home only too ready to try to destroy his reputation both as player and coach.

O Fenômeno

The conservatism of *futebol-força*, allied to the occasional flash of brilliance from a striker: it was a plan which took Brazil only as far as a quarter-final defeat against Argentina in Italy, a World Cup excoriated at home as the worst for a *Seleção* since 1966. Criticism of the team was only tempered by low expectations beforehand and the resignation afterwards of Sebastião Lazaroni, a manager plainly out of his depth. Four years later, though, under a new and altogether cannier coach – Carlos Alberto Parreira – very similar tactics led to Brazil winning the World Cup for a record fourth time.

Having argued with Romário early on during a tricky qualifying campaign, Parreira left the Barcelona striker out of the team until a crucial final fixture against Uruguay – who else? – at the Maracanã. Reinstated, Romário proved inspirational and scored the two goals which secured Brazil's safe passage to the US. At the tournament, in tandem with the elusive Bebeto, the same player gave a team built around the discipline of Dunga and the defensive solidity of centre backs Aldair and Márcio Santos just enough invention further forward to manoeuvre Brazil into the Final. Played in the sweltering heat of Los Angeles, the game against Italy was dismal, finishing 0–0 after extra-time, and eventually decided by Roberto Baggio's penalty miss. Perhaps it summed up the *Era Dunga* and its legacy: 1994 was a triumph for substance over style.

In the aftermath of the US World Cup – a victory remembered in Brazil with less affection than the failure of 1982 – change was inevitable. To progress, however, Brazil stepped backwards and the team travelled to France as holders in 1998 under a previous winner, both as player and coach: Mário Zagallo. Furthermore, they had a player who truly belonged in the company of Friedenreich, Leônidas, Pelé, Garrincha and the nation's other all-time greats. Ronaldo, FIFA World Player of the Year in 1996 and 1997 – and, eventually, the World Cup's all-time leading goalscorer – had honed his talent playing *futebol de salão* as a boy. Quick feet and close control, allied to prodigious physical power and deceptive pace, made him a player to build a team around. Just 22 in France, he was already laying waste the defences of clubs across Europe and being lauded at home in Brazil as *o Fenômeno*, 'the Phenomenon'. Ronaldo, one way or another, dominated the 1998 World Cup and, indeed, the one that followed it.

Brazil had an exceptional centre forward, Ronaldo, previous winners like Cafu and Bebeto and future winners such as Rivaldo and Roberto Carlos in their ranks. They went off to France, though, with little expected of them: the controversial omission of an injured Romário, certainly, was seen as a huge blow to their chances. As it was, with a bit of luck, Ronaldo's goals and some penalty shoot-out heroics from goalkeeper Cláudio Taffarel along the way, Brazil found themselves in another Final, this time against hosts France. There the story of the 1998 World Cup took a bizarre turn for the worse: the details are still mired in accusation, counter-accusation and conflicting conspiracy theories. The fact is that, on the morning of the game, Ronaldo was taken ill, rushed to hospital for tests and then left out of the starting line-up, only to be reinstated at the very last moment. The game kicked off with Brazil's team selection a mystery and whispers of dark deeds already in the air. Ronaldo wandered rather aimlessly through proceedings and an apparently shell-shocked *Seleção* were comprehensively beaten, 3–0.

Exactly what happened at the Brazil team's hotel and then in the corridors of the Stade de France remains a matter of conjecture: was Ronaldo's well-publicised crisis ahead of the game physical or mental? What did the hospital tests show? Who made the decision to leave him out of the team? And who decided, after all, that the talisman would play? The reasons behind Brazil's failure in the 1998 Final have exercised journalists, fans and conspiracy theorists ever since. Even Brazil's team sponsor, the sportswear giant Nike, found themselves dragged into the maelstrom of rumour after a partnership agreement, signed in 1996, cementing a relationship unlike any other in the history of the game. Whatever else, that deal proved Brazil had outgrown national borders as a footballing brand; they had become an international team which, literally now as well as metaphorically, belonged to the world.

★ ★ ★

In 1989, one of the more controversial figures in the history of Brazilian football, Ricardo Teixeira – then the son-in-law of FIFA president João Havelange – was elected president of the *Confederação Brasileira de Futebol*. Just as his father-in-law had been ruthless in exploiting the commercial opportunities presented by World Cups, the CBF on Teixeira's watch threw itself wholeheartedly into the business of profiting from the prominence of the national team around the world. The Nike partnership was the standout deal: with so many Brazilians playing abroad, the *Seleção* began using Europe as a home base for prestigious friendlies to ensure the availability of star names for games organised in consultation with sponsors Nike. Such was their international profile and popularity Brazil could draw capacity crowds even to exhibition games organised wherever the CBF's busy commercial schedule demanded. Particularly in the wake of World Cup victory in the US in 1994, Brazil's players became clothes-horses, helping to drive the phenomenal success of the sportswear brand to which the CBF was now hitched.

The dramatic narrative that played out its first act in Paris in 1998 reached an equally extraordinary conclusion at the 2002 World Cup in Japan and South Korea. Again, Ronaldo was the leading man and this time his redemption – after the breakdown in France had been followed by four years dogged by a succession of injuries – was spectacular. Many had written off the man previously hailed as the world's greatest player. And many had also written off Brazil's chances after

a stuttering qualification campaign which saw them through only in third place in the South American group behind Argentina. The coach was another pragmatist from Rio Grande do Sul, the avuncular figure also leading the team on home ground in 2014, Luiz Felipe Scolari: known in Brazil as *Felipão* and worldwide as 'Big Phil'.

The 2002 winners have perhaps never received the plaudits they deserved. The team may not have had the swagger or the flamboyance of favourites past; certainly they were organised defensively, three centre halves expertly protected from midfield by Gilberto Silva and Kléberson. But they had what Brazilians call *jogo de cintura*, a quality best understood as 'flexibility', the ability to adapt to changing circumstances even when things aren't going well. They had classical full-backs in the raiding Brazilian style: Roberto Carlos and the captain – Brazil's most capped-ever player – Cafu. And they had the outstanding outfield stars of the tournament in the attacking trio of Rivaldo, Ronaldo and Ronaldinho. On the way to the Final against Germany, all three had their own match-winning moments. Ultimately, in Yokohama, it fell to Ronaldo to bring down the final curtain, his two goals crowning a Man-of-the-Match performance, earning him FIFA's Player of the Tournament accolade and securing a place in history for the *Seleção: Pentacampeão*, 'five time champions'. Brazil's best player had given a memorable World Cup its inspirational twist in the tale.

If 2002 afforded a reminder of the heights reached by Brazilian teams on the world stage, 2006 saw a World Cup campaign which appeared to hit a new low. The tournament in Germany, if nothing else, exemplified the degree to which Brazilian football had taken on a life of its own around the world. All but three of the World Cup squad were playing their club football in Europe, where eye-watering salaries could be paid to players competing in a tournament which was beginning to rival the World Cup for glamour and technical quality: UEFA's Champions League. Just as significant, perhaps, was the number of Brazilians involved with other competing

International Stadium, Yokohama 2002

teams: Francileudo Santos, for example, born in the north eastern state of Maranhão, was Tunisia's star player; the *Paulistano* Marcos Senna anchored Spain's midfield and would go on to win the European Championship with them, two years later. Costa Rica and Saudi Arabia were both coached by Brazilians, as had been Japan – by the great Zico – in 2002. Most galling, perhaps, was the sight of Luiz Felipe Scolari, who coached a battling Portugal team to the semi-finals in Germany, by which time Brazil had already packed their bags and scattered to the different corners of Europe they were now calling home.

As holders, Brazil were among the favourites in Germany. All was not well, though. *Felipão* had resigned and been replaced as manager by the coaching team which had masterminded victory in the US a decade previously, Carlos Alberto Parreira and Mário Zagallo. Preparations were overshadowed by an eager commercialism which saw the CBF sell tickets for training sessions at the team's base in Switzerland and then schedule warm-up games, like a fixture against New Zealand in Geneva which might have made sense as a money-making exercise but proved ineffective as a test for the players ahead of the tournament. Parreira's preference, before and during the World Cup, was for experienced players ahead of promising newcomers and for organisation ahead of flamboyance. It was an approach which put him in more or less open confrontation with Brazil's travelling press corps and an alienated Brazilian public at home. The sharpest focus settled on Ronaldo, injured and overweight, who played – and scored, to become the World Cup's top goalscorer of all time – despite a popular clamour for the inclusion of Brazilian football's rising young talent, Robinho. After a series of unconvincing performances in Germany, Brazil were eventually dispatched 1–0 by France in the quarter-finals.

Four years later in South Africa a cycle was brought, rather ignominiously, to its close: Dunga, Brazil's

winning captain in 1994, returned to coach the team in 2010. The World Cup is now a groaning behemoth, 32 teams competing on a stage cluttered by the demands of broadcasters and sponsors who behave – understandably given that they, along with the host nation, foot FIFA's very large bill – as if the tournament, in fact if not in spirit, is hosted solely for their benefit. In 2010, Brazil found themselves somehow on the periphery of the important narratives. Here was a first World Cup on the African continent, the end result of a process begun, in footballing terms and to the governing body's very great credit, by FIFA's banning of apartheid South Africa from the world game in the early 1960s. Here, too, it transpired, was a team that could be spoken of in the same breath as the great Brazilian sides of 1958, 1962 and 1970. 2010 was Spain's tournament. Brazil's elimination by Holland at the quarter-final stage, losing 2–1 despite scoring first through the mercurial Robinho and dominating the first half, was merely a footnote. This was a script written by Casillas, Puyol, Xavi, David Villa and Andrés Iniesta: suddenly it seemed as if the world had discovered a new way for football to be played and, with it, a new favourite team.

★ ★ ★

Football evolves, and with it the culture around the game. Perhaps as significant a development as any, off the field at least, has been the widening gap between top players and the men and women who pay to watch them play. Subscription television has been a driving force behind that. So, too, the arrival of a commercial expertise sufficiently inventive to maximise profits from our fascination with the sport. Agents and players' unions have ensured that more of the money coming into the game has gone into the pockets of those who play it. In the world's major leagues, a footballer can earn as much in a month as an ordinary fan in the crowd can expect

Ellis Park Stadium, Johannesburg 2010

to earn in a lifetime. That's as true in Brazil – maybe more so – as it is anywhere. Alongside that economic chasm between those who play and those who watch has grown a cultural divide, too. Our heroes are somehow distant despite in many cases their backgrounds having been humble or challenging, or both. They are no longer men of the people – the most celebrated players seem more like movie stars, privileged and glamorous beings from another world. And for Brazilians, there's a further disconnect: geography. The twenty-first-century *Seleção*, by and large, is made up of players who earn their livings thousands of miles away. Even international fixtures – apart from those in continental competitions – happen, as often as not, in European or Middle Eastern cities rather than in São Paulo or Rio, Porto Alegre or Salvador.

Another thing to look forward to: the 2014 World Cup summer being one bringing the *Seleção* home. With host nation status come extra pressures, of course: heightened expectations and even more frenzied media attention. But the tournament is a chance to welcome players back to represent their country in the cities where they were born, to the clubs where they learnt the game, putting them back within touching distance of the football-mad supporters whose aspirations they share and whose identity they represent. Since 2002, the national team – individually and collectively – has come up short. Who wouldn't get excited at the prospect? 2014: the perfect time – and the perfect place – to rekindle the country's love affair with the *Verde-Amarela*, the boys in 'Green and Yellow'.

2013's Confederations Cup tournament served only to up the ante. History suggests the winners of the dress rehearsal tend not to match up when the real show begins. Brazil, after all, lifted the trophy in both 2005 and 2009. In 2013, though, there appeared to be a lot to admire in the current generation assembled by the old favourite, Luiz Felipe Scolari: a solid defensive base, marauding full-backs, a balanced blend in midfield, infectious team spirit and, up front, a young man

apparently destined for great things. Sooner rather than later is every Brazil fan's fervent wish: Neymar da Silva Santos Júnior – better known just as *Neymar* – has already captured the imagination of a nation. Born and raised on the fringes of São Paulo and now playing alongside Lionel Messi at Barcelona, he is every inch the modern star and yet Neymar draws us in: here is a player who plainly delights in the game, all tricks, invention and the promise of the unexpected. He plays *futebol* in the way only Brazilians play it; the way Brazilians want to see it played. At 22, he may be a little young to have the weight of 200 million people's hopes and fears resting on his shoulders. Then again, this World Cup may be one that Neymar – like Pelé, like Garrincha and like Ronaldo before him – can claim as his very own.

These are challenging times for Brazil, under a successor to the adored President Lula da Silva, Dilma Rousseff, who sometimes struggles to achieve the widespread popularity her predecessor enjoyed. Rousseff was da Silva's choice but lacks his common touch. And she hasn't had his experience, shared and celebrated by so many Brazilians, of a long journey from extreme poverty into the corridors of power. Indeed the nation's first female president was brought up in upper middle-class comfort, her father a successful entrepreneur, in Belo Horizonte.

Staging a World Cup, the biggest live event on earth and watched on television by hundreds of millions, brings its own potentially overwhelming challenges, too: stadium construction, infrastructure development, logistics management, security control and the rest. It may help Rouseff, though – indeed, it may help Brazil – that, come kick-off, only one thing will matter from Manaus to Curitiba, from Brasilia to Recife, from São Paulo to the *Cidade Maravilhosa*: for the sixth time in the glittering history of the world's greatest footballing nation, is this a World Cup that Brazil are going to win?

São Cristovão de Ipirango, Bahia

SOURCES

1. THE FIRST TIME

'Football will never catch on, you can be sure of it…'
Graciliano Ramos, *Traços a Esmo*, 1921; quoted in Leandro
Narloch, *Politically Incorrect Guide to the History of
Brazil*, São Paulo: Leya, 2009.

'You, players who in less than a few hours will be hailed
as champions by millions of compatriots…' A speech on
the pitch quoted by Jonathan Wilson in 'Uruguay's 1950
World Cup triumph a testament to the spirit of garra',
Sports Illustrated, 4 July 2010.

'It seemed that we had a collective drop in pressure…'
Tim Vickery, personal interview with Zizinho.

'Bigode was having problems…' Tim Vickery, personal
interview with Zizinho.

'A silence which terrorised our players…' Tim Vickery,
personal interview with Zizinho.

'Gigghia's goal was received in silence…' Alex Bellos,
Futebol: The Brazilian Way of Life, Bloomsbury, 2003.

'I played for 19 years and won titles…' Zizinho, *O Mestre
Ziza*, SUDERJ (Edicoes de Maracana), Rio de Janeiro,
1985 (translation: Tim Vickery).

3. *CARIOCAS E PAULISTANOS*: A STORY BEGINS

'A travelling newspaperman reported…' 'Almost Like
Watching Brazil', Chris Freddi, *When Saturday Comes*,
Issue 157, March 2000.

'The green-eyed mulatto…' *Soccer in Sun and Shadow*,
Eduardo H. Galeano, Verso, 1998.

'Unlike the British style…' *Inverting the Pyramid: The
History of Football Tactics*, Jonathan Wilson, Orion, 2008.

4. THE RUBBER MAN

'Getúlio Vargas wrote in his private diary…'
WWW.FIFA.COM/CLASSICFOOTBALL

'Leônidas, meanwhile, remembered…'
WWW.FIFA.COM/CLASSICFOOTBALL

5. *BRASILIDADE*

'Our *Mulatto* football…' 'Football Mulato', *Diários Associados*, Gilberto Freyre, 17 June 1938 (author's translation).

'Under Brazilian law…' *Barbosa: Um Gol Faz Cinquenta Anos*, Roberto Muylaert, RMC Editora, 2000.

'I was totally disillusioned…' Alex Bellos, *Futebol: The Brazilian Way of Life*, Bloomsbury, 2003.

'There were a few players in the national team…' Ibid.

'The Brazilians were the main offenders…' *Brawling in Berne: Mediated Transnational Moral Panics in the 1954 Football World Cup*, Gerd von der Lippe and Malcolm MacLean, *International Review for the Sociology of Sport*, 2008.

'the man who kept his cool…' Ibid.

'convinced that the infamous Battle of Berne…' *Refereeing Around the World*, Arthur E. Ellis, The Sportsmans Book Club, 1956.

'more refined than the primitive and hot-blooded…' *Brawling in Berne: Mediated Transnational Moral Panics in the 1954 Football World Cup*, Gerd von der Lippe and Malcolm MacLean, *International Review for the Sociology of Sport*, 2008.

'fifty years of progress in five'… *A Concise History of Brazil*, Boris Fausto (trans. Arthur Brakel), Cambridge University Press, 1999.

'a modern capital…' *The Curves of Time: The Memoirs of Oscar Niemeyer*, Oscar Niemeyer and Ana Luiza Nobre, Phaidon Press, 2000.

'football which was technically great…' *The Brazil Book of Football*, Stratton (ed), Smith (author), Soccer Book Club, 1964.

'teamwork from the head of delegation… Ibid.

'the players needed and were entitled to…' Ibid.

'The 24-year-old Garrincha's absence…' *Garrincha: The Triumph and Tragedy of Brazil's Forgotten Footballing Hero*, Ruy Castro, Yellow Jersey Press, 2004.

'Interestingly, the same psychologist…' Ibid.

'Garrincha's incomparable swerve…' *The Story of the World Cup*, Brian Glanville, Faber, 1997.

'They showed football…' Report in *The Times* of London, June 30 1958.

'The stadium stood to them…' Report in *The Times of London*, June 30 1958.

6. IN COLOUR

'European football in general…' *The Brazil Book of Football*, Stratton (ed), Smith (author), Soccer Book Club, 1964.

'Didi treats the ball lovingly…' WWW.FIFA.COM/CLASSICFOOTBALL

'I make no secret of the fact…' *The Brazil Book of Football*, Stratton (ed), Smith (author), Soccer Book Club, 1964.

'Spanish fans, I got to learn…' Ibid.

'A determined campaign…' Ibid.

'It is the ball that needs to run…' Ibid.

'I was burning…' Ibid.

'Moreira was convinced…' Ibid.

'no Queens…' Nelson Rodrigue's column for *O Globo* newspaper during the 1962 World Cup.

'Everything about Garrincha was Brazilian…' *À Sombra das Chuteiras Imortais: Crônicas de Futebol*, Nelson Rodrigues, Ruy Castro (ed.), Companhia das Letras, 1994.

'The build-up to the Brazil-Portugal game…' *The Story has Been Told*, Milile Kraba, Xlibris Corporation (Sep 16 2010).

'the Mongrel complex'… *À Sombra das Chuteiras Imortais: Crônicas de Futebol*, Nelson Rodrigues, Ruy Castro (ed.), Companhia das Letras, 1994.

'We were mutts again…' Brazil World Cup blog, Igor Natusch: http://brasilcopasmundo.blogspot.com/2010/07/1966-se-nao-esta-quebrado-nao-conserte.html

'Havelange would continue to insist…' *Folha de São Paulo* newspaper, June 25 2008.

'was too busy scoring goals…' Private interview with Tim Vickery.

'I'll tell you what, Mr President …' *How They Stole the Game*, David Yallop, Constable (2nd edition), 2011.

7. *CARNAVAL!*

'It's better to do Carnival…' (TW) *Joao Ternura*, Anibal Machado, Livraria José Olympio Editora (1976).

'great, creative and generous, having a glorious future'…' *Carnavais, Malandros e Heróis*, Roberto DaMatta, Editora Rocco, 1979.

'Carnival is an absolutely wondrous enigma…' Ibid.

'It is Carnival that…' Ibid.

8. *TENHA FÉ*: BELIEF IN BRAZIL

'Pope Francis conducting a mass…' http://www.bbc.co.uk/news/world-latin-america-23483478

9. CLUB, COUNTRY, *FUTEBOL!*

'If you hang a black and white shirt…' From Roberto Drummond's football column for the *Estado de Minas* newspaper, quoted at http://www.galoforte.net

10. A BRAZILIAN PLANET: 2014

'We shouldn't worry about the Dutch…' Quoted at: http://www.v-brazil.com/world-cup/history/1974-Germany.php

'When I was born…' Quoted at: http://www.fifa.com/newscentre/features/news/newsid=1107035/index.html

BIBLIOGRAPHY

BOOKS

Including:

A Concise History of Brazil, Boris Fausto, Cambridge (1999).

A Death in Brazil: A Book of Omissions, Peter Robb, Bloomsbury Publishing PLC (2005).

À Sombra das Chuteiras Imortais: Crônicas de Futebol, Nelson Rodrigues/Ruy Castro (eds), São Paulo: Companhia das Letras, (1993).

Aesthetics in Performance, Angela Hobart/Bruce Kampferer (eds.), Berghahn Books (2005).

'Almost Like Watching Brazil,' Chris Freddi, *When Saturday Comes*, Issue 157, (March 2000).

An Entirely Different Game: British Influence on Brazilian Football, Aidan Hamilton, Mainstream Books (1998).

Barbosa: Um Gol Faz Cinquenta Anos, Roberto Muylaert, RMC Editora (2000).

'Brawling in Berne: Mediated Transnational Moral Panics in the 1954 Football World Cup', Gerd von der Lippe and Malcolm MacLean, *International Review for the Sociology of Sport* (2008).

Brazil, Michael Palin, Weidenfeld & Nicolson (2012).

Brazil: Five Centuries of Change, Thomas Skidmore, OUP USA (2009).

Brazil on the Rise: The Story of a Country Transformed, Larry Rohter, Palgrave Macmillan (2012).

Carnivals, Rogues and Heroes: Interpretation of the Brazilian Dilemma, Roberto DaMatta, University of Notre Dame Press (1992).

Football Against the Enemy, Simon Kuper, Orion (2003).

Football: Brazil Player by Player, Liam McCann, Demand Media (2013).

Futebol: The Brazilian Way of Life, Alex Bellos, Bloomsbury Publishing PLC (2003).

Garrincha: The Triumph and Tragedy of Brazil's Forgotten Footballing Hero, Ruy Castro, Yellow Jersey Press (2005).

Globalised Football: Nations and Migration, the City and the Dream, Nina Clara Tiesler/Joao Nuno Coelho (eds.), Routledge (2008).

God Is Brazilian: Charles Miller, The Man Who Brought Football to Brazil, Josh Lacey, Tempus Publishing (2005).

How They Stole the Game, David Yallop, Poetic Products Ltd (1999).

Inverting the Pyramid: The History of Football Tactics, Jonathan Wilson, Orion (2009).

João Ternura, Anibal Machado, Livraria José Olympio Editora (1976).

O Mestre Ziza, Zizinho, SUDERJ (Edicoes de Maracanã), Rio de Janeiro (1985).

Passion of the People?: Football in South America, Tony Mason, Verso Books (1994).

Pelé: His Life and Times, Harry Harris, Robson Books (2001).

Pelé: The Autobiography, Pelé, Pocket Books (2007).

Politically Incorrect Guide to the History of Brazil, Leandro Narloch, Sao Paulo: Leya (2009).

Refereeing Around The World, Arthur E. Ellis, The Sportsmans Book Club (1956).

Rodar: The Circulation of Brazilian Football Players Abroad, Carmen Rial, Horizontes Antropologicos (2008).

Soccer in Sun and Shadow, Eduardo H. Galeano, Verso (1998).

Soccer Madness, Janet Lever, Tempus Publishing (1984).

The Ball is Round: A Global History of Football, David Goldblatt, Penguin (2007).

The Beautiful Team: In Search of Pelé and the 1970 Brazilians, Garry Jenkins, Simon & Schuster (1998).

The Brazil Book of Football, Stratton Smith (ed.), Souvenir Press (1963).

The Brazilian Sound: Samba, Bossa Nova, and the Popular Music of Brazil, Chris McGowan & Ricardo Pessanha, Temple University Press (2009).

The Color of Sound: Race, Religion, and Music in Brazil, J John Burdick, New York University Press (2013).

The Curves of Time: The Memoirs of Oscar Niemeyer, Isabel Murat Burbridge (trans.), Phaidon Press (2000).

The Footballer's Companion, Brian Glanville (ed.), Eyre & Spottiswoode (1962).

The Gilberto Freyre Reader, Gilberto Freyre (trans. Barbara Shelby), Random House Inc. (1974).

The Human Tradition in Modern Brazil, Peter M. Beattie (ed.), Scholarly Resources Inc. (2004).

The Story Has Been Told, Milile Krabba, Xlibris Corporation (2010).

The Story of the World Cup, Brian Glanville, Faber & Faber (2005).

Understanding Brazil, the Country of Football, Mouzar Benedito (trans. Phil Turner), Liz Editora (2013).

WEBSITES (HOME PAGES)

Including:

www.4dfoot.com

www.acertodecontas.blog.br/artigos/70-anos-de-foot-ball-mulato

www.anpocs.org.br/portal/publicacoes/rbcs_00_25/rbcs25_10.htm

www.band.uol.com.br

www.bbc.co.uk/religion/religions

www.bbc.co.uk/sport/0

www.brasilcopasmundo.blogspot.co.uk

www.brazilcarnival.com.br

www.brazilian-football.com

www.brazilianfootball.org/soccer/history cafefutebol.net

www.comciencia.br/comciencia/handler.php

www.copa2014.gov.br/en

www.dailymail.co.uk/sport/football/index.html

www.dc.itamaraty.gov.br/imagens-e-textos/carnaval01ing.pdf

www.fifa.com/classicfootball/history/index.html

www.fifa.com/classicfootball/matches/index.html

www.fifa.com/classicfootball/players/index.html

www.imortaisdofutebol.com

www.inbedwithmaradona.com

www.independent.co.uk/sport/football

www.liv.ac.uk/~rory/Football%20Introduction.pdf (studying football in the americas, Rory Miller)

www.lyricalbrazil.com

www.mg.co.za/section/news-sport

www.nytimes.com/2013/10/20/sports/soccer

www.oglobo.globo.com/pais/noblat/posts/2010/07/03/football-mulato-305261.asp (Football Mulatto, Gilberto Freyre, *Diario de Pernambuco*, 17 June, 1938)

www.revistabrasileiros.com.br

www.roadfoggy.com

www.sambafoot.com/en

www.sites.duke.edu/wcwp

www.soccerlens.com
www.soccerex.com/
www.tardesdepacaembu.wordpress.com
www.telegraph.co.uk/sport/football
www.theguardian.com/football
www.tracingthetree.wordpress.com
www.twohundredpercent.net
www.v-brazil.com/world-cup
www.veja.abril.com.br/historia
www.vibrant.org.br/downloads/v6n2_damatta.pdf
www.vibrant.org.br/downloads/v6n2_damo.pdf
www.whc.unesco.org/en/list
www.world-football-legends.co.uk
www.worldsoccersource.com
www.youtube.com/user/FIFATV
www.youtube.com/user/FIFATV/videos
www.youtube.com/watch?v=6jL6vZXKI4w
www.zocalopoets.com

PICTURE CREDITS
Getty/Popperfoto images, pages:
Alinari Archives: 61
Almeida, Vanderlei: 182, 225
Alves, Ormuzd: 163
Andrade, Edu: 197
Andreassi, Eduardo: 49
Banagan, John W: 31, 57, 149
Blanco, Levi: 171
Borba, Alfredo J G A: 44
Bueno, Fernando: Cover image; 40
Chiba, Yasuyoshi: 50
Contursi, Dud: 19
Crawford, Eric Marc: 231
Da Silva, Leonidas: 87
Edmonson, Paul: 106
Felton, Herbert: 70
Garcia, Daniel: 218

Griffiths, Laurence: 127
Guatelli, Caio: 159
Haynes Archive: 92, 109
Heavey, Scott: 101
Heck, Celia: 32
Heffernan, Michael: 154
Karger, George: 83
Mendes, Buda: 147, 232
Melo, Thiago: 79
Morales, Gabo: 161
Nacinovic, Marcelo: 27
Outram, Steve: 43
Popper, Paul: 63
Robinson, Alex: 53
Schincariol, Miguel: 181, 194
Scorza, Antonio: 167, 175
Severin, Kurt: 64
Simon, Christophe: ii, 150, 221
Suenaga, Helio: 187
Tama, Mario: 177
Thomas, Bob: 25, 85, 86, 103, 121, 214
Underwood Archives: 76
Uebel, Lucas: 198
Zambotto, Priscila: 64

Stuart Roy Clarke/The Homes of Football, pages:
74, 104, 185, 187, 190 and 201

ACKNOWLEDGEMENTS

Oscar's Brazil would not have been written without the help,
advice and diligence of a lot of other people. I'd particularly like to thank:

Oscar for his patience and clear memory.

Tim Vickery and Fernando Figueiredo Mello for their enthusiasm
for the project, their punctuality, their first-hand insight and, of course,
their considerable skills as writers.

Andrew Dart and Fritz Stockler for putting Oscar and I
together and introducing the idea of this book for helping to fund
the work of Casa do Zezinho.

Pascal Lafitte for making practical arrangements.

Caroline de Moraes for selfless and expert translations.

Melanie Michael Greer for guidance and perspective.

And everyone at Blink Publishing, especially Clare Tillyer, Clive Hebard,
Jane Donovan, Richard Johnson and Perminder Mann.